Reprints of Economic Classics

POPULAR DISTURBANCES AND PUBLIC ORDER IN REGENCY ENGLAND

POPULAR DISTURBANCES AND PUBLIC ORDER IN REGENCY ENGLAND

BEING
AN ACCOUNT OF THE LUDDITE AND OTHER DISORDERS IN ENGLAND DURING THE YEARS 1811–1817 AND OF THE ATTITUDE AND ACTIVITY OF THE AUTHORITIES

BY

FRANK ONGLEY DARVALL
(B.A. Reading; M.A. Columbia; B.A., Ph.D. London)

REPRINTS OF ECONOMIC CLASSICS

AUGUSTUS M. KELLEY · PUBLISHERS
NEW YORK 1969

First Edition 1934

(London: Oxford University Press, 1934)

Reprinted 1969 by

AUGUSTUS M. KELLEY · PUBLISHERS

NEW YORK NEW YORK 10010

By Arrangement With OXFORD UNIVERSITY PRESS

LIBRARY OF CONGRESS CATALOGUE CARD NUMBER

68-58973

PRINTED IN THE UNITED STATES OF AMERICA

by SENTRY PRESS, NEW YORK, N. Y. 10019

PREFATORY NOTE

THE research upon which this book is based was chiefly done in the years 1928 and 1929 in London, when the author was a graduate student of University College, London, and a member of the Institute of Historical Research. During part of that time he was the holder of a University Post-graduate Studentship. The results of this research were included in a thesis, *The Luddite Disturbances and the Machinery of Order*, accepted by the University of London in 1932 as an approved thesis for the External Degree of Doctor of Philosophy in History. Copies of the thesis, which contain most of the material included in this book, some of it in a more detailed form, are available for reference in the Libraries of the Universities of London and Reading.

The author desires to express his obligation to the many people and institutions without whose help this work could not have been done. He is particularly indebted to Dr. Sidney Peyton of the University of Reading, at whose suggestion he commenced research in this field and whose continual interest and inspiration have been invaluable; to Mr. H. L. Beales of the London School of Economics, who has served as his academic adviser and has generally supervised his work; to the University of London, on whose Studentship the work was commenced, and which has made a generous grant in aid of publication; and to the Commonwealth Fund, on whose Fellowship the writing of the thesis was completed. He also wishes to take this opportunity of thanking the Librarian and staff of the Institute of Historical Research, the British Museum, the Public Record Office, and other places in which he was collecting material, for their courtesy and assistance.

Amongst living authors whose books have been a

particular help he would wish to mention Mr. and Mrs. J. L. Hammond and Lord Passfield and Mrs. Sidney Webb, upon whose work all students of this period and this sort of subject are accustomed heavily to rely.

FRANK DARVALL

LONDON
May 30, 1934.

CONTENTS

INTRODUCTION

THE popular disturbances in England towards the end of the Napoleonic Wars and in the immediate post-war period are worthy of a greater attention than they have yet received. If for no other reason than that the most serious of these, the disorders in some of the manufacturing districts in the winter and spring of the year 1811–12, required for their suppression the use of an army larger than that with which Wellesley set sail for Portugal in 1808,[1] or than those with which he won many of his victories in India, these Regency disturbances are surely a matter of some importance. Disorders in England which required unprecedented measures, including the use of a military force more than six times as large as had ever previously been needed for such a purpose throughout the whole history of England,[2] cannot be passed off as if they were a merely local, industrial phenomenon.

The most important of these disturbances, and disturbances of a kind were endemic in England throughout the whole period from the American Revolution to the final collapse of Chartism, were those to which the name Luddite has been given. These disorders were originally restricted to a campaign against stocking frames and lace machines in the midland counties of Nottingham, Derby, and Leicester. They were given the name 'Luddite' because of the tradition in the hosiery industry that a certain Ned Ludlam, a Leicester stockinger's apprentice, when reprimanded on one occasion, and ordered to square his frames, had lost his temper and taken up a hammer and beaten the offending frames into pieces.[3] His name was

[1] Wellesley set sail with 9,000 men (*Camb. Mod. Hist.*, vol. ix, p. 440). About 12,000 were employed against the Luddites (see Chap. XIII).

[2] Ryder in the House of Commons in Feb. 1812 said that the force sent to Nottingham between Nov. 15 and Dec. 9, 1811, which amounted to 1,800 men, was larger than had ever before been used for quelling a purely local disturbance (*Parl. Debates*, xxi. 11. 808).

[3] Blackner, *History of Nottingham*, p. 402.

given by common custom in the trade to any one who broke stocking frames for any reason, and therefore, by natural transfer, to those disorderly mobs of framework knitters who in March 1811, and on various occasions thereafter, attacked the frames of unpopular hosiers. Since this disorder, starting in Nottinghamshire in 1811 and continuing into 1812, extended from the midlands and the hosiery and lace trades into Lancashire, Cheshire, and Yorkshire and amongst the croppers and the cotton weavers, and since the rioters proceeded from mere attacks upon machinery to raids for fire-arms, or for lead, and to attacks upon provision shops and grain dealers, the name Luddite, which was originally purely a midland and hosiery term, became attached to the whole range of disorders which characterized the years 1811–12, and to similar outbreaks during the next five years.

These disorders, in which attacks upon machinery were the major, and the most significant, though not the only, acts of the rioters, were very destructive. They resulted in the loss of, probably, upwards of one hundred thousand pounds' worth of machinery and other property. They placed the persons and property of more than a million people, the merchants, manufacturers, and labourers of the disturbed districts, temporarily at the mercy of the disorderly Luddites. They were suppressed with great difficulty, by the use of tremendous and hitherto unprecedented military and civil force, including an army of 12,000 soldiers,[1] and only after a great deal of damage had been done.

While this outbreak of Luddism in 1811–12 was the most serious it was not the only instance of disorder during these years. There were further outbreaks of Luddism, though of a more restricted kind, in the winter of 1812–13, in the summer and early autumn of 1814, and in the summer and autumn of 1816. There were riots in London on the occasion of the passage of the Corn Bill in 1815. There

[1] Chap. XIII, p. 260.

were serious agricultural disturbances in the spring and early summer of 1816. There were widespread apprehensions of disorder in the winter of 1816–17, apprehensions which lead the Government to suspend the Habeas Corpus Act. There were three so-called 'risings' in the spring and summer of 1817, 'The March of the Blanketeers', the 'Pentridge Revolution', and the 'Huddersfield Rising'. There were other minor and local riots and disorders.

These minor and confused disturbances, and this liability to sudden popular outbreaks like 'Peterloo', continued throughout the Regency, and indeed throughout the reign of George IV. But there was not after 1817 any major disorder such as Luddism. The situation of the working classes, the ebb and flow of popular distress and discontent, the recurrent occasions of riot or more widespread disorder, and the measures and reforms into which they forced those responsible for the maintenance of internal order, remain matters of great interest and importance. But more striking than they, and offering, perhaps, a clearer example of the strength and weakness of public order in early nineteenth-century England, are the disturbances of the years 1811–17, and especially that which was called Luddism.

They are interesting for a number of reasons, apart altogether from the unusual damage they caused and the unprecedented measures into which they forced the authorities. They were an early and striking example of 'direct action' as an instrument of labour policy. They were a definite, and initially and temporarily a successful, attempt to apply pressure to certain employers, and to force them to grant the body of employees various concessions which they were demanding, and which they had been unable to obtain by pacific means. Had they been successful they might have made a policy of 'sabotage' a more popular substitute for trades union or political action, as a means of obtaining a redress of grievances for manual labour, than in fact it was to be.

They were also, though only to a limited extent, and less than has been suggested, an attempt on the part of manual labour to prevent the introduction of labour-saving machinery. They were largely provoked by the pressure of technological unemployment, by distress occasioned, as it was thought, by the introduction of new machinery throwing hand-workers out of employment and forcing down the level of hand-worker's wages. They were, in certain districts and instances, a definite attempt to put back the clock of industrial advance, to protect the old position of the hand-workers even at the expense of their ultimate good, and of an immediate gain to the trade and the country as a whole, which the orthodox economists suggested, though the workers doubted, would follow the introduction of labour-saving machinery. Had they been successful they might have encouraged other workers to repeat the experiment, and thus effectively have retarded the advance of the new industry.

It is an interesting question, though one in which few contemporary critics had any concern, whether such a result would have been an unmixed disaster. It would, of course, probably have operated, as opponents of Luddism suggested that it must, to drive industry to other districts and countries where manufacturers were free to employ the new, and cheap, methods of production. But it might also have lead to a greater planning of industry, to the gradual, controlled introduction of machine and factory production in such a way, and at such times, as not to cause undue suffering to any class of workers, instead of the heedless, headlong, competitive race which actually took place, and which, whatever its ultimate value to the community, caused untold and unnecessary suffering to great groups of men.

An important aspect of these disturbances, however, and one on which there has been a great deal of misunderstanding, is the extent to which Luddism was an opposition to labour-saving machinery as such. In the cropping industry of the West Riding, which was the seat of a violent Luddite campaign in the months of February, March, and April 1812, it was. In the attacks upon steam looms at Stockport, Middleton, and Westhoughton, which were a feature of the disorder in Lancashire and Cheshire in 1812, such opposition to new machinery was certainly one, though not the only, factor. But in the main seat of Luddism, and that in which the greatest damage was done, there was no such opposition to labour-saving machinery. The midland Luddites, as all the best informed local and contemporary witnesses emphasized, were not fighting against new machinery. They were using attacks upon machinery, whether new or old, as a means of coercing their employers into granting them concessions with regard to wages and other matters.

This fact, and the other characteristic of these Regency disturbances, including Luddism, that they were the product of extreme distress, a release of pent-up feelings under pressure of intolerable suffering, which might have taken place whether or no there was new machinery, are aspects of this problem which have often been overlooked but which are of fundamental importance. Many people have completely misunderstood the whole Luddite movement, and much of British economic history during these years, because they have wrongly thought that opposition to new machinery was a general and permanent characteristic of workers during the Industrial Revolution, and the main cause of Luddism. The Luddites in the midlands, and they were the most numerous and persistent of the rioters, did not object to new machinery. The Luddites elsewhere, some of whom did object to new machinery, would not have undertaken their campaign unless they had had other causes, and objects, for disorder. Opposition to new machinery, which was by no means an invariable phenomenon of the industrial advance, even when it was present, very often showed itself, as in these years, not when the labour-saving machinery was first introduced, but later, when a severe depression, due largely to other causes, caused distress and discontent, and thus made labour-saving machinery appear to be a needless aggravation of what would in any case have been a difficult situation. It was not labour-saving machinery as such to which workers objected. It was unemployment and low wages which provoked them to riot, and they only recognized machinery as a cause of such things, and therefore as an evil to be opposed, upon occasions of general unemployment and trade depression.

In some ways a more interesting and important aspect of these disturbances to the general critic than that of 'direct action', which should interest the student of trades unionism, or than that of opposition to labour-saving machinery, which would appeal to technologists and 'technocrats', is this connexion which they establish between distress and disorder. It is a significant fact, and one which should do much to reassure people who are terrified to-day by bogies, such as Technocracy or Communism, as it did to calm contemporary authorities, that disturbances seemed to occur in England, upon the whole, only when and where there were, in addition to particular causes of industrial or political discontent, evidences of sudden, sharp, unrelieved distress. Where there was no special distress, or where distress was adequately relieved, new machinery was safe and Jacobin doctrines were at a discount. Only where there was the double cause of trouble, a coincidence of special causes for discontent, like a rise in the price of provisions, with general causes, like unemployment due to the introduction of new machinery, was there likely, in Regency England, to be any serious disorder.[1]

These disturbances are important, also, in showing how

[1] A similar coincidence of distress and disturbance was noticed at other, previous, occasions of disorder, for instance in 1778 at the occasion of a previous outbreak of framebreaking. For a general discussion of this subject see Chap. X.

dependent England was growing upon conditions in the outside world. The distress and depression, which were the major cause of the Luddite and other disturbances, were due far more to the breach with the United States than to any other single cause. It was the closing of the American market, far more than the introduction of new machinery or the spread of Jacobin doctrines, which provoked the disorders of 1811–12. Similarly it was the post-war depression, far more than any spread of sedition throughout the country, which created the post-1816 disturbances. Industrial England was growing very vulnerable to foreign conditions. She had given many hostages to fortune in her growing dependence upon foreign markets. She was in an odd position indeed for a mother country when the closing of the market of a small nation, created by the rebellion of '13 of her colonies, could stir her industrial districts into riots requiring an army to suppress them. Madison in America, like Napoleon in Paris, could, though he knew it not, have taken comfort from these English disturbances, which were, as truly as any captures by sea or land, part of the price that England was paying for the war.

It was to external causes, such as the sudden boom and collapse in the trade to South America in the years 1807–10, following the capture of Buenos Aires, or the American Non-Intercourse Act, or the ending of the war, which occasioned sudden, severe distress, and precipitated a general business depression; rather than to domestic ones, such as the introduction of new machinery, that disturbances may generally be traced at this period of English history. It was largely, though not solely, to external causes, such as the reopening of the continental market, following Napoleon's breach with the Tsar, rather than to domestic ones, such as the concessions made by the employers to their riotous workpeople, that the cessation of disturbances was often due.[1] Industrial, and indeed, to

[1] As in 1812.

a lesser extent, agricultural England, had already, at the beginning of the nineteenth century, become so dependent upon world conditions as to have their internal order varying with the progress of events abroad. Already then, 100 years before the world was ready to recognize the interdependence of nations, England at any rate had so far ceased to be self-sufficient as to see her workpeople goaded into riot by the acts of foreign governments. Washington even then, as the close connexion between the American Non-Intercourse Act and the Luddite disorders so clearly shows, had the power to make or mar even the domestic policy of its one time mother country.

Equally important, as a reason why greater attention should be given to this period and to disturbances such as these, is the light that they throw upon the stability of English society and government. It was then, and has been ever since, a matter of some uncertainty, whether or no there was any real danger in England of a revolution such as the French. While it is impossible to give a final answer to such an hypothetical question from any such study as this, it is possible by examining the actual disorders which happened at this time, and the efforts that were made to put them down, to get a very fair idea of the elements in early nineteenth-century England which were making for disorder, and of the strength and weakness of the forces of order. It is possible, by a study of the most serious of the disorders from which early nineteenth-century England suffered, to say with some degree of assurance that there was at that time no real danger of a general collapse of order, or of a violent overturn of government or society. English society at the time of the Napoleonic Wars, though subject to great and hitherto unprecedented strains, was, like English society at the time of the last Great War, far more stable and secure than that of the continental countries in which revolutions occurred or were threatened.

These disorders, which a few alarmists thought apt to

issue in revolution, were, however, very serious. And they exhibit in a new light the essential weaknesses of, on the one hand, the system of order, and on the other of the economic and social organization, of Regency England. That such profound and protracted disturbances should have happened, and that they should have been found so difficult to suppress, is convincing evidence that there was something radically wrong with the England in which such events were possible. The absence of any regular system of police, the archaic system of local government, the unrepresentative character of Parliament, were all shown to be serious causes of instability in early nineteenth-century England. The difficulties of these war and post-war years did a tremendous amount to awaken contemporary authorities to the necessity of taking reform earnestly in hand. It was more than a coincidence that the foundation of the new police, the reform of Parliament, and the creation of new efficient organs of local government should have followed within twenty years of these grave national disturbances. There are few ways in which a better conception can be obtained of the problem with which the governing class was faced in nineteenth-century England, so far as the machinery of order and the internal government were concerned, than by a study of that system in action at the time of these disorders.

Similarly there are few ways in which it is possible more clearly to grasp the industrial and economic problem which faced England in the nineteenth century, the problem of using state action to prevent the readjustments of the Industrial Revolution bearing too hardly upon the working population, than by a study of these Regency disturbances, which were so largely provoked by the readjustments that the Industrial Revolution was causing, and by the absence of any court of appeal save force to which the aggrieved workers could look for help. The legalization of Trades Unions, the conversion of Parliament from a rigid *laisser-faire* attitude towards industry to a willingness to intervene successively, by way of Factory Acts and other state regulations, to redress the abuses connected with the new industry—the creation, that is, of legal, pacific, industrial, and political outlets and instruments for discontent amongst the working classes, outlets and instruments which did not exist in 1811—were, hardly less than the creation of the new police, the consequence of these disturbances. England was not safe while she bottled up the discontent of her working population. A merely negative policy towards industrial distress, leading to disputes between masters and men, was an unsafe policy. It almost inevitably caused, as it did in these years, serious disorder, leading to calls upon the Government and upon the military. It was necessary, and the Regency disturbances did something to teach the governing class that it was necessary, if disorder was to be avoided, to do something to relieve distress. And relief of distress, though few contemporaries realized that fact fully or consciously, inevitably involved the far-reaching state regulation of industry that was established during the later nineteenth century.

A study of Regency disturbances, and of the attitude and activity of the authorities in relation thereto, should be more than a mere record of local riots and police measures. It can be, as this book tries to be, an introduction to some of the major problems of nineteenth-century England. It can be a new window through which to look, from a different angle, upon the Napoleonic Wars, upon the Industrial Revolution, and upon the situation which both were creating. This study is hardly more than an introduction to the larger study that is needed. The record of disturbances, and of state and industrial action thereto, should be carried from 1817 to the end of the Regency, and beyond. Luddism should be tied up with Chartism, by filling in the period between the two. It is hoped, however, that this book, limited though it is to the years 1811–17, and to a portion only of the field, may be of some value. It is, at any rate, a full study of some hitherto neglected aspects of English history at that intensely interesting time, when the country was at the cross-roads between the new and the old, after it had outgrown its eighteenth-century suit of government and social order and before it had been given a new one. It should be of some interest to people in another period of transition, when social and political machinery and thought is once again lagging behind the advance of industry, and when the social cost of war is once again being appreciated. The Luddites, poor victims of war and of industrial advance, should receive the sympathy of our modern unemployed, paying a similar price for similar events. The March of the Blanketeers, feeble expedient though it was, should be worth a little attention at a time of similar attempts, of 'hunger marches' and 'bonus armies'.

Disorder to-day, like disorder in England a hundred years ago, is often, like the bubbling of boiling water, a sign of changes which are taking place within a body, whether it be of people or of matter, and which are promoting some elements and reducing others. It is also often a sign that something radical is wrong with the society in which it happens. It is, like the symptoms of disease, a warning to the patient to alter his habits of life. It is unfortunate that nations should require overt acts, such as disorder, as individuals require physical suffering, such as disease, before they recognize and take in hand the readjustments that are needed in their way of life. It is because of that, however, that disorders, such as those dealt with in this book, are worthy of particular study.

I

ENGLAND IN 1811

ENGLAND in 1811 was still largely a rural and agricultural country. Well over half the population was living in the country.[1] Many even of those who were living in the towns were still in contact with the country, with the outlook and interests of country people. They were living in small towns rather than in large ones and were accustomed to travel not, like town dwellers to-day, from one town to another, but from their little country towns out into the country villages in which society as well as industry was still chiefly situated.

There were very few large towns, although the urban population of the country was increasing rapidly, both absolutely and in relation to the rural population. London,[2] including the other cities and suburbs in the metropolitan area, had now for the first time more than one million inhabitants, one-tenth of the entire population of England and Wales. Two other towns had more than 100,000 inhabitants, Manchester and Liverpool, and three more, Birmingham, Bristol, and Leeds, more than 60,000. No other English towns had as many as forty, and not more than a handful as many as thirty, thousand inhabitants. A number of new, industrial towns were developing, especially in the north, and were beginning to challenge the supremacy of the older county towns, Norwich, Nottingham, Leicester, Derby, which had been considerable towns for many years. But few of these places, which are great cities to-day, had in the early nineteenth century as many as 20,000 inhabitants. The typical English town was still a small one, more likely to consist of a few thousand than of tens of thousands of people. It was very dependent upon its immediate countryside, very local in its outlook,

[1] *Parl. Papers*, 1812, ii; Census Returns for 1811.

[2] *Population Returns for 1831*, E. Moxon (London, 1832), p. 25.

still very much of a self-contained, self-satisfied, little country town.

Industry was still situated chiefly in the country. Even the newer industries, like the great and growing cotton manufacture of the north, were still seated more in the country than in the town. They still, in all but a small minority of cases, used water power rather than steam, when they used any non-human source of power at all. Not even in the cotton industry,[1] that in which the Industrial Revolution had made its greatest advance, was machine or factory production yet supreme. In the spinning branch factories dependent upon water power had largely superseded the old system of working by hand at home. But even in this branch some hand-work in the home or in very small, country workshops survived, and few large, steam-driven factories had been established. In the weaving branch hand-work was still almost universal, factories were only beginning to come in, steam looms were very, very rare. The other great textile industry, the staple trade of Tudor England, the woollen and worsted manufacture,[2] was even less advanced than the cotton trade, and was still busy adapting the simplest jennies to its use. The typical worker in 1811, in the new, industrial north as well as in the older, more rural south and east, worked at home or in a small country workshop by hand on a simple machine.

There were as yet, except upon one or two collieries, no railroads. Canals were carrying the major part of the heavy goods traffic, and the canal system was being completed and made national in its extent. But the road was still for personal transportation and for much light or local goods

[1] The following works on the cotton manufacture were written by contemporary witnesses: *History of the Cotton Manufacture*, by E. Baines; *The British Cotton Manufacture*, by Richard Guest; *Compendious History of the Cotton Manufacture*, idem; *Cotton Manufacture of Great Britain*, by D. Ure.

[2] See *The History of the Woollen and Worsted Industry*, by E. Lipson, and *The Woollen and Worsted Industries*, by J. H. Clapham.

traffic the only available route. And the roads, despite the multiplication of turnpike trusts, and the stimulus that their example had given to the local and parish authorities charged with the care of the highway,[1] were still, except upon a few main routes, extremely bad. Trade was becoming national. Local industries were becoming dependent upon agents and financial houses in the major provincial towns and in London. Coastwise shipping was developing fast and was breaking down local isolation. Imports and exports were expanding rapidly, despite the pressure of the war and the operation of Napoleon's Decrees and of the Orders in Council, the value of goods imported into or exported out of the country now normally exceeding £40,000,000 a year.[2] The great industries of the country, textiles, hosiery and lace, iron, ship-building, coal-mining, and their newer subsidiaries, were increasingly dependent upon the state of foreign trade, having to draw many of their raw materials, wool, cotton, lumber, and sell from one-third to one-sixth of their products abroad.[3] The population that they employed had given even greater hostages to the state of world affairs, the British farms being less and less able every year to supply even the staple articles of food in adequate quantities,[4] and the taste for non-British luxury goods, tea, coffee, spices, tobacco, dried fruits, and wines, being rapidly on the rise, so that ships loaded with wheat from Odessa were becoming as necessary to British well-being as ships loaded with spices and other luxuries from the Levant and the Orient had long been. And all this growth of foreign trade was naturally playing into the hands of the London houses which so largely

[1] See *The King's Highway*, by S. and B. Webb. Robert Lowe, in his *General View of the Agriculture of the County of Nottingham* (London, 1798), p. 135, says that roads in that district were much improved, parish officers having profited from the example of the turnpikes.

[2] *Social England*, H. S. Traill and J. S. Mann, i. 828.

[3] See evidence before House of Commons Committee on Petitions for the Repeal of the Orders in Council, 1808 and 1812.

[4] See *The Industrial and Commercial Revolutions in England in the Nineteenth Century*, by Lilian Knowles, p. 365.

monopolized it and obtained through it an increasing control over local industries and provincial business.

Even so the outstanding currents of life were still local ones. Local small town banks abounded, and still issued their own notes, and dominated the business of their localities. Partnerships rather than companies were the typical business unit, and one at least of the partners even in the great metropolitan houses was probably resident in and a respected citizen of the provincial town serving the trade in which the house dealt, Bristol, Norwich, Nottingham, Stockport, Leeds.[1] In most cases indeed the local influences were still more pronounced, the trade of the country being dominated by bankers and merchants in the smaller towns, in Stroud, Mansfield, Halifax, or some such smaller place, to whom even the great provincial centres were still somewhat remote. The Cloth Hall or Exchange in these small country towns, especially in the clothing trade in the west country and the West Riding, rather than the wholesale market in Manchester, Liverpool, Bristol, or London, was the meeting-place of the solid, responsible, but small, provincial business men, with personal businesses and close relations with their workpeople, who were still the backbone of the country.

Agriculture was still the major industry. More than 35 per cent. of the population was directly engaged in it,[2] and an even greater proportion had some interest in it. The countryside had undergone great changes. Agriculture was further advanced than most other industries in the transformation from medieval to modern conditions. Open field agriculture was growing very rare. Enclosure had proceeded apace, and was proceeding especially rapidly in the first two decades of the nineteenth century, in each of which more than a million and a half acres was enclosed, 3,110,000 acres being converted from common field tillage between 1800 and 1820 as against a total of only 3,400,000

[1] Felkin, *History of Machine Wrought Hosiery and Lace*, p. 437.

[2] *Population Returns for 1831*, E. Moxon, p. 2.

in the preceding 40 years from 1760 to 1800.[1] The Squire had taken the place of the Lord of the Manor. The triple division of functions in agriculture between landlord, tenant farmer, and agricultural labourer, had been established in a thousand villages. The tendency under enclosure, which was an expensive process, to squeeze out the small man, particularly the leaseholder under the old system with only a few strips in the common fields and pasture for a pig or cow, had thrown many an extra family upon the Poor Law, or forced them to make the hard choice between staying in the country as a labourer on another man's land or going into the city or to the new industrial districts, to become a hand in another man's factory.[2] The appearance of the typical village had changed, the old common fields being divided into a patchwork quilt by the new hedges and ditches separating one man's farm from another's, and new, larger, brick and stone houses and barns taking the place of the old, poor buildings of mud and wood and thatch.[3] The new rich, enjoying the fruits of trade to the East and West Indies, had bought themselves into Society, as they had into politics, and had become landowners, covering the English countryside with new, square, red brick, Georgian residences. The new scientific agriculture, profiting from the experiments of pioneers like 'Turnip' Townshend, Coke of Holkham, and Bakewell, who saw the profits that were to be realized by putting money into their land and by farming upon a great scale, was altering the course of country life, and making it increasingly difficult for small, poor farmers to make a living and a profit. The spirit of change was at work creating a new England. It had not yet entirely enclosed the village fields,[4] or eliminated the small man's

[1] Porter, *Progress of the Nation*, new ed. by Hirst, p. 188.

[2] For a good account of the effect of the new changes on the workers of all classes, see J. L. and B. Hammond's books, *The Skilled Labourer, The Town Labourer, The Agricultural Labourer.*

[3] Robert Lowe, op. cit., p. 9.

[4] Porter, op. cit., p. 188. More than 2 million acres was enclosed after 1810.

rights of common, or destroyed the yeoman and the peasant farmer. But it had created a great ferment of opinion in the country, a range of new and often unrecognized problems.

Particularly had it, coming at a time when industry was beginning to be affected by the introduction of machinery, and to draw its workers into factories and to the town, destroyed the old partnership between industry and agriculture whereby the village craftsman was also a small cultivator in the village fields, with a cow and pigs on the common pasture, and the village labourer also, in the winter or in his wife's spare time, a spinner of wool or a knitter of lace and stockings. The country folk in the nineteenth century were being increasingly forced to choose between their two professions, in neither of which was it becoming possible for the unskilled, propertyless handworker to make a decent living. They were being drawn from the south-east, the old seat of England's industries and population, to the north and west, its future seat of wealth and power (and ugliness), and from the country to the town. They were hanging on, struggling on, not yet conscious that the old way of life was doomed. Several times in the years between the overthrow of the old system in France in 1789 and its overturn in Britain following the Reform Bill of 1832, conditions in the countryside became so desperate that the agricultural labourers, now so well behaved a population, broke into riot and revolt.[1]

It is not necessary to assume that their previous situation had been ideal to admit that their present situation in 1810 and 1811 was worse than it had been. Every class of the population was having to pay a part of the price of the war and of the Commercial, Agricultural, and Industrial Revolutions, all of which were acting and re-acting upon one another at this time. They were being forced unawares into a situation in which they would have to

[1] e.g. in East Anglia in the spring of 1816 and sporadically throughout this whole period.

resort also, in order to deal with their new problems, to political and social innovations far-reaching enough to be called revolutionary. It is difficult, since so many changes were happening at once, to determine which were the prime cause of the prevailing distress. It is, however, impossible to ignore the extent or the severity of the popular distress existing in 1810–11, or to deny that the impact of the new industrial changes upon an unprepared society was, at any rate partly, responsible for the sufferings of the people.

The major, and most immediate, cause for distress in 1810 was, however, the war and the course of foreign trade.[1] The Continental System, despite the loopholes that wily British and neutral merchants and smugglers were able to drive in it, and that Napoleon was ready to tolerate, was bound to have a restrictive effect upon British exports. The mere fact of the war also, and the destructive effect of the continuous marching and countermarching upon the continent of Europe, was bound to limit at the same time the capacity of the European peoples both to buy industrial products from and sell agricultural products to Great Britain. Even more serious, because of the importance of the United States as Britain's major customer, was the closing of the American market in retaliation for the Orders in Council. For a year or so the occasional open periods in the American market, and the market in South America which was opened in 1807 after the British occupation of Buenos Aires, together with the great British war demand, prevented a general collapse.[2] By 1810, however, the shipments to South America had ceased, no payments having been received on account of those sent

[1] See *Parl. Papers*, 1817, xiv. 243: 'An account of the Official Value of Exports from Great Britain, 1792–1816.'

[2] For effects of the boom and consequent collapse in exports to South America, see evidence of witnesses before the House of Commons Committee on the Orders in Council and also statements by Ministers in Parliament during the debates on the Framework Knitting Bill and the Nottingham Peace Bill, Feb. 1812.

out in 1807–9. Partly because of this, and as a reaction from the excessive speculative orgy that had followed the opening of this new mysterious market, there was in 1810 a financial panic. Banks failed. There were a tremendous number of commercial and industrial bankruptcies. The Government had to obtain authority to issue £6,000,000 worth of Exchequer Bills before the panic could be stayed.[1] An industrial depression of great severity, which had been delayed before only by the speculative prospects of this new market, was precipitated.

The situation was already serious when the American Non-Intercourse Act came into force in February 1811. This completely closed the vitally important American market, upon which many firms, especially in the midlands and the north, had depended for the disposal of sometimes as much as one-third of their product.[2] British exports fell from £48,000,000 in 1810 to £32,000,000 in 1811, a catastrophic decline of 33⅓ per cent., and imports from £39,000,000 to £26,000,000, an equally serious relapse.[3] The fall in exports to the United States, which had normally absorbed almost one-quarter of the entire volume of British exports, was even more sudden and complete. Exports, which in 1810 had reached a value of £11,217,685, fell in 1811 to the paltry figure of £1,874,917.[4] No industrial or social structure could be expected to stand such shocks.

The distress was naturally great. Petitions poured in to Westminster from every manufacturing district in the country.[5] Everywhere there was talk of unemployment, part time, diminished wages, shrunken earnings, terrible distress. The expenditure upon the Poor Law, which in 1801, a previous year of very great depression and distress, had been £4,017,871, amounted in 1811 to £6,656,105, an increase of 65 per cent., whereas the population had only

[1] Traill and Mann, op. cit., p. 828.

[2] See evidence before House of Commons Committee on the Orders in Council, May 1812.

[3] *Parl. Papers*, 1817, xiv. 243.

[4] *Accounts and Papers*, 1812, x. 25.

[5] *Parl. Debates*, xix. 1017, and xx. 608 et seq.

increased from 8,872,981 to 10,163,676, an increase of just under 15 per cent.[1] It was said in 1812 that one-fifth of the population in most of the towns of Lancashire was in the condition of requiring charitable relief.[2] Wages were variously said to have declined by 15, 30, 33, and even 50 per cent.[3] Some trades talked of half work only,[4] others even of having shrunk to one-fourth of what they had been.[5]

To aggravate this already sufficiently distressing situation was the high and rising level of prices. Throughout the whole period from 1790 to 1810 prices generally were rising fast, faster even than wages which were also, on the average and except for times of depression like 1810–12, on the rise.[6] According to Silberling's index figure,[7] taking 1790 as the base year, prices had risen by 1812 to a maximum height of 87 per cent. above their pre-war level. The price of wheat, which averaged 107*s.* 3½*d.* per quarter for the period 1800–13, but which in good years, even during the war, fell as low as 90*s.* a quarter, rose in August 1812 to a ghastly maximum of 160*s.* a quarter.[8] The price of a quartern loaf of bread, and bread was the staple diet of a working-class population which could seldom afford meat[9] and was never very attracted to vegetables, apart from potatoes, which had only been 1*s.* 3½*d.* even in the famine years of 1800 and 1801, and which fell as low as 1*s.* 1*d.* in 1805, was 1*s.* 2½*d.* in 1810, 1*s.* 2*d.* in 1811, 1*s.* 5*d.* in 1812, and even, at one time during that year, 1*s.* 8*d.*[10] Life at such a time was very hard for working-class families which were often getting only from 7 to 9 shillings,[11] or at the most

[1] Porter, op. cit., p. 64. [2] *Leeds Mercury*, Feb. 22, 1812.

[3] *Parl. Papers*, 1812, iii. 265 and 273.

[4] Fletcher to H.O., Feb. 25, 1812, in H.O. 42. 120.

[5] *Parl. Papers*, 1812, ii. 213.

[6] Palgrave, *Dictionary of Political Economy*, Appendix, p. 801, quoting Bowley.

[7] Quoted in J. H. Clapham, *Economic History of Modern Britain*, i. 602. [8] Knowles, op. cit., p. 366.

[9] Maitland to H.O. in H.O. 40. 1. [10] Knowles, op. cit., p. 366.

[11] e.g. at Stockport (Lloyd to H.O. in H.O. 40. 1) and Nottingham (Felkin, op. cit., p. 231).

from 13 to 15 shillings, a week, despite the long hours they had to work. General Maitland, Officer Commanding in the north in 1812, estimated that in that area prices had risen and wages fallen on an average almost one-third by 1812 as compared with conditions a year or so before.[1] Conditions were worse in Lancashire than elsewhere, for reasons which are discussed later. But even the lesser fall of wages which was reported for the country as a whole was serious enough, especially at a time of such famine prices.

The latter were due partly to the war, which had been driving prices up continually, thus providing a great impetus to the expansion of trade and the introduction of new methods. But they were due primarily to the terrible succession of bad harvests. The British crop failed in 1809, 1810, 1811, and 1812.[2] In the last two of these years, in 1811 and 1812, the years of the most extreme British industrial depression and commercial stagnation, the continental crop failed also and the British scarcity could not be relieved, as usual, by importation. For a time of depression, the trough of the business cycle, to be also a time of high prices is almost unprecedented. It naturally added enormously to the sufferings of every class of the people.

The stagnation of trade was somewhat relieved by the repeal of the Orders in Council in June 1812.[3] Although the American Declaration of War, news of which was received immediately thereafter, abruptly halted the boom in trade that news of repeal had set in motion, the defeat of Napoleon in Russia, and the break up of the Continental System, to prevent which the Russian expedition had been embarked upon, served to revive it. Industries were in the autumn of 1812 again working full time.[4] In 1813 also,

[1] Maitland to H.O., May 4, 1812, in H.O. 40. 1.
[2] Tooke, *History of Prices*, p. 326.
[3] Maitland to H.O., June 19, 1812, in H.O. 40. 1.
[4] Lloyd to H.O., Oct. 1812, in H.O. 40. 1.

at last, there was again an abundant harvest. Although the Peace was followed by several difficult and distressing years,[1] there was not again for some time such a coincidence of general and particular causes of distress as that which made 1811 and 1812 such terrible years in Britain. There was, however, throughout this period, indeed throughout the whole decade of the Regency, a state of strain in England, extended by the longest of its wars, giving birth to a new industrial system.

Population was growing so fast, 15 per cent. every decade.[2] Industry and agriculture were developing and undergoing the most complicated mutual readjustments even more rapidly. Some classes, industries, localities were rising, both absolutely and at the expense of others. Some few were declining, not merely relatively to the general advance, but even, to some extent, absolutely. Even had the framework of government,[3] national and local, and the knowledge, sympathy, and foresight of industrial and political leaders[4] been adequate, which they were not, to the varied needs of the time, English society in the early nineteenth century would have been extended to the uttermost in order to solve its unprecedented problems. England in 1811, towards the end of a costly war, at the beginning of a tremendous series of revolutions, was a fit setting for a stirring drama of social protest.

[1] There was particularly a severe agricultural depression.

[2] *Population Returns for 1831*, E. Moxon, p. 9.

[3] See Chap. XII and also *History of English Local Government*, by S. and B. Webb.

[4] See Chap. XVI.

II

THE MIDLANDS IN 1811

THE chief seat of the Luddite disturbances lay in the three midland counties of Nottingham,[1] Derby, and Leicester. This pleasant and typically English countryside[2] was in the early years of the nineteenth century going through the same process of transformation that was affecting the country as a whole. Midway between the old, populous, and previously dominant south-east and the new, hitherto neglected, and now rapidly developing north-west, this low-lying country in the valley of the river Trent, shut off from the north-west by the mountain ridge of the Pennines, which splits Derbyshire in two, had been previously more akin in character to the south than to the north. Like the south it had always been able to mix agriculture with industry, there being a sturdy proportion of craftsmen among its, for those days, ample population. Like the south it had recently been feeling the pressure of competition from the rising north, which was tempting away its workers and some of its industries.[3] Like the south it was undergoing a process of rapid enclosure.[4] The industrial revolution had come to it and stirred up a thousand currents of change, like an urban radical in a sleepy country village. But it had not yet fundamentally altered its rural, eighteenth-century character.

This area had once contained a great proportion of forest and other waste land. Parts of the once extensive Sherwood Forest, famous since the days of Robin Hood, were still surviving, to shelter beneath the sturdy trunks of their old oaks further adventurous, unorthodox defenders of the

[1] For a description of Nottinghamshire just before this time, see J. D. Chambers, *Nottinghamshire in the Eighteenth Century*.

[2] Topography and agriculture of Nottinghamshire *circa* 1800 described by Robert Lowe, *General View of the Agriculture of the county of Nottingham. . . .*, London, 1798.

[3] Felkin, op. cit., p. 299.

[4] Robert Lowe, op. cit., p. 19.

poor. A great stretch of Nottinghamshire, some 30 miles long and from 7 to 10 miles wide, was still listed at the end of the eighteenth century as being 'forest', though it now contained the homes of a numerous population and was divided up into a thousand separate farms and estates, both large and small.[1] The actual number of trees still standing, and particularly of old trees, was not large, and was being rapidly diminished by the pressure of war time needs. But a considerable area was wooded to some degree and was still felt worthy of being called 'forest' on more than historical grounds. The rest of the district, with the exception of the Derbyshire mountains, which were really outside it, was even, pleasantly undulating, with only gentle hills to divide one locality from another. It had a good soil and was, as it had long been, a prosperous farming country.

Despite the progress of enclosure, which was proceeding very fast throughout the reign of George III,[2] and despite the unusual number of large estates and gentlemen's houses,[3] the district was predominantly one of small farms of 300, 100, and even 20 acres. By 1811 very little land, especially in the 'forest' area, which was also the chief industrial district of the region, was still unenclosed. The amalgamation of holdings and the gradual elimination of the smaller cultivators, which was happening here, as elsewhere in the country, and for the same reasons, was turning the inhabitants, perforce, either into farm labourers or artisans, and was ending the old custom of families being both agricultural and industrial, farming some strips of land in the common fields and working a frame for a Nottingham hosier. Particularly had this process been happening during the war years, under pressure of the high prices then prevailing. An observer in 1811 would not have said, as Robert Lowe did in 1798, that most families still possessed not merely a garden but a few acres

[1] Robert Lowe, op. cit., p. 14.
[2] Porter, op. cit., p. 188.
[3] Robert Lowe, op. cit., p. 9.

of ground upon which to keep a cow and some pigs.[1] But even so this midland area was not, as were other districts in the south and east, the scene of particularly severe agricultural distress or discontent. The many small farmers in the three counties were a source of stability to society and were profiting from the unusually high prices of agricultural products.

The typical houses[2] were of brick and tile, though in Derbyshire and on the Derbyshire borders they were sometimes made of local stone. Some of the older, poorer cottages and barns were made of mud, but it could be said in 1798 that no recent buildings had been of these materials. New houses and barns were sometimes thatched, but less often than before. The ground floors were laid with stone or brick and the upper floors with plaster. Except in the case of gentlemen's seats, which, as we have seen, were especially numerous in this area, the buildings and offices were usually small, though by prevailing standards neat and well built. They were usually surrounded by a garden and sometimes by a larger meadow or pasture.

A large proportion of the country population, larger than was general in the country as a whole, was employed not at agriculture but at some trade. The chief trade of the district was that of framework knitting,[3] a trade associated with the counties ever since the Rev. Mr. Lee had invented the process in the reign of Queen Elizabeth. There were, however, also other trades, chiefly coal-mining, brewing, and, to a declining extent, cotton. The latter trade, and the woollen and worsted industry, which had had a minor seat in the district, had been driven away from it in the last two decades of the eighteenth century, largely because of the riotous opposition that had been manifested against

[1] Ibid., p. 140. [2] Ibid., p. 9.

[3] The standard authority for all problems connected with the Framework Knitting Industry is William Felkin's *History of the Machine Wrought Hosiery and Lace Trades*. Especially full on the technical side, Felkin's work is a contemporary and first-hand authority with regard to the period 1800 to 1850.

new machinery. Several Leicester firms which had been experimenting in the 1770's with new methods of spinning wool into worsted yarn had been driven by disturbances amongst their workpeople to Worcestershire and Yorkshire and even Aberdeen.[1] In the early nineteenth century Leicester hosiers had to be content to buy their yarn and other raw material in a distant market. By 1811 a visitor to the midlands would not have listed, as Robert Lowe did a dozen years earlier, cotton as a major local manufacture.[2]

The pre-eminent local manufacture by far was that of framework knitting. This industry, which was divided into two main branches, the hosiery and lace trades, had become increasingly centred in these three midland counties. In the early eighteenth century the chief seat of the industry had been London, where the old Stuart incorporated Framework Knitters Company[3] had had its head-quarters. There had been riots in London in 1710 and angry apprentices had broken more than 100 frames, the property of masters who disregarded the traditional limitation upon taking too many apprentices.[4] There must have been further similar trouble later, or the threat of it, though we have no records on the point, for the legislature in 1727 passed an act making framebreaking in the stocking industry in the metropolis an offence punishable with death.[5] Partly to escape legal and other limitations, and partly because production was cheaper there, the trade had moved during the first half of the eighteenth century from London to the region around Nottingham. By 1780 out of 20,000 frames in the country no less than 17,000 were said to be situated in the midlands.[6] This localization of the industry had become even more marked by 1812. In that year nearly 90 per cent. of all the frames in the

[1] Felkin, op. cit., pp. 229–30.
[2] Lowe, op. cit., p. 179.
[3] See 'The Framework Knitters Company', by J. D. Chambers, *Economica*, Nov. 1929.
[4] Felkin, op. cit., p. 227.
[5] Ibid., p. 228.
[6] Chambers, *Nottinghamshire in the Eighteenth Century*, p. 99.

United Kingdom, and more than 60 per cent. of the frames listed as being at work anywhere in the world, were said to be in the midlands.[1]

Of these frames 45 per cent. were in Leicestershire, 36 per cent. in Nottinghamshire, and 19 per cent. in Derbyshire.[2] Between them there was a certain amount of specialization. The Leicestershire trade was chiefly in wool. The cotton trade was concentrated in Nottinghamshire. The silk trade was divided between Nottingham and Derby.[3] The manufacture of the finer qualities and more expensive fashions was also increasingly carried on in Leicestershire, thereby giving that county an advantage over the others in the depression, which affected the cheaper branches of the manufacture most severely.[4]

No more than one frame in five, out of those in this area, was to be found in the three county towns.[5] The largest number of frames in any town, and the largest in proportion to that in the surrounding country districts, was to be found in Nottingham, which contained 2,600 frames, or 28 per cent. of those in the county as a whole. The proportion of Leicestershire frames in the town of Leicester was smaller, six frames being worked in the country to every one in town, and in Derby smaller still, hardly more than one frame in twelve being worked in the county town. Preponderantly the industry was a rural one, more than 82 per cent. of the frames in the three counties being scattered throughout the 253 manufacturing villages. Some of these local centres of the industry were large, Mansfield, for instance, having a population of more than 7,000,[6] and Sutton-in-Ashfield, another prominent centre of the industry, of more than 5,000. There were other considerable villages, Arnold, Basford, Bulwell, and a few

[1] Felkin, op. cit., p. 437, quoting Blackner.

[2] Ibid.

[3] Porter, op. cit., p. 383.

[4] Felkin, op. cit., p. 436.

[5] Ibid., p. 437.

[6] Lowe, op. cit., p. 177 et seq. gives the population of some Nottingham towns and villages in 1797. Census of 1811 shows growth in population since then.

more, with considerable numbers of stockingers, and with populations of 1,000 and upwards. The typical manufacturing village was, however, a small one, the 100 centres of the hosiery trade in Leicestershire in 1812 having only 96 frames, on the average, apiece, while the 74 in Nottinghamshire had only 89, and the 83 in Derbyshire only 52.[1]

This widely scattered manufacturing district, though distributed throughout this large number of villages in the three midland counties, had, nevertheless, a unity of its own. The framework knitting industry had a particular portion of each county for its own, and Nottingham for its industrial capital. Most of the frames in Nottinghamshire were to be found in the district to the north-west of the county town, in the two hundreds of Broxtowe, and particularly in the north hundred, and in the contiguous district over the Derbyshire border, which was really a part of the same manufacturing region.[2] The frames in Derbyshire were to be found mainly in the south-east corner of the county, near the Nottinghamshire border, between that and the county town. The frames in Leicestershire again, though less concentrated into a particular region, were still chiefly to be found in the northern part of the county, between the town of Leicester and the river Trent. The hosiery villages in each county were largely dependent upon the county town, in which the hosiers' warehouses were situated, from which the master stockingers received their raw material, and to which they took their finished goods for sale. The county towns were the centres in which hosiers and stockingers alike met for discussion of their common affairs,[3] the regulation of frame rents, wages, prices, &c. And of the three county towns Nottingham was industrially the most important.[4]

[1] Felkin, op. cit., p. 437.

[2] *Census Returns*, 1811; *Parl. Papers*, 1812, xi. 246 et seq.

[3] See advertisements frequently appearing in the local papers, especially the *Nottingham Journal* and *Review*.

[4] It was the seat of the committees of hosiers and stockingers con-

The industry not merely had two distinct branches, hosiery and lace; its personnel was divided into two distinct groups, hosiers and stockingers. The hosiers were the capitalists and dealers, the stockingers the craftsmen. The hosiers, who very often maintained offices in London as well as in Nottingham or one of the other county towns, one partner specializing in selling the finished product, the other handling relations with the master stockingers,[1] varied in wealth and status, some being wealthy merchants and exporters, long since advanced from the status of small town craftsmen, others being small men, recently working stockingers themselves, launching out in a modest way upon the business of selling as well as making hosiery and lace. They purchased the raw material, often, as we have seen, in a distant market. They gave it out to the master stockingers and lace workers to be made up into stockings and other hosiery products and lace. They received back the finished product in their warehouses or sent their agents around the country villages to collect it, deducting so much for wastage or for faults in the workmanship, and paying so much a piece or a dozen. They shipped the finished goods to London dealers, or to their London office, to be sold to consumers in the United Kingdom, on the Continent, or, as was increasingly the case, in the United States.[2]

The hosier was often, perhaps usually, also a large owner of frames. The stocking frame was a relatively simple machine, substantially unaltered in many years, and costing from ten to thirty pounds apiece.[3] Lace machines, of which a new and more complicated type was coming in around 1809–16, were more expensive.[4] Originally the stockingers had usually owned their own frames, though there had always been some large hosiers with numbers of

cerned with the Petitions and Bill of 1812 and 1819, and also of the more permanent Union of the men and Committee of the hosiers.

[1] Felkin, op. cit., p. 437.

[2] See Inquiry of 1812, op. cit.

[3] Coldham to Newcastle, Nov. 28, 1811, in H.O. 42. 119, and Becher to H.O., Feb. 11, 1812, in H.O. 42. 120.

[4] Ibid.

frames to let out to individual master stockingers. Even as late as 1800 it was said that very many Leicestershire stockingers did own their own frames.[1] But increasingly, especially in Nottinghamshire and Derbyshire, this was not the case. The master stockinger rented his frame or frames from a hosier, or from an independent owner of frames. He paid a varying rent per frame per week, sometimes whether the frame was at work or not. A typical figure for frame rent in these years was 1*s.* per frame per week.[2] Some hosiers, such as Mr. Hayne, one of the witnesses before the 1812 Parliamentary Committee inquiring into conditions in the industry, who owned £20,000 worth of frames, were said to wish to make no profit upon their frames, only to cover the cost of maintenance and depreciation.[3] It was generally desired that frame rents should be stabilized at some such figure as 7 per cent. on the value of the frame, or, as Gravener Henson, a great authority upon the industry, suggested, at 5 per cent. plus the cost of repairs or 8 per cent. in all.[4] But, despite the general feeling that the situation was intolerable, and despite the fact that frame rents, unlike other things, had universally been fixed in the industry by a regulation of the manufacturer,[5] no progress was made in getting such a standard generally accepted. Some frames paid as high a return as 30 per cent. on their real value.[6] Outsiders, with no previous or other connexion with or knowledge of the industry, were attracted to it and became large investors in machinery, which they let out at exorbitant rates to the unfortunate workmen. Particularly was this true after 1805, in which year by general agreement frame rents had

[1] Felkin, op. cit., p. 118, quoting Gardiner, *Music and Friends*, ii. 810, for state in 1814. See Report of Law Officers on application of hosiers as to their right to damage against the Hundred (H.O. 42. 141). 'Frames generally the property of the manufacturer, very seldom of the Labouring Mechanic.'

[2] Inquiry of 1812, op. cit., pp. 246–8.

[3] Ibid. and Hayne to H.O., Feb. 12, 1812, in H.O. 42. 131.

[4] Inquiry of 1812, pp. 246–8. [5] Ibid. [6] Ibid.

been raised, as a preferable method to a reduction of wages of meeting the exigencies of a declining market.[1] So far from benefiting the industry this agreement hurt it, outsiders being attracted by the large profit that was possible under the new frame rent, and a great speculation in frames, and consequent over-production, taking place.

This problem of frame rents, and the power over the worker that it gave to the frame owner, was one of the most bitter sources of grievance to the workers, and to the better hosiers, in the early years of the nineteenth century, and for long afterwards. Frame owners compelled stockingers who possessed machines of their own to rent others on threat, if they did not, of withholding work from them, so that their own frames would have to stand idle. Master stockingers were often compelled to pay rent on all their frames whether they had a workman upon them or no, and to rent more frames than they needed or could keep at work. When work was short they were often compelled to put their workmen on the hosiers' frames rather than on their own, so that the hosier, who had the whip-hand since he could give or withhold work at pleasure, could get his full rent, no matter how severe the depression in trade. Lace frame rents were especially exorbitant and machine frames generally were much more highly rented than plain frames.

Whether he owned his own frames or rented them from a hosier, or from an independent speculator in frames, and most master stockingers did both, the craftsman kept the machines in his own workshop, situated usually, in the midland area, at the top of his house.[2] It was estimated as late as 1845, when there was another parliamentary inquiry[3] into the condition of the framework knitters, that there were no less than 4,621 separate shops in Nottinghamshire,

[1] Felkin, op. cit., p. 436.

[2] See reports of outrages in Home Office Papers, particularly H.O. 42. 129 et seq.

[3] *Parl. Papers*, 1845.

with an average of only 3·25 frames per shop.[1] This average probably was true of 1811 as well as of 1845, though the condition of the more than 50,000 framework knitters[2] and their families was continuously declining throughout the fifty years from 1800. The typical master stockinger in 1811 lived in a midland village, in which there were 22 other master stockingers,[3] and, like them, had, on an average, from three to four frames at work in the shop on the second floor of his modest cottage, which, like that of his fellow villagers engaged in agriculture and other crafts, was a simple building of brick and tile, with floors of brick or, upstairs, of plaster.[4] He and his family and one or two apprentices or journeymen worked on these frames, when there was work to be had, from early morning to late at night, from dawn to dark, and, when necessary, also by candlelight.[5] They slept, masters and workmen often, though not always in the same building, in bedrooms adjoining or beneath the workshop.[6] They were less and less apt to have the time or the opportunity to cultivate a garden or tend to the pigs and cows that would once have surrounded their cottages and given them a subsidiary source of income. Agriculture was increasingly having less place for such survivors of the day of the open field village, and industry, with its declining earnings, was making year by year greater demands upon its workmen.

Earnings, not merely per workman or per frame but per family, were very small. Evidence given before the Parliamentary Committee in 1812 went to show that at that time in the plain silk branch average earnings were only 12*s.* clear of all deductions,[7] and that many families,

[1] Chambers, op. cit., p. 88.
[2] Felkin, op. cit., p. 239.
[3] Figure arrived at by dividing number of frames at work by number of villages and the average number of frames per shop (original statistics in Chambers, op. cit., p. 88, and Felkin, op. cit., p. 437).
[4] Lowe, op. cit., p. 9.
[5] See reports of Luddite attacks in H.O. 42. 129 et seq.
[6] Ibid.
[7] *Parl. Papers*, 1812, ii. 225.

especially in Nottingham, were not receiving more than 13*s.* a week.[1] Blackner, the local historian and himself a framework knitter of many years standing, stated that wages in the lace trade were no more than 14*s.* 6*d.* a week.[2] Felkin, at that time connected with a large Nottingham firm of hosiers, and the foremost authority upon all problems connected with the industry for the period 1800–50, gives an even lower estimate of average earnings in the cheaper and more crowded branches of the industry doing plain work, stating that many workers were only getting 7*s.* a week.[3] Although some of the hosiers presented rather contrary evidence, and proved that full earnings per frame per week in several firms had not declined since the opening of the century,[4] they were not able to controvert the general statement that wages on the whole were not merely low but lower, on the average, by about one-third, than they had been in the period 1806–7, and before.[5] For even when nominal wages were the same as they had been a deficiency of work kept down the actual earnings of the stockingers to a distressing level.

When it is remembered that the prices of every necessity of life were rising fast, so that even people whose nominal wages were rising found themselves with declining real wages,[6] it will be understood how very difficult was the situation of the framework knitters with nominal wages which were so much less than they had been before. A wage of 7*s.* or even 14*s.* 6*d.* per week was little enough for a stockinger and his family at a time when a quartern loaf of bread, which had once sold for 1*s.* 1*d.*, was selling for 1*s.* 5*d.* and even 1*s.* 8*d.*[7] It is difficult to see how these midland families, dependent upon this one industry, were able to maintain life upon so small a sum, which had often

[1] Ibid.
[2] Ibid., p. 232.
[3] Felkin, op. cit., p. 231.
[4] *Parl. Papers*, 1812, ii. 261.
[5] Ibid., pp. 225, 232 et seq.
[6] Bowley, in *Dictionary of Political Economy* (edited by Palgrave), p. 801.
[7] Knowles, op. cit., p. 366.

to be spread over the 5–6 mouths that the average household in England at that time contained.[1]

To make matters worse even these small wages were often paid not in money but in kind. The system of 'truck' or payment in goods,[2] which was an abuse present in many industries in the early nineteenth century, and which had been legislated against, so far as this particular industry was concerned, back in the previous century,[3] was still widely present, especially amongst the women employed as runners in the lace trade, and around Sutton-in-Ashfield. Many hosiers, like other employers, kept not merely a warehouse for the receipt of hosiery but a shop for the sale of provisions and other household necessities, and they paid their workpeople not in money but in orders upon this shop, which, as one might expect, often charged exorbitant prices for its goods. Others contented themselves, like one Nottingham hosier, whom the Committee of Framework Knitters in Nottingham investigated, with paying their stockingers in such articles as cloth and buttons. One man, who was owed £2 8*s*. (a fortnight's wages), by this hosier, was given cloth and buttons valued at £2 12*s*. 6*d*., but he could only sell them for 10*s*. 6*d*.[4] Stockingers were forced to all sorts of extremities, to paying local shopkeepers and even the doctor in the goods they received from the hosier, which they could only dispose of with difficulty and at a discount. The system of barter which thus developed was inconvenient and expensive. The hosier, to whom such a method of payment was cheaper, especially at a time when his stocks were a glut upon the market, than payment in money, was the only person who stood to gain by it. The workman found himself defrauded out of a large part of his earnings, since no shopkeeper would accept, and no pawnbroker lend money upon, the goods which were the stockingers only currency at their full value. In Nottingham, in

[1] Porter, op. cit., p. 90.
[2] *Parl. Papers*, 1812, ii. 239 et seq.
[3] Ibid.
[4] Ibid.

Sutton-in-Ashfield, in Skegby, in Mansfield, and in other towns and villages in this district in which this method of payment was employed, it was one of the major grievances of the population.[1]

Akin to it were the other frauds and abuses[2] of which the stockingers (and many of the better hosiers) complained. The hosier had the whip-hand over the worker. Schedules of prices and deductions were seldom published and were frequently changed. The worker could seldom know at the time he was given his raw material to work up into stockings just how much he was going to get for his labour when he took the finished goods back to the warehouse of the hosier. A certain allowance, ¼ of an ounce per pound, was traditionally allowed the workman for the shrinkage and wastage of material during manufacture.[3] Certain deductions were also traditionally allowed from the price he received per piece of lace or per dozen stockings on account of poor workmanship and of defects of one kind or another in the finished product and of late delivery. But it was at the discretion of the hosier what deduction was allowed the stockinger and what was charged to him. Many stockingers complained that they were defrauded, raw material being given out wet so that it might weigh more, and register a greater shrinkage than that allowed, for which the worker could be charged. They complained that wholly unreasonable deductions were made from the standard price on account of imaginary imperfections in the finished product. Hosiers were said to pay the price appropriate for simple, plain varieties of work, quickly and cheaply manufactured, for full fashioned and complicated work, which ought to be paid for at a higher rate.

This latter abuse was particularly complained of in the lace trade, where the measurement of the finished article, and determination of its quality and value, was a complicated process. The workmen claimed that there was an

[1] Hayne to H.O., Feb. 12, 1812, in H.O. 42. 131.

[2] *Parl. Papers*, 1812, ii. 22 et seq.

[3] Chambers, op. cit., p. 122.

infallible instrument of measurement, the rack,[1] which counted the number of holes, or courses, in the lace, which they wished the hosiers to be forced to employ. The latter, without giving any very good reason for their policy, were unwilling to make wide use of this machine, and clung to their prerogative of fixing arbitrarily the value and the price of the articles brought in to them by the master craftsmen.

An added source of grievance to the master stockinger was the amount of time he had to spend in coming into town to get his supplies of material, and to dispose of his finished goods at the warehouse of the hosier, and the long hours he was often kept hanging about the warehouse, waiting his turn and having his stockings and lace counted and valued. Some hosiers had agents who travelled around the country villages, distributing raw material and orders for goods and collecting the finished articles. Some had offices and warehouses in the larger country towns. There was also a class of middlemen, or 'bag' hosiers, in existence, who had no established business or warehouse of their own, but who went about the country peddling hosiery, buying goods from small stockingers and selling them to the larger hosiers. In these various ways it was possible for the master stockinger to save the time he would otherwise waste going into Nottingham, or Leicester, or Derby, to deal directly with a large hosier. Unfortunately, however, these smaller men were often the most unscrupulous; one did better, in spite of the waste of time and the expense of the journey, by going directly to a large, responsible Nottingham hosier. Many a small, innocent stockinger found himself cheated by a 'bag' hosier, who had talked so cunningly to him in the ale-house of his local village, and learnt that it was better after all to deal with the distant, superior, formal hosier in the county town. Many a large hosier, anxious to deal fairly by his men, found himself hurt by the competition and undercutting of these lesser,

[1] *Parl. Papers*, 1812, ii. 216.

irresponsible, unscrupulous hosiers and 'bag' hosiers, and had to lower his own standards and deal hardly and unfairly with his stockingers, or go under, such was the pressure of competition.

For it is clear that by 1810 and 1811 conditions in the trade were growing chaotic.[1] Not merely was the condition of the stockinger worse than it had been in the not so distant past, the condition of the hosier was serious also. With regard to the situation of both it is important not to fall into the easy mistake of imagining that that past had been any sort of 'golden age'. The conditions revealed in the parliamentary inquiry of 1778,[2] when midland stockingers had appealed to Parliament for an alleviation of their sufferings and regulation of the industry, and when, following the defeat of the consequent Bill, there had been a great frenzy of frame breaking in Nottingham,[3] alone should prove that all talk of the 'easy prosperity' of the framework knitter in the eighteenth century was exaggerated. From 1750 onwards for more than thirty years there had been distress in the industry, and discontent, which issued, at periods of especially poor trade, like that from 1776 to 1778, in disturbance. Even after these continual disputes between hosiers and stockingers over wages had been temporarily settled by an agreement to abide by a list of prices that was drawn up in 1787[4] there had been many stockingers whose situation was distressing, and many periods of poor trade and low earnings. Some few, lucky stockingers for a period of years, and a larger, though still a minority, section of the industry in years of good trade, might have been as prosperous as those of whom the Rev. Mr. Becher talks,[5] who developed profligate habits, and rioted away their ample

[1] Every witness so agrees, Newcastle, Coldham, Cartwright, Becher, Felkin, Henson, and many of the witnesses before the Parliamentary Committee on the Stockingers Petitions in May 1812.

[2] See *Journals of the House of Commons.*

[3] Felkin, op. cit., p. 228.

[4] Ibid., p. 232.

[5] Becher to H.O., Feb. 1812, in H.O. 42. 120.

living at the ale-house, with no thought of putting by for old age and bad times. The fact that the trade expanded so much, and that agriculture was almost denuded of labourers, as some witnesses say was the case,[1] is some evidence that the trade of stockinger was, at any rate by the standards of the time, considered an enviable one. But it is a mistake to think of it, even in its most lush periods of prosperity, as being in any way idyllic.

It had, however, obviously been better off in the latter years of the eighteenth century than it was in 1811. The decline in trade had set in even before the turn of the century,[2] though its effects were not obvious until a year or two afterwards. The decline in the number of different fashions manufactured was one of the first signs of the coming depression. Ever since 1780 the number of varieties had been diminishing. By 1800, however, there were still seventeen different varieties left.[3] The decline continued much more rapidly in the next decade and by 1810 a great number of workmen, originally employed at full fashioned, highly skilled work, had been thrown back into the manufacture of plain hosiery, a more crowded and less well paid branch of the trade. Partly this decline was due to a simple change of fashion, to the coming in of boots and even long trousers in the place of stockings and knee breeches. Partly it was due to the war, and the need for personal and public economy. Whatever its cause its effects upon the hosiery industry were disastrous.

To make matters worse there had, in the years of good trade before the turn of the century, been an alarming over-expansion of the industry.[4] Not merely had out-

[1] *Parl. Papers*, 1812, ii. 239.

[2] Felkin, op. cit., pp. 434 et seq.

[3] Ibid., p. 434.

[4] Mr. Becher (to H.O., Feb. 11, 1812 in H.O. 42. 120) says 'the reduction of the standard and structure to normal would in any case have caused trouble'. Mr. Cartwright (letter to *Nottingham Review*, Jan. 3, 1812 in H.O. 42. 119) says 'even when the trade was good, it was always rather overstocked with hands which kept wages low'. Mr. Coldham (letter to H.O. undated but evidently late in December 1811, in H.O.

siders been attracted into the trade as speculators in frames, they had been drawn in as apprentices. Master stockingers, who received a premium for every apprentice they trained, found it profitable to take a large number of apprentices, who could, also, while learning the trade, help the stockinger keep his frames at work. A framework knitter at Nottingham in the early years of the nineteenth century is reported by Felkin to have had twenty-four apprentices.[1] Two framework knitters at Hinckley had done even better (or worse) than this and had 100 between them.[2] The trade could not absorb, even at the best of times, such an unreasonable influx of new recruits, nor could any stockinger really give an adequate schooling to so many. Many of these new pseudo-stockingers had no real mastery of their craft. They gave to their own apprentices a knowledge and competence still more inadequate. The whole trade suffered by the bad character and the bad workmanship of many of these new recruits.

In other ways, also, the trade had become top-heavy.[3] Many hosiers had, in order to meet the demands of a boom market, resorted to old, cheap, shoddy methods of production. Five different and discredited such methods were listed by the petitioners from the industry to the House of Commons in 1812:[4]

Single-press cotton lace.
Two course hole warp net.
Single cotton, single or double spun.
Single worsted from one roving.
Cut-up stockings, made in one piece and cut to the shape.

Single press was lace looped once only and so loosely knotted and easily unravelled.[5] Single cotton and single thread, like single worsted, was yarn of a single strand, a weak material long since discarded by all the better

42. 118) agrees that even in prosperous times there had been 'too many frames and too many hands'.

[1] Felkin, op. cit., p. 435.

[2] Ibid.

[3] See p. 37, n. 1, and p. 38, n. 4.

[4] *Parl. Papers*, 1812, ii. 206.

[5] Ibid., p. 288.

hosiers in favour of double or triple thread, several strands intertwined to make a stronger thread. Two course hole, like single press, was a cheap, easy way of looping the strands in the manufacture of lace. All these various frauds were difficult to distinguish upon first glance, especially for laymen with untrained eyes. When stiffened with starch and gum for the market it was very difficult to distinguish the fraudulent article from the good. Introduced at first to take an easy advantage of an expanding market these cheap goods had for a time the effect of expanding the trade. Once their inferior quality became known, however, they had the effect of destroying the confidence of the consumer, with the result that the trade very rapidly declined. Particularly in the lace trade had this process extended so far that it could be said in 1812 'there (was) not one fourth of the lace frames at work'.[1] People would sooner give seven shillings for a yard of thread or Buckinghamshire lace than give a midland hosier sixpence for his best lace, though the latter, when it was not fraudulent, was generally considered nearly as good as Buckinghamshire lace (which was hand-made upon the old pillow system).[2]

Cut-up stockings were manufactured of large pieces of knitted material, manufactured on large frames, and cut out and sewn to the shape of the foot. If the stockings were sewn too near the seam they split easily, if too far from it, then there was a bulge up the back of the stocking and they were bulky and uncomfortable. In any case they soon lost shape. They were, however, easily and cheaply made and, so long as there was a demand for them, they returned a good profit to the hosier and to the worker. So much was this the case that not merely were old, wide frames, once used for the manufacture of pantaloons, turned to the manufacture of knitted goods by the piece (the market for knitted pantaloons having declined)[3] but a new species

[1] *Parl. Papers*, 1812, ii. 288. [2] Ibid.

[3] Felkin, op. cit., p. 435.

of wide frame[1] was introduced to take advantage of the great demand. These wide frames, which were still in 1812 felt to be new, though they had been in operation for a dozen years, had since 1803–4 largely superseded the narrow frames previously most commonly employed. Both sorts of wide frame, new and old, were, mainly because of the cut-up goods manufactured upon them, bitterly unpopular.[2]

The objection of the workers to these new, and, as they felt, fraudulent methods of production was twofold. They noticed, and resented, the decline in the market for lace and hosiery products, which they felt to be mainly due to these poor quality goods which were destroying the confidence of the consumer.[3] They resented also the displacement of skilled labour that resulted from these practices, poorly trained stockingers being able to make these articles, and poor prices being paid for them. The pride of the workman in his craft, which was felt both by the better hosiers and by the leading stockingers, was insulted by these frauds, which were besides an added opportunity for unscrupulous hosiers to defraud not merely the consumer but also the workman, who, as fashions were taken out of the hose, and fewer varieties were manufactured, was thrown back upon poorly paid hack work.

The hosiers were divided in their feelings about these things.[4] Some of them resented them and tried their hardest to get their colleagues to discontinue them. A group of hosiers in 1809 announced that they would have to reduce wages 3*s*. a dozen if the workers could not or would not secure a reduction of frame rents and the cessation of cut-up spurious work.[5] Attempts to secure the same end continued throughout the next three years.[6]

[1] Ibid.

[2] See *Declaration of the Framework Knitters* and *General Ludd's Triumph*, anonymous pamphlets sent to H.O. by Coldham, Jan. 14, 1812, in H.O. 42. 119.

[3] See *Parl. Papers*, 1812, ii. 213 et seq.

[4] Ibid., pp. 288 et seq.

[5] Felkin, op. cit., p. 232.

[6] See *Nottingham Journal* and *Review* for these years.

In 1811 a leading Nottingham firm, that of Brocksopp and Parker, agreed with their men to pay unabated wages provided the latter could get other hosiers to pay the same price and to discontinue the manufacture of cut-up articles.[1] Such hosiers were as convinced as any of the stockingers of the damage that cheap, fraudulent methods of production were doing to the trade. Other hosiers, however, felt differently. They argued that there was a demand for cheap goods.[2] The American market, for instance, and especially the Canadian, had taken large quantities of cut-up goods, particularly gloves and mittens, and orders were repeated. The Mediterranean and Levant trade positively preferred single thread articles, they did not want expensive articles which lasted a long time. The large Leicester cut-up trade was said to be chiefly for the export market and orders were repeated. If cheap methods of production were to be put down such hosiers felt that even the little trade there was left to the industry would disappear. Even the hosiers who objected to cut-ups as a general rule, and particularly in the case of stockings, were inclined to condone them in certain cases, as for instance gloves, mittens, and pantaloons. Most hosiers would have agreed with the petitioners against the Framework Knitting Bill which was before Parliament in the summer of 1812, that all that was really necessary was that the cheap or fraudulent article should be clearly marked as such; if the customer could know at once what he was buying the manufacturer of better and more expensive varieties would not be penalized. The trouble was that it was impossible to secure such a regulation and in the absence of it the poor article undersold the better and drove it out of circulation just as bad money drives out good.

The result of these various abuses, all of which economized labour and cheapened production, was to accentuate still further the existing over-expansion of the trade.

[1] Felkin, op. cit., p. 240. [2] *Parl. Papers*, 1812, ii. 288 et seq.

Every one was agreed that some reduction was necessary,[1] that somehow or other the output of the industry must be cut down, the number of frames and the profit per frame reduced, the number of stockingers and apprentices limited. As the market declined after 1800 conditions went from bad to worse. These new methods, introduced to take advantage of an expanding market, were continued to minimize the losses consequent upon a declining one. To deal with one, and that the oldest of these abuses, that of 'colting' or taking too many apprentices, a cause of frame breaking as long ago as 1710, an attempt was made to secure the intervention of Parliament[2] to enforce the old regulation that no stockinger could take more than two apprentices at a time. The petitioners were recommended to appeal to the old Framework Knitters Company, which had fallen on lean and evil days and had even neglected to elect overseers and other officers. The old organization took on a new lease of life. Officers were elected, two each for Nottingham and Leicester, one each for Mansfield, Sutton, Hinckley, Leake, and Loughborough, in 1804.[3] Men joined the company in many midland villages at the, for them, heavy subscription rate of £1 13*s.* 6*d.* a head. A test action was brought by the Company against a stockinger, a Mr. Payne of Burbage, near Leicester, who had disregarded the Company's regulations and taken too many apprentices. After a long, bitter, expensive case the courts awarded 1*s.* damages, which was equivalent really to a verdict for Payne and against the Company.[4] The attempt to secure regulation in this manner broke down.

A second attempt to deal with a different aspect of the matter was made in 1805.[5] By mutual agreement between hosiers and stockingers it was, as we have noticed above, decided, rather than reduce wages, to increase frame rents. This merely accentuated the difficulty, more speculators, not being genuine members of the trade, and not therefore

[1] See p. 37, n. 1, and p. 38, n. 4.
[2] Felkin, op. cit., p. 435.
[3] Ibid.
[4] Ibid., p. 436.
[5] Ibid.

affected by the agreement to keep wages above what would have been the otherwise necessary level, coming into the business and letting out frames in order to make a cheap profit in this way.

The situation in the industry became still more chaotic after 1807, in which year the old agreement with regard to wages, negotiated in 1787 and continued for the next twenty years, expired.[1] There was now nothing to prevent wages finding their natural, economic level, nothing to hold the more unscrupulous hosiers in check. And all attempts to negotiate a new wage scale for the industry, which were widely supported by responsible hosiers as well as stockingers, broke upon the rock of the impossibility of getting the lesser hosiers to agree to any regulations whatever, for the limitation of apprentices, the reduction of frame rents, the elimination of cut-ups and other fraudulent work, the maintenance of a fair wage and other conditions of work, the restriction of the trade and of frame owning to people with a real interest other than purely speculative and financial in it. A considerable, general decline in wages, amounting to about 33 per cent., and an even greater decline in the amount of work available, took place in the ensuing years.[2] The disputes between stockingers and hosiers, and between different sections of hosiers, took on an increasingly bitter, desperate tone.

The general decline in trade due to causes other than a change in fashion and the effect of poor quality production, due that is, like the decline in other industries, to the high taxation and the diminishing general purchasing capacity of the country, and to the restriction of foreign markets consequent upon Napoleon's Continental System, was somewhat offset by a sudden expansion of the South American trade.[3] When the British occupation of Argentina in 1806 opened up the markets of South America to

[1] Felkin, op. cit., p. 232 and *Parl. Papers*, 1812, ii. 225. [2] Ibid.

[3] Ibid., and speeches of Ministers in Parliament, Feb. 1812; in Hansard.

British commerce there was a great excitement of trade. Great shipments went out in 1807 and were repeated in 1808. It was then seen that the whole trade had been a dead loss, payments were not being received for the first shipments, even fifteen and eighteen months after dispatch. For the hosiery industry, as for other industries, the brief opening of the United States market, which was very important, especially to Leicester,[1] and to other midland districts dependent normally upon an export demand, was a welcome respite. The complete closing of this market by the Non-Intercourse Act in February 1811 had the effect of upsetting the whole top-heavy structure of the trade. Warehouses were glutted. Demand was non-existent. For more than a year, until the repeal of the Orders in Council, being quickly followed by the break-up of the Continental System and Napoleon's Russian defeat, an almost unexampled depression rested upon the hosiery districts with even greater severity than upon the rest of the country.

The distress was very real. The number of hands out of work was very great, amounting probably, for months at a time, to more than a fifth of those normally engaged in the industry.[2] Many other workers, a majority of the whole number, were able to get only irregular and inadequate employment. The wages, as we have seen, even of those in full employment were less than they had been. And the price level was unprecedently high, affecting the midlands fully as much as it affected the rest of the country, this area being less able even than others to profit by importations, and being, as a great agricultural area, severely affected by the terrible run of bad harvests, of which that of 1811 was one of the worst. The hosiery villages, with their 80–100 stockingers, masters, journeymen, and apprentices, and their families, fully as depressed as their fellow villagers, small farmers and farm labourers feeling the effects of a long succession of bad seasons,

[1] *Parl. Papers*, 1812, ii. 285.

[2] Conant and Baker to H.O., Feb. 6, 1812, in H.O. 42. 120.

were the scene of very great distress. No one had accumulated any reserves for such an emergency, the high prices and high taxes of these years making such a policy difficult, even if it had not been alien to the temperament of the average framework knitter. The Poor Law, with its now general habit of paying allowances to workers whose wages fell below a certain standard, or who were unemployed, had pauperized the population, keeping down wages and discouraging thrift. In a time of distress like that which the hosiery districts, even more than the rest of the country, were experiencing in 1811, the great mass of the population had nothing to look to other than charity, public or private.

Private charity there was forthcoming in considerable, though hardly in adequate, measure in the following year, 1812.[1] But the wealthier classes, themselves hard pressed by the pressure of trade depression and bank failures and bad harvests, not to mention war taxes and prices, were a little slow to recognize the pending emergency. They needed to have their attention brought to the condition of the workers by something more dramatic than silent suffering. They were not quick enough with their help in 1811 to ward off disturbances. The Poor Law also, strained beyond all precedent, was a somewhat inadequate solvent to distress. It was not organized to take care of such a tragic situation, of emergencies such as that which confronted it in the winter of 1811, and even more in that of 1812, when more than 15,000 persons, or almost one-half of the population, were in receipt of public relief in the three parishes of Nottingham alone.[2]

There was therefore in the years from 1807 onwards, and especially between February 1811 and June 1812, a situation in the hosiery districts which contained the seeds of widespread disorder. The industry upon which a great part of the population depended was not merely, like other

[1] See *Nottingham Journal* for May 1812.

[2] Felkin, op. cit., p. 231.

national industries, affected by the general depression, it was slipping from its former position in any case, and was riddled with disputes. Some sections of it were better off than others, and some neighbourhoods; the manufacture of various finer varieties, raised cords, braces and cravats made on Dawson's wheels, special worsteds, &c., which was largely confined to Leicester and its environs, paying from 5 to 50 per cent. better wages,[1] as well as affording more adequate employment, than other less skilled sections of the industry, in the neighbourhood of Nottingham, depending upon plain work. Unemployment and under-employment, which were general, were worse in the district to the north of Nottingham than elsewhere in the region.

It was in this area also that negotiations between hosiers and stockingers with regard to wages, frame rents, and cut-ups and other fraudulent work, had been carried especially far. It is clear that for several years prior to 1811 there had been continual meetings in Nottingham between different representatives of the industry[2] in order to try to end these causes of friction and sources of grievance. Time and again agreements appeared to be in sight, only to break-down because a minority of the trade, consisting of small, unscrupulous hosiers, would not come into line.[3] Things had reached a pass when hosiers and stockingers alike might have been forgiven for losing patience and for thinking that negotiations would never get anywhere; recalcitrant hosiers would never listen to reason. Some of the better hosiers, hard pressed by the competition of this irreconcilable minority, were being forced to tell their men that their ability to continue to pay the old wages and employ the old methods was dependent upon the whole trade being brought into line and forced to maintain the same standard. The stockingers were finding them-

[1] Ibid., p. 436.

[2] See issues of Nottingham Papers and also *Parl. Papers*, 1812, ii. 222 and 259; also Felkin, op. cit., p. 240.

[3] Felkin, op. cit., p. 230.

selves faced with an extension of the evils of which they complained, with wage-cutting even on the part of the better hosiers, with whom they had always been able to agree, unless they should be able to coerce the minority to come into line. There was a positive inducement to the distressed operatives to forsake negotiation for violence, peaceful methods having so patently failed to secure any improvement of conditions. Parliament, the Framework Knitters Company, and agreements within the trade, all had been tried in order to bring to an end these long-standing abuses, 'colting', 'truck', 'cut-ups', wide frames, excessive frame rents, speculation in frames, reductions in wages, &c. All had failed.

The midlands, and especially the Nottingham hosiery district, contained in 1811 fuel for a dangerous conflagration.

III

THE NORTH OF ENGLAND

North-west of the hosiery districts, across the Pennine chain of hills, which separated southern from northern England, lay the other main seat of Luddism, and the chief centre of the new industrial England of the later nineteenth century. The rough, hilly moorlands of Yorkshire and Lancashire and that part of Cheshire bordering upon Lancashire had been largely deserted in the Middle Ages, and even on into Stuart times. Their population had been small. Industries had been lacking and the soil was adequate only for a poor, sparse agricultural population. Communications had been very bad and towns were small, self-contained, and widely separated from one another. There had been nothing to indicate the future importance of this long-neglected region, with only the sheep who wandered up and down its many lonely, lovely dales to keep it from being forgotten by the rich, populous, easy-going south. Life in the north was hard, both because the land was barren and because the weather was damp and cold. A peculiar, sturdy, persistent character was developed by the hardy northern people, shepherds and woollen merchants and men-at-arms, but it had not yet been given an opportunity of dominating the rest of the country.

The rise of this region was indeed one of the outstanding results of the industrial revolution, which completely transferred the balance of power as of population from the south-east to the north-west. It had by no means been completed by 1810. Lancashire was only just passing Middlesex in point of population.[1] But it had gone far. First the woollen, then the cotton, and finally the coal-mining and other industries took a hold of this district. The wool, for which the Yorkshire dales had always been famous, began even in Tudor times to be made up at home,

[1] Smart, *Economic Annals of the Nineteenth Century*, p. 289.

instead of being shipped to Norwich or Bristol or London for manufacture in those southern regions in which the medieval clothing industry of England had had its chief centres. As the eighteenth century advanced more and more the clothing industries of East Anglia, whose speciality was worsted, and of the west country, Gloucestershire, Wiltshire, and Somerset, which produced chiefly woollen goods, lost ground as compared with that of the West Riding of Yorkshire. By 1810 the woollen industry of the north was definitely predominant. Cotton also, a new industry, took hold of the north. Lancashire and the adjacent parts of Cheshire became as famous for their cottons as Yorkshire was for its woollens and worsteds. A third textile industry, that of silk, for which Cheshire was to be famous, was beginning to take on. Chemical, dyeing, and other finishing trades subsidiary to these great textile industries, and also coal-mining and canal and road building, those essential servants of the industrial advance, were pushed forward. A great network of trades, with its own banks, and merchants and even shipping, was growing up in the north, centring upon the major northern towns, Manchester, Liverpool, and Leeds, and being less and less dependent upon London and the south.

By 1811 almost one-sixth of the entire population of England lived in this area. It contained a great number of large and growing towns. Manchester and Liverpool, the largest cities in the country, except for London, had each more than 100,000 inhabitants. Leeds had more than 60,000.[1] Other towns, Huddersfield, Bolton, Stockport, had populations of 15,000 and upwards. And there were many more towns, Macclesfield, Oldham, Middleton, and others, in close contact with these larger centres and already themselves well started on that phenomenal period of growth which was to cover this whole region with a forest of chimneys. The older towns, Chester, Lancaster, and even York, for long the metropolis of northern England,

[1] Moxon, *Population Returns for 1831*, p. 25.

were being left behind by the newer, drabber industrial towns, many of which had not yet been given any official recognition at all, and were, like Manchester, just overgrown manors. Far more than was the case in the midlands, or elsewhere in the country, was the tendency in this area for the population, and for industry, to become urban, especially in the district between Manchester and Stockport, which was fast becoming one continuous manufacturing area.

This tendency was not yet, however, by any means complete. The woollen industry was still mainly a rural, as well as a domestic or small workshop, industry. Even the cotton manufacture was carried on more often than not in small establishments rather than in large ones, and in the country rather than in the town. The chief source of power was still water rather than steam, and water power was to be found in the rural valleys, along the banks of the many tumbling streams which ran down from the Pennines, rather than in the towns. The factory system also had not yet come in at all widely, except in cotton spinning. The typical Lancashire man and lass had not yet become a labourer in a great urban mill. He was in 1811 still just as likely to be a hand weaver working at home, in a damp cellar or a dark shed, in what used to be a country village and had not yet become, for all the dreary extension of bricks and mortar which had shut it off from the open country, legally or from the point of view of administration, a town. He was still, even if he were living in one of the larger of these mushroom towns, likely to be a countryman in outlook, not yet used to the conditions of city life. He was still near enough to open country, to the moors which surrounded each of these towns, and in which discontented mobs could gather and hold secret meetings,[1] to be able to escape from the monotony of

[1] It is noteworthy how many disturbances in the north originated in the moors, as those in Nottinghamshire originated in the forest, outside but near the main towns.

hard streets. He was still able to breath clean air and to see green fields, since factory chimneys were very few and far between.

This great manufacturing district, becoming increasingly industrial and urban, and already more so than most other parts of England, was drawing in its rapidly increasing population from many parts of the country, but especially from Ireland.[1] These immigrants, and again especially the Irish, were often undisciplined, little used to the conditions of city or factory life, an easy prey to the agitator and the demagogue. Perhaps because so many of them were new-comers to the area, and had already travelled so far, they seem to have been less rooted to one place, and more ready to travel from one town to another,[2] and to keep up a regular contact with their fellow workers elsewhere, than were the inhabitants of the midlands. Again and again in connexion with these northern towns is it reported that people from out of town[3] were the prime movers in some disturbance, or that delegates of the trade societies had been coming and going between one town and another.

More than other parts of the country also this region seems to have been dependent upon a foreign market. The cotton industry, of course, got its raw material from abroad, and it was also accustomed to sell abroad a large part, from one-third to one-sixth of its products.[4] Even the woollen industry, drawing much of its raw material from domestic sources and selling a considerable proportion of

[1] Lloyd to H.O., Feb. 26, 1812, in H.O. 42. 120. Lloyd is also a witness to the share of the Irish immigrants in the disorders of the time. There was also much talk, some of which he repeats, of delegates from Ireland visiting the north in 1811 and 1812, and again later.

[2] There was obviously contact between the 'committees' of the disaffected in Bolton, Stockport, and Manchester. See confession of Thomas Whittaker in H.O. 42. 121.

[3] e.g. at Macclesfield, April 1812; see *Manchester Exchange Herald*, April 21, 1812.

[4] See petitions to Parliament 1811 and 1812 and evidence before the Committee to consider petitions for the repeal of the Orders in Council, *Parl. Papers*, 1812, iii.

its products at home, was increasingly, both as regards supplies of wool and sales of cloth, dependent upon foreign conditions. Witnesses before the House of Commons Committees upon the Orders in Council in 1808 and 1812 speak emphatically of the vital importance of a foreign market to all these northern industries, which were accustomed to sell a great proportion, and the vital margin, of their production abroad, on the continent of Europe, in the Mediterranean or Levant, and in North and South America. Conditions abroad, the closing of the Continent by Napoleon's decrees and of North America in retaliation for the Orders in Council, even more than the pressure of war taxation at home, affected the well-being of the northern, manufacturing population, even more markedly than they did that of the country as a whole.[1]

Evidences of depression of trade and of distress throughout this area in 1811, and for a year or two before, are easy to find. Petitions poured in from the cotton districts to Parliament every year. An address from Bolton in 1811[2] tried to attract the attention of the Government 'to the frightful situation of that valuable part of the people the COTTON WEAVERS'. The Stockport weavers, having applied to the magistrates for redress, had been advised by them to apply to the Government. A deputation went up to London and interviewed the Home Secretary, but returned only with the melancholy advice to the men that they should have patience.[3] In February 1812 there was said to be 'not more than half work in the cotton trade'.[4] Conditions had been almost as bad for a full year. A similar state of things existed in the woollen industry around Leeds. A leading manufacturer there talked of 'numbers of hands being out of employment'.[5] At the same

[1] Ibid.

[2] In letter from Hamill to Ainsworth, April 19, 1811, in H.O. 42. 115.

[3] Pamphlet, *The Beggar's Complaint against Rack-Rent Landlords . . . also some observations on the Conduct of the Luddites*, Sheffield, 1812, pp. 106–7.

[4] Fletcher to H.O., Feb. 25, 1812, in H.O. 42. 120.

[5] Oates, Wood, and Smithson to Ryder, Jan. 22, 1812, in H.O. 42. 119.

time in Liverpool there was an increase of the number on the Poor Rate of from 8,000 to 15,350, showing an alarming growth in the extent of unemployment.[1] In Bolton, according to Brougham, no less than 3,000 individuals out of a population of 17,000 were in the spring of 1812 in need of relief, and only 300 were able to obtain it.[2]

Unemployment and under-employment were not the only source of distress, the rise in prices and the decline in wages which were reported were in themselves enough to cause unprecedented suffering. It was reported in Stockport that a cotton weaver in full work could only get 9*s.* clear earnings per week upon which to support his family, after working 16 hours a day for six days a week in order to earn that pittance.[3] According to General Maitland prices throughout the north had risen on an average one-third and wages had fallen in the same proportion. A weaver who could once have got 31*s.* 6*d.* a week could now often get only 10*s.*, for which he had to work 'six days in the week and hard'. Potatoes and oatmeal were the staple diet of the workers, who could seldom if ever afford meat, and potatoes now (in May 1812) cost 1*d.* a pound as against the old price of 3 pounds a 1*d.*[4]

It is clear that this decline in wages was not wholly due to the war and to the cessation of the American demand, which were the major causes of the depression so far as the country as a whole was concerned. There is some evidence that wages of hand-loom weavers, facing the competition of the new steam looms, were continuously declining from about 1805 onwards. Some figures quoted by Porter[5] give as an average weekly wage for hand-loom weavers at Bolton for 1805 25*s.*, 1806 22*s.*, 1807 18*s.*, 1809 16*s.*, 1810 (due, probably, to the improved American demand) 19*s.* 6*d.*, 1811 and 1812 14*s.* This steady decline, though

[1] Tooke, op. cit., p. 330. [2] *Parl. Debates*, xxiii, 1014 et seq.

[3] Lloyd to H.O., March 3, 1812, in H.O. 40. 1.

[4] Maitland to H.O., May 3, 1812, in H.O. 40. 1.

[5] Porter, op. cit., p. 49.

arrested for a year or two after 1813, wages picking up again in 1814 to almost their original figure of 25*s*. per week, was continued again afterwards, so that a nadir of 9*s*. a week was reached in 1818.

The later inquiries into conditions of the hand-loom weavers show that this drop was permanent and was largely due to the competition of machine weaving. Similar figures are available for Stockport,[1] where the price for weaving 24 square yards of cambric fell from 25*s*. in 1802 to 10*s*. in 1811 and 1812, a tremendous fall which was clearly partly, if not chiefly, due to the competition of the new steam looms, and which was continued.

Even so, and in spite of the fact that there were further causes to bring distress upon particular classes of workers, the general situation was obviously very serious, and would have caused trouble quite apart from such matters as the introduction of new machinery. Lancashire and Yorkshire were particularly hard hit by the Continental System and the Orders in Council, and even more by the depression of 1810 and the cessation of the American trade in 1811. Merchants could not dispose of their goods. Mills were running half time and middlemen giving out half work. Great numbers of men were out of work and prices were so high, and wages so much reduced, that even those in work could not earn enough to keep their homes together and their families fed. As the principal of a Manchester firm writing to a London business house in 1812 well said, when 'an honest, industrious fellow by hard labour cannot get bread much less clothes for himself and children' things are getting to 'the point beyond which human nature cannot bear'.[2]

Employers and employed, magistrates and newspaper-men, all recognized the gravity of the situation, though no one knew how to handle it. The Bolton magistrates toyed with the idea of reviving the old Statute of Artificers,[3] soon

[1] Ibid., p. 298. [2] J. Meyer, Feb. 11, 1812, in H.O. 42. 120.
[3] Fletcher to H.O., April 11, 1812, in H.O. 40. 1.

to be repealed for ever, and rating wages. The manufacturers admitted that a 5 per cent. increase in prices would not affect the demand and it would allow a 15 per cent. increase in wages. The necessities of the workman, caught between the upper and nether millstones of declining wages and advancing prices, might thus be relieved 'without injury to his employer'. The Stockport magistrates,[1] though not daring to go so far, apparently used their influence to help the distressed workers in any way they could, and forwarded their petitions to the Home Secretary. The latter,[2] however, like the Council of Trade[3] in dealing with similar petitions from Bolton weavers a year before, was strongly opposed to any interference in the normal working of the laws of supply and demand, wages must be left to find their own level.

Meetings of masters and men, together and separately, were held in the leading towns.[4] There were public meetings, like that in Manchester, to protest against prevailing conditions, which was dispersed by the constables and the dragoons, Colonel Hanson, a prominent sympathizer with the operative's cause, being actually imprisoned for his share in the affair.[5] Meetings of a more secret nature of delegates from the different towns and trades were held to discuss the possibility of a general 'turn out' or strike.[6] The various trade societies, which had existed for many years, and had tried to keep up the standard of manufacturing wages,[7] were especially active but entirely unsuccessful.

It was against such a background of general distress and discontent, from which all the trades of the country, but

[1] Lloyd to H.O., Feb. 26, 1812, in H.O. 42. 120.

[2] H.O. to Fletcher, April 14, 1812, in H.O. 79. 2.

[3] *Parl. Debates*, xix. 1017 and xx. 339, 608 et seq. See also letter from James Hamill in H.O. 42. 115.

[4] See deposition of Humphrey Yarwood in H.O. 40. 1.

[5] Baines, *History of the County Palatine*, p. 231, and Prentice, *Historical Sketches of Manchester*, pp. 31–3.

[6] See depositions of Yarwood, Bent, and others in H.O. 40. 1.

[7] Maitland to H.O., May 3, 6, and June 22 in H.O. 40. 1.

especially of the midlands and the north, were suffering, that the situation of two particular classes of northern workers was to be noticed. The hand-loom weavers were, and were for long to remain, among the most depressed classes of the new industrial population, able, to a most surprising extent, to hold their employment in face of the advance of machine and steam production, but not able to hold their relative economic position, or their former rate of wages. The shearmen or croppers in the woollen industry had been among the most prosperous of hand workers. But they were one of those few classes of hand workers whose elimination was to proceed most rapidly.

The unemployment and under-employment amongst the cotton weavers, and the steady decline in their earnings, we have noticed. As yet there were very few steam looms at work. In 1806 four factories had been erected to use the new steam looms, two at Stockport and one each at Manchester and Westhoughton.[1] The introduction of this new machinery even though, unlike most of that previously introduced, it necessitated a shift of production from the home or the small workshop to the factory, and from the country to the town or to the neighbourhood of a colliery, did not seem to provoke at first any opposition. Hand workers were not displaced, the new looms being barely able to take care of the extra demand of an expanding market. The new methods of production spread slowly, there being in 1813 still only fourteen such factories in this area, between Manchester and Stockport, employing between 2,000 and 2,400 looms together.[2] It was after rather than before 1815 that the rapid spread of power-driven machinery in the cotton industry took place, and later still before the new methods were widely employed in wool. Even in 1820, when there were some 12,000 power looms at work, there were still 240,000 hand looms, the

[1] Baines, *History of the County of Lancaster*, vol. i, p. 118, and *History of the Cotton Manufacture*, p. 235.

[2] Ibid.

new machines having apparently merely supplemented and not replaced the old ones and domestic production.[1] The unemployment and under-employment from which these cotton towns were suffering were clearly not to be attributed to the very few steam looms that there were at work in 1812. Even the decline in wages, which was clearly partly due to the competition of a cheaper method of production, was due also to other causes. Even so it was a natural delusion on the part of the distressed weavers to think that their recent sufferings were due to this new method of production.[2] Many of the other workers in the district, colliers, navvies, cotton spinners shared the same idea,[3] so much so that pamphleteers thought it worth while to publish exhortations to the working class not to think machinery the cause of their sufferings.[4] At a time of deep distress in the district the fourteen new factories with their more than 2,000 steam looms were a source of added and bitter discontent to the thousands of suffering hand workers in and around Stockport, Bolton, and Middleton, in which neighbourhood these new machines were concentrated.

A somewhat similar situation existed in the area to the north of Leeds.[5] The cropping or shearing branch of the woollen industry, whose function it was to finish off cloth by raising the 'nap' or fluff on its surface and shaving it off sheer, was concentrated in the district between Leeds and Huddersfield. The whole of the great wapentakes of Agbrigg and Morley, with their numerous industrial popula-

[1] Porter, op. cit., pp. 298–9.

[2] Baines, *History of the Cotton Manufacture*, p. 235.

[3] It is noted that all these different classes of men took part in such disturbances as those at Middleton, Westhoughton, and Macclesfield, in April 1812.

[4] See examples enclosed in letters from Manchester in H.O. 40. 1 and H.O. 42. 123.

[5] A very readable account of conditions in the neighbourhood of Huddersfield at this time is to be obtained in Peel, *Risings of the Luddites*; Charlotte Brontë's *Shirley* is also good, as is a later novel *Inheritance* by Phyllis Bentley.

tion, the whole country between the rivers Aire and Calder, was dotted with little clothing villages. All of them, like the rest of the West Riding and of Lancashire and Cheshire, were, as we have seen, feeling the effects of the national trade depression to an unusual degree, because of their especial dependence upon the American export market. There was there, as elsewhere and to an even greater extent, unemployment and diminished earnings, aggravated by famine prices. Especially was this true of the Spen valley, the seat of the cropping trade.

This valley, and some of the other dales which ran parallel to it, was thickly dotted with cropping shops. The latter were usually small, seldom employing more than ten to fifteen workmen.[1] The master cropper, owning a small number of simple hand frames, which he kept in a workshop adjoining or behind his house,[2] worked to the orders of wealthier clothiers, meeting them at the Cloth Halls and Exchanges of Huddersfield, Heckmondwike, Halifax, and other local towns.[3] He employed a handful of apprentices and journeymen, most of whom could at one time have hoped themselves in time to own a cropping shop of their own. These latter workmen lived in cottages scattered about the hill-sides of the district and had ample opportunity to come and go unseen, and to meet for any secret purpose. They did not differ too much in status from their masters, with whom they were often on the friendliest of terms.[4]

Always a small class in relation to the total number of workers in the industry, they had until recently been a

[1] It was from just such a small shop, that of John Wood, master cropper of Liversedge, that some of the outstanding Yorkshire Luddites are known to have come.

[2] See depositions from persons suffering from Luddite attacks in H.O. 40. 1. and H.O. 42. 119 et seq.

[3] John Horsfall, one of the leaders of the Huddersfield Committee for the suppression of the disturbances, was murdered on his way back from the Huddersfield Exchange, which he always attended on Tuesdays.

[4] See Peel, op. cit., for an account of conditions in Wood's workshop. See also opening chapters in Phyllis Bentley, op. cit.

favoured one. They had, as it was reported by the *Manchester Exchange Herald*,[1] 'from time immemorial rendered their craft a species of monopoly by limiting the number of apprentices'. Better off than their fellow workmen in the ordinary and more crowded branches of the industry they were wont to expend 'twice or three times as much money at the ale house than the weaver, the dresser or the dyer'.[2] They were notoriously independent and high spirited, 'the least manageable of any persons employed in this important manufacture'.[3]

It was many years since machinery for shearing had been invented. In 1802 there had been riots in Wiltshire and Somerset on the introduction of gig-mills and shearing frames.[4] These machines, superseding hand labour in this favoured branch of the trade, had been violently opposed. Introduced in Gloucestershire they had been prevented by the animosity of the workmen from extending to other countries. There were, when the Parliamentary Committee upon the woollen industry presented its report in 1806,[5] already a few factories recently introduced in Halifax, Huddersfield, and Leeds. But factories and improved shearing frames were still very much the exception. There was a powerful association amongst the shearmen of the district, which was said to have relations with other trades and even with Scotland.[6] They are reported to have issued a warning in 1805 to manufacturers not to introduce new machinery. They boasted 'If Parliament would not grant them their rights they would grant them themselves'.[7] They were so far successful that in 1812 it could be said that 'until within a very recent period but few individuals had the temerity to shear cloth in the North of England by machinery'. For many years the manufacturers of the West Riding had been intimidated

[1] April 21, 1812, quoting from the *Alfred*, London evening paper.

[2] Ibid.

[3] Ibid.

[4] Report of the Committee on the Woollen Manufactures, *Parl. Papers*, 1806, iii.

[5] Ibid.

[6] Ibid., p. 605.

[7] Ibid.

'by the characteristic violence of the Croppers' from using a 'species of machinery so useful'.[1]

The machine[2] in question was not an elaborate one. It consisted merely of a double pair of shears working on a frame. It had this advantage that while the pair of shears was working across the cloth the worker had merely to watch the operation until the cut was completed, then run the shears off the cloth to a resting-place on the shear-board, unhook the cropped portion, pull forward the rest, hook again to the boards, raise the 'nap', run in the shears to the position necessary for cutting, and the operation could re-continue. It was easier, quicker, and less painful than the hand operation.

Despite the opposition of the croppers a few such machines had been introduced in the years immediately preceding 1812. Especially in 1810 and 1811 a number of shearing frames had been put on the market by Messrs. Enoch and J. Taylor of Marsden.[3] They had been installed in a number of shops, and some quite large mills had been established, notably by Mr. William Cartwright at Rawfolds, and by some other manufacturers in the neighbourhood of Huddersfield and Leeds. The displacement of hand labour was continuing gradually, as it was to continue with rather greater rapidity after 1813. The number of gig mills in the north of England, which was said to be 5 in 1806, had increased to 72 by 1807, and the number of new shearing frames from 100 to 1,462.[4] Even by 1812 there were few villages in the Spen valley which did not contain at least one shop in which an enterprising, though often rather fearful master was using the new methods. Though the number of large establishments, some of them in Leeds[5] and other towns but mostly in the

[1] *Manchester Exchange Herald*, April 21, 1812.

[2] Peel, op. cit., p. 29.

[3] Ibid., p. 30.

[4] E. Lipson, *History of Woollen and Worsted Industries*, p. 191.

[5] For example, one of the first to be attacked by the Luddites, that of Messrs. Oates, Wood, and Smithson (letter from firm to H.O., Jan. 22, 1812, in H.O. 42. 119).

country,[1] was limited, the number of smaller shops with a few new shearing frames was large.[2]

The new methods were, however, unpopular, not merely amongst the displaced croppers, or amongst the smaller masters who were unwilling or unable to install the new and more expensive machinery, and who were feeling the competition of their fellows who had done so, but amongst the populace generally, and even amongst substantial manufacturers in other lines of business. The General Officer Commanding in the district commented[3] with surprise in the spring of 1812 upon the disturbing phenomenon:

> 'how much the opinion and wishes of even the more respectable part of the Inhabitants are in unison with the deluded and ill-disposed populace with respect to the present object of their resentment Gig Mills and Shearing Frames and this extends also to persons having Mills of a different description employed in the Manufacturing branch. . . .'

Most people in 1811 and 1812 found it difficult to appreciate the value of new machinery economizing labour at a time when goods were a glut upon the market and when there was, in any case, a surplus of labour available. When shop after shop was having, unwillingly but necessarily, to turn off one employee after another, when every master craftsman was compelled by restriction of demand for his products to work his frames part time, it seemed a needless innovation to introduce new, expensive machines increasing productive capacity and enabling one man to do the work of several. The croppers who had fought the introduction of new machinery even in good times, when the market was expanding and they were having to work overtime to fill orders, could hardly be expected calmly to sit by and see it introduced in bad times, when orders were

[1] For example the large mill of William Cartwright at Rawfolds (Peel, op. cit.).

[2] See numerous depositions in H.O. 40. 1 and H.O. 42. 119 et seq.

[3] Grey to H.O., April 16, 1812, in H.O. 42. 122.

few and far between and old frames and hand workers were standing idle.

The cropping villages, scattered all over the lonely moors and dales of this region, were seething with discontent as the bitter autumn of 1811 gave way to the even more distressing winter of 1812. There was not a village in which unemployment was not heavy, not a worker to whom low earnings and high prices had not brought distress. There was not an ale-house bar but around which of an evening some recently turned off cropper was to be heard bewailing his fate and cursing the new shearing frames, which, whether or no they were really responsible for his ill fate, were a more concrete and immediate, and therefore intelligible, cause of it, than so distant a matter as the American Non-Intercourse Act, or so vague a one as the war, which had been continuing so long that one had almost forgotten there had ever been a time of peace. There was not a workman in employment who was not sympathetic to such tales, and scared of a similar fate. There was not a cropping shop in which the men, and few in which the masters, did not grumble, as they tended their old machines, about conditions in the trade, and argue about the value or justice of introducing the new machinery. There was not a day when some little group of Yorkshiremen, returning home from work, or going out to look for it, did not pass with angry glances and muttering words some new mill or old workshop employing the new, hated frames.

The neighbourhood of Leeds, like the neighbourhood of Manchester and of Nottingham was in 1811 and 1812, a seething mass of distress and discontent, liable at any moment, in the bitterness of its apparently insoluble disputes, to break out into disorder.

IV

DISTURBANCES IN THE MIDLANDS 1811–13

THE break-down of negotiations between the Nottingham hosiers and the discontented framework knitters in the early part of 1811 caused widespread ill feeling. The employees of such firms as that of Brocksopp and Parker, threatened with a further reduction in their already much diminished earnings, felt that their only remedy was to coerce the recalcitrant hosiers into line.[1] Only so could better firms, such as their own, which were being driven unwillingly and by the force of competition into wage-cutting and other malpractices, avoid copying the example of the worst employers, whose frauds and economies were enabling them to undercut their fellows. There was much muttering amongst the men, as indeed amongst the better and more responsible hosiers. People were afraid of what might happen, with unemployment and distress so universal.

In Arnold, a small town just outside Nottingham, and in which many 'wide' frames were employed upon 'cut-ups',[2] little groups of angry framework knitters broke into the workshops in which the frames of unpopular hosiers were situated and took the jack-wires[3] out of the frames. Deprived of these wires, a minor but an essential part of the machinery, the frames could not be worked. They were not permanently damaged and could be worked again as soon as the wires had been replaced. But removal of the wires was an effective method of coercing their owners. The example of these Arnold stockingers was widely followed throughout the villages and towns of the district

[1] See evidence of T. Lathom before the Committee on Framework Knitters Petitions, *Parl. Papers*, 1812, ii. 222, and also 'Statement of several Hosiers of Nottingham to the Framework Knitters of that town, respecting the reduction of their Wages, etc.' Ibid., p. 259.

[2] Felkin, op. cit., p. 236.

[3] Ibid.

in the ensuing weeks, during February and the first week of March. A rude warning was given to all irreconcilable hosiers, to those paying low wages or in 'truck', to those using wide frames or making cut-ups, and otherwise annoying or defrauding their workpeople, and to stockingers taking too many apprentices, that they had better join with the better part of the trade in putting an end to such abuses. The dismembered frames were left idle and useless in the workshops, not to be used again until concessions had induced the angry stockingers to bring back the wires, which were meanwhile deposited in the churches, as hostages for the good behaviour of their owners. The spirit of negotiation was obviously giving way to a spirit of violence, favouring direct action. But even so the undercutting hosiers held firm.

So strongly was the public stirred that noisy assemblages of workpeople began to gather in the district, to protest against the general distress, and the abuses which were thought to occasion it. On March 11 a particularly large mob of framework knitters, some hundreds strong, gathered in the market-place at Nottingham. Angry speeches were made and the crowd was 'vociferous in condemning their Employers and clamouring for work and a more liberal price'. So ugly a situation appeared to be developing that the military were called out and the mob was dispersed late in the afternoon.[1] Its members, who were mostly country stockingers, dispersed to their homes.

The trouble, however, so far from being ended, was only just begun. That night at Arnold,[2] between dusk and dawn, no less than sixty stocking frames were broken by the mob, swarming around the town, entering the houses of

[1] Account in report of Conant and Baker to H.O., in H.O. 42. 119. This document, which is a complete report of the disturbances in the midlands up to the first week of February 1812, submitted by two experienced police magistrates sent down from London to assist the local authorities, is the best source of information with regard to the overt acts of the Nottinghamshire Luddites.

[2] Ibid.

unpopular stockingers, and breaking the frames of special, hated hosiers. The general populace so far from preventing actually aided and abetted the disturbance, cheering on the frame-breakers and obstructing the authorities. It was necessary to call out the Dragoons the following morning in order to clear the town. The whole neighbourhood had been fired by these riotous outbursts. For several weeks the same disturbances continued. Night after night in the surrounding villages mobs collected and entered various workshops in order to break the frames of unpopular hosiers.[1] All over the north-western part of Nottinghamshire, in the various hosiery villages, often in several different places on the same night, and sometimes even by day, cases of framebreaking were reported. So general was the public sympathy with the rioters that no arrests were possible, though hundreds of people were witnesses to many of the attacks.[2]

The authorities quickly took what precautions were possible. The Nottingham magistrates established a regular nightly watch of six regular and six special constables.[3] Special constables were enrolled in the town and in the county. Parties of the military, of necessity small, were stationed in some of the disturbed country villages.[4] A regiment of regular militia, on the march from Worcester to Hull, was diverted at Derby.[5] A troop of Dragoon Guards was brought over from Lichfield. A large detachment of troops was sent to Mansfield and smaller bodies, which were increased as forces were available, were sent to other neighbouring places. Liberal rewards were offered for the detection of offenders, and some active, intelligent officers from Bow Street Police Court, London, were brought down to the district and put to work in the disturbed villages.[6] The riots, which had resulted in the destruction of more

[1] Conant and Baker, op. cit., and *Nottingham Journal*, March 23, 1811.
[2] *Journal*, April 20, 1811.
[3] Conant and Bakers' report in H.O. 42. 119.
[4] Ibid.
[5] *Journal*, March 20, 1811.
[6] Ibid.

than 200 frames, were gradually put an end to. By the beginning of April everything was quiet again.

These disturbances had in any case been localized. No frames had been broken in the town of Nottingham itself,[1] despite the distress there, nor had the disturbances extended over the county borders to Derbyshire or Leicestershire. The damage had been confined to a small number of populous villages in the country to the north-west of the town of Nottingham. It had ended almost as quickly as it had begun. It had, however, been very serious while it lasted, and it had greatly inflamed the body of stockingers and alarmed the authorities.

Throughout the summer, despite the bad harvest and the deepening depression of trade, all was quiet. It was not until November that the disturbances were renewed, again almost without warning and to the surprise of the authorities. On the 4th of that month during the night there was a riot in the village of Bulwell and six frames were broken.[2] It was noted that they were wide frames making cut-ups. On the ensuing nights other similar small attacks took place. On the night of the 10th a much more widespread and alarming spirit of riot showed itself. Eight or ten frames, said to belong to a man who was teaching the art of framework knitting to people who were not bound apprentices, were broken at Kimberley.[3] Another mob from Arnold, collecting in Bulwell forest, where they were joined by other detachments from neighbouring villages, was drawn up in line by a commander calling himself 'Ned Lud'.[4] When their numbers reached about 70 they were ordered to march off to Bulwell, a town of some 2,000 inhabitants, and a noted centre of the framework knitting industry, where Edward Hollingsworth, a particularly unpopular hosier, had a great number of

[1] Ibid. and Conant and Baker, op. cit.

[2] *Nottingham Review*, Nov. 9, 1811.

[3] Conant and Baker, op. cit.

[4] As reported in ibid.

frames.[1] Hollingsworth had apparently been expecting trouble and had already removed a number of his frames under guard to Nottingham. He was not, however, prepared to beat off such an attack as he was to experience this night. The mob of Luddites advanced in order to the village, placed guards around the house, and sent men ahead with great hammers and axes to break open the doors. Hollingsworth was ready for them and there was a spirited defence. Shots were fired on both sides and one of the assailants, a man of the name of Westby from Arnold, was killed. Retreating to carry off his body the mob of Luddites was not deterred by this set-back and they advanced again, overbore all resistance, and entered the house. Having broken a number of frames they retreated and dispersed. Similar attacks, by large mobs and small, and usually without resistance, took place every night in one or more villages in the district between Bulwell and Sutton-in-Ashfield. On the night of the 13th there was another great attack.[2] A crowd collected at Hucknall, the rumour having gone around that frames were to be broken in Sutton-in-Ashfield, a great centre for manufacture of 'cut-ups' and payment in 'truck'. Being joined by men from Kirkby and Bulwell this mob moved off, having stopped to collect money at the houses of one or two masters, whom the mob intimidated into subscribing to their cause. They collected some arms at Kirkby and just beyond there they joined up with another detachment from Arnold, who had been waiting at an ale-house for the other contingents to arrive. The whole force, gathering itself together at the seventh milestone between Nottingham and Mansfield, moved on to Sutton. Its members, many of them armed with muskets and pistols as well as axes and hammers, made no attempt to conceal their purpose. Word of their advance spread rapidly. The Mansfield Volunteers were

[1] Conant and Baker, op. cit., and *Nottingham Journal*, Nov. 16, 1811.

[2] Ibid. and depositions of J. Cooper Kirk and John Amos in H.O. 42. 124 and 125. See also depositions of arrested Luddites in H.O. 42. 117.

called out and were joined by some dismounted dragoons, the whole force marching rapidly through the night towards the scene of the disturbance. They arrived too late, however, to prevent the attack. The Luddite mob had already broken open the great doors of the house, and gone upstairs to the workshop, where they had broken a great number of frames. The troops were able to make some arrests, eight or a dozen people being apprehended, of whom four were later committed to the county gaol. But they had not been able to prevent some seventy frames from being broken at Bett's workshop (he being a large, hated hosier) and elsewhere in the town of Sutton.

Night after night, despite all military and police precautions, similar attacks took place. Night after night mobs of Luddites collected in the forest, word of their intentions having spread abroad throughout the surrounding villages, and attacked the frames of particularly unpopular hosiers. More often than not no attempt was made to warn the military or to resist the attack. The stockingers who guarded the frames seldom had any more love for the hosier who owned them than had the assailants. The neighbours, who knew of the attack, who watched the Luddite gang march through the village, who came out to gaze at the framebreaking, sympathized rather with the framebreakers than with the hosiers or the authorities. Frames were broken on the same night in towns and villages twelve or fifteen[1] miles, or even farther, apart, so that the authorities knew not in which direction to go. There seemed to be several different gangs[2] at work.

There was much system in the attacks.[3] Particularly unpopular hosiers were selected as the victims.[4] The attacking group was well organized and well lead, men with hammers and muskets going ahead, guards being placed to give an alarm, every man having his appointed task, to

[1] Felkin, op. cit., p. 231. [2] Ibid.

[3] See letters from Newcastle, Coldham, Sherbrooke, &c., in H.O. 42. 118 and 119. [4] Coldham to H.O. in H.O. 42. 119 (Jan. 14, 1812).

break the doors, to watch out for the police and militia, to look after the householder and his family, to break the frames, to guard the retreat. The members of the attacking parties, gathered from several different villages, numbering from six to sixty, meeting in the forest at some spot convenient to all, knowing one another by number and not by name, were obedient to a common leader, the 'General Ned Ludd' of famous memory.[1] They acted quickly and surely, knowing in each house to which they came just which frames they were to break and which to spare, for only the frames of unpopular hosiers, paying low wages or in goods, or doing fraudulent, cut-up work, were broken, other frames of the same construction, even wide frames, doing good work for fair wages, being spared.[2]

Precautions were immediately taken to prevent this campaign of destruction continuing. A squadron of dragoons was ordered from Lichfield.[3] The area commander, General Dyott, was told to hold himself ready to give more assistance as needed.[4] The Mansfield Volunteers and two troops of Yeomanry were called out on the 13th. On the 14th the entire county force was called out.[5] The 1st or Nottinghamshire Regiment was kept on duty until the 27th when it was relieved by the 2nd or Southwell Regiment, of which two companies had already been out for a week.[6] Four companies of Yeomanry Cavalry were kept on duty. Four hundred special constables were enrolled in Nottingham and a nightly watch of six regular and six (later twelve) special constables was established.[7] A strong guard of military was posted at the Exchange with orders to be in instant readiness by day or night. Guards were stationed

[1] Blackner, *History of Nottingham*, p. 403.

[2] Descriptions of actual attacks can be found in the issues of the *Nottingham Journal* and *Review* and of the *London Times* and *Courier* for these months.

[3] Beckett to Wright, Nov. 15, 1811, in H.O. 42. 119.

[4] Ibid.

[5] Conant and Baker, op. cit.

[6] Particulars of military and police arrangements in H.O. Domestic Letter Books, particularly H.O. 42. 119 and also in the local papers.

[7] Conant and Baker, op. cit.

about the district, where they were needed, so far as troops were available.[1] Others were employed to guard the wagons that were coming daily into the town of Nottingham, bringing in the frames of hosiers who were afraid of their safety in the country.[2]

Despite such precautions the disturbances continued. There was something of a riot at Arnold on the 14th on the occasion of the funeral of Westby, the Luddite killed on the night of the 10th at Bulwell.[3] There were even cases of framebreaking during daylight, almost within eyesight and earshot of the military. On the 27th there was even a case of a Luddite attack upon some frames being brought into Nottingham under military guard, a frame being broken on Reed Hill, near Nottingham, at midday, in the sight, and in spite of the efforts, of its escort of hussars.[4] Threatening letters[5] were circulating widely, not merely around Nottingham but also in the surrounding counties, warning hosiers to discontinue the unpopular methods, urging magistrates and militiamen not to obstruct the Luddites. Here and there ricks were fired, and even plantations, and the cattle of prominent magistrates and officers of militia were houghed.[6]

Cases of force collections of money began to be reported.[7] This offence, which was to be common during December, especially in Leicestershire, where there was practically no framebreaking, was noted from the very beginning of the disturbances in the Nottingham area. Stockingers would call and offer for sale copies of the Framework Knitters Act[8] (as a protection against prosecution for vagrancy) or would ask for money for unemployed workmen. Others

[1] Ibid.

[2] The disturbances had hardly started in November before hosiers started bringing their frames into Nottingham for safe keeping. Reckless attacks on such parties were continually reported as taking place, often in broad daylight.

[3] Conant and Baker, op. cit.

[4] *Nottingham Journal*, Nov. 30, 1811.

[5] See examples in H.O. 42. 117 et seq.

[6] Conant and Baker.

[7] See depositions in Rutland's letter to H.O. of Jan. 5, 1812, in H.O. 42. 119.

[8] Becher to H.O., Feb. 11, 1812, in H.O. 42. 120.

would make a round of the leading stockingers, and even of some of the hosiers, threatening a Luddite attack if they would not subscribe to the Luddite funds. Men in work were continually forced to contribute to the support of those out of work and of the Luddites.[1]

On December 5 three strangers were reported to have been calling on the stockingers of Osgathorpe.[2] They let it be known that unless the head stockingers called at the house at which they were and contributed to the funds of the Luddites 'worse would come of it'. In one case they visited a leading framework knitter and read to him a letter:

'Gentlemen all, Ned Ludd's Compliments and hopes you will give a trifle towards supporting his Army as he well understands the Art of breaking obnoxious Frames. If you comply with this it will be well, if not I shall call upon you myself. Edward Ludd.'

Several stockingers seem to have contributed amounts from 6*d.* to 1*s.* each, being alarmed at such letters and at the talk of a list in the possession of the strangers marking down certain frames for destruction. The next day the men were at Hugglecoat and visiting various houses on a similar errand. At one place they got 1*s.* on the excuse that 'there had been a mobbing and they belonged to the mobbers and that some had been thrown into prison and they wanted to collect some money to pay Counsel'. At Ibstock their purpose was to raise money for the unemployed. 'Several people in the neighbourhood of Nottingham had not anything to do and they wished to collect something for them.' Such charitable collections were easy. Even when there was no sympathy for the distressed stockingers for whom nominally the money was sought, or when the stockingers and hosiers called upon had no guilty conscience or special fear of attack, the general alarm the Luddites had occasioned was sufficient to make it difficult for any one to

[1] Coldham to H.O., Jan. 14, 1812, in H.O. 42. 119.

[2] Depositions in Rutland to H.O., Jan. 5, 1812, in ibid.

refuse a Luddite, or a stockinger who might be a Luddite, anything.

Great bodies of troops were being concentrated in the area. No less than nine troops of cavalry and two regiments of infantry were brought into the midlands between November 15 and December 15, 1811.[1] On December 7 the midland area commander, General Dyott, was ordered personally to Nottingham to take command.[2] He found himself in possession of a force of between 800 and 900 cavalry and 1,000 infantry, 'a larger force than had ever been found necessary in any period of our history to be employed in the quelling of a local disturbance'.[3] Squadrons of cavalry were dispatched to Derby and to Loughborough, to give confidence to the local magistrates who had requested reinforcements.[4] Six companies of the Berkshire Militia were cantoned out in the various Nottinghamshire villages in which the magistrates apprehended disorder.[5] The Nottingham nightly watch was increased from twelve to thirty-six constables.[6] Specials were also sworn in in the surrounding country villages, where that was possible.[7] Public houses were ordered to be closed at 10 p.m., after which hour no one was to be abroad.[8] Proclamations were issued by the town and county magistrates warning the public that forcibly to enter a house at night time for the purpose of breaking a frame amounted to the crime of burglary and was punishable as a felony, exhorting them not to contribute money to the support of the disaffected, declaring that all who, being entrusted with the care of frames, should aid the framebreakers either overtly, or by leaving their doors open, or by not calling assistance, or in other ways, would be proceeded against as accomplices,

[1] See records in local papers, Conant and Baker's report, Sutton and Blackner's histories, &c.

[2] Conant and Baker.

[3] Ryder in House of Commons, Feb. 14, 1812, in *Parl. Debates*, xxi. 11. 808.

[4] Conant and Baker.

[5] Butt to Torrens, Dec. 7, 1811 and Dec. 10, in H.O. 42. 119.

[6] Conant and Baker.

[7] Ibid.

[8] Conant to Beckett, Dec. 7, in ibid.

and calling on all loyal citizens to join in the suppression of the disturbances. Finally an appeal was made to the Government to send down Bow Street officers to apprehend offenders.

All these precautions were bound to have their effect. They were successful in preventing a spread of the trouble throughout Leicestershire and Derbyshire, where disturbances began to be reported towards the end of November and in the first week of December. Except for the district on the Notts.–Derby. borders, which was part of the Nottinghamshire hosiery district, there was little trouble in these other counties, except for the removing of jack wires from the frames.[1] This offence, with which the Nottinghamshire disturbances had started, the circulation of threatening letters, and the collection of money, were almost the only overt acts of disorder from which the other counties, and especially Leicestershire, were to suffer. The latter county had very little unemployment. The manufacture of finer qualities afforded more regular work and better wages. Despite the prevalence of 'cut-ups' there was not the same general distress or cause for disagreement between hosiers and stockingers.[2] Derbyshire, although it suffered from the same depression and distress as Nottinghamshire, had fewer frames and a more scattered industry. Its hosiers, being smaller men, were also noted as being among the first to make concessions. A 'mixture of coercion and conciliation' was quickly successful in restoring order.[3] Derbyshire and Leicestershire also, not being troubled with disorders so soon as Nottinghamshire, were able to profit by the warning and concert adequate defence measures promptly before matters got out of hand.

In Nottinghamshire it was less easy, despite every possible precaution, to restore order. The populace was too generally sympathetic to the objects of the Luddites. Though the slow moving military and the inadequate

[1] Felkin, op. cit., p. 236.
[2] Ibid., p. 437.
[3] Conant and Baker.

police, as they were reinforced, were able to prevent attacks by large mobs, such as those we have noted and with which the disturbances opened, they were unable to prevent the sudden, isolated attacks of two or three Luddites upon a handful of hated frames, into which the disorder rapidly degenerated. Cases of framebreaking continued to be reported, more frequently in some weeks and regions, and less frequently in others, but at the average rate of 200 frames a month, during the months of November and December 1811 and up to February 6, 1812, throughout the hosiery district in north-west Nottinghamshire. Hardly a night occurred in which there was not at least one Luddite attack. Alarm was very widespread. Many householders would not dare, apart from the law on the matter, to venture out of doors after 10 p.m. or even after dark. Villagers took it in turns to sit up all night and watch one another's cottages. Some stockingers did not get a full night's sleep for three months. A general watch was kept and many a village made arrangements such as that made at Lord Middleton's Hall, where a tar tub was placed on the roof, ready to be lighted in case of alarm, and where a guard was posted on seventeen successive December nights.[1]

Partly as a result of this alarm a number of new offences began to be reported. There were cases of robberies of lonely farm-houses, especially upon the Derbyshire border.[2] Whereas the Luddites in all their previous attacks had confined themselves rigidly to the one object, the destruction of obnoxious frames, avoiding all temptation to steal, these new pseudo-Ludds did not break frames at all but were merely common robbers. There were, as the *Nottingham Journal* remarked,[3] now two classes concerned in the disorders:

1. 'Luddites who broke frames under the mistaken idea that they would therebye benefit trade and who confined themselves to that species of offence.'

[1] *Times*, Dec. 16, 1811. [2] *Nottingham Journal*, Dec. 28, 1811.
[3] Ibid., Jan 10, 1812.

2. 'The yet more numerous class who adopted the nomme de guerre "Nedd Ludd's men" as a cloak for the commission of almost every crime.'

The thing which seemed to be bringing Luddism properly so called to an end was not the military and police arrangements but the concessions that violence had provoked. Quite early in the disturbances hosiers had begun to give in to their offended workpeople, to announce that if their frames were spared they would pay higher prices, discontinue cut-ups, &c. As early as November 23, Derbyshire hosiers are noted as having staved off framebreaking by concessions.[1] Felkin records[2] an interesting experience of his youth:

'It was in the last week of November, 1811, that the writer of these lines, then a youth of scarcely seventeen, was required by his masters to get into the saddle and make a long round, to convey the information that if their frames, of which they employed about 3,000, were spared from the destruction with which they were threatened, one shilling per dozen advance would be paid on the following Saturday, and be continued whether others paid it or not. It was a dreary afternoon with heavy rain and winter sleet. He rode hard, and at Basford, Bulwell, Eastwood, Heanor, Ilkeston, Smalley, Sawley, Kegworth, Gotham, and Ruddington, delivered to the head framework knitters the joyful news of the offered advance. The wintry storm, though uncomfortable enough to the messenger, tended greatly to the success of his message. It prevented for the night the marauding parties employing themselves; these frames had been undoubtedly doomed, for an example, as belonging to one of the most influential houses in the trade. The promise made was faithfully performed; not one of their frames was injured, and no further fears were excited as to the safety of their property.'

At the same time Messrs. Lacey and Seals, a prominent firm of Nottingham hosiers, announced that they would pay the regular price in the hope of terminating the

[1] Conant and Baker.

[2] Felkin, op. cit., p. 233.

disturbances.[1] They admitted they had been paying inferior wages but they had done so on the entreaty of their workpeople, who were eager for work at any price, and because others had done so, but they were reversing their policy, lest their motives might be misunderstood. Other firms copied their example and promised to pay the standard prices and discontinue making 'cut-ups'. *The Times* reports[2] a meeting of the trade in Nottingham in order to secure a general agreement to pay the usual prices, an attempt at compromise which failed because the men demanded also that only certain work, of the best sort, should be done. Various firms did, however, carry out this agreement, no less than fifty firms, for instance, being reported by the *Nottingham Journal*[3] to have given an advance of 6*d*. per pair for black silk hose.

The town and county magistrates also attempted to mediate. They held a meeting with certain leading hosiers on December 4 and proposed to meet deputations from the masters and the men in order to work out 'some plan of conciliation which might at once and for ever put an end to the present Spirit of Discontent acting in attacks upon the property of the Hosiers'.[4] Unfortunately the hosiers did not take kindly to the suggestion, the magistrates were rebuffed, and did not again attempt this species of interference in a trade dispute. Negotiations did, however, continue between delegates and committees of the framework knitters and the hosiers. Several meetings were held. On the 13th a meeting[5] of hosiers agreed upon a new list of prices appreciably in advance of the prevailing rate. On the 14th some of the leading hosiers advertised[6] to the workmen that the latter should bring in any complaints they had in writing to an attorney who was named. So well did negotiations proceed that towards the end of the month the press and the authorities both expected the

[1] *The Times*, Nov. 29, 1811.
[2] Ibid., Nov. 30.
[3] *Nottingham Journal*, Nov. 30.
[4] Conant and Baker.
[5] *Journal*, Dec. 14.
[6] *Times*, Dec. 14.

disturbances to come to an end. At Mansfield everything was reported settled.[1] 'At Nottingham only and immediately around it (did) any appearances of discontent now prevail.'

Unfortunately, however, all these attempts at peaceful settlement broke upon the same rock as that upon which previous trade negotiations, before framebreaking commenced, had been wrecked. It was impossible to get all the hosiers to come into line. Only about half the trade would sign an agreement to pay higher prices. The others, many of whom were personally favourable to the idea, would not bind themselves to pay higher rates so long as other manufacturers were outside the agreement, free to pay the old prices and undersell hosiers paying the new and higher ones.[2] A small, adamant minority was able to prevent the majority of the trade from concluding a satisfactory agreement.

Even so the many individual concessions that were made by fearful hosiers, the many firms which paid higher prices, or discontinued making cut-ups, even though they were not willing to sign an agreement binding themselves to do so, had an appreciable effect. It not merely checked the framebreaking for several weeks while negotiations were proceeding, so that the week December 13–20 was almost entirely free from attack, and the whole month of December much quieter than either November or January, but it encouraged the peaceful elements amongst the stockingers to take up again the negotiations that had been carrying on before framebreaking started. And it had the temporary effect of raising the average rate of wages in the trade by about 2*s*. a dozen.[3]

The break-down of negotiations for a general agreement, which was reported on December 30, precipitated, however, a serious recrudescence of disorder. The first fortnight of January was as full of attacks as the period of the first and

[1] Dec. 29, Newcastle to H.O. in H.O. 42. 119.

[2] *Times*, Dec. 27.

[3] Felkin, op. cit., p. 439.

greatest disorder in November. Not a night passed without at least one attack, and there were usually several. While the perpetrators of these sudden, effective raids upon isolated houses and individual frames were little, rapidly moving groups of men, one or two, or at the most six or seven, in number, and not great mobs, such as had been out in March and November, they were just as destructive to property. They were, indeed, more difficult even than large mobs to deal with. They could plan, commence, and conclude an attack in a few minutes of time. Long before the alarm could be given, or the police or military summoned, the Luddite party would be far away again.

Guards were placed in most of the disturbed villages, and even, where possible, in individual houses where an attack was feared.[1] Especially in the town of Nottingham the continual parading of constables and soldiers throughout the night would have been thought sufficient to deter the most adventurous, reckless Luddite. The daring of the framebreakers was, however, amazing. One Luddite escaped from the back of a house, where he had broken a frame, while the police contingent, under the command of Felkin, was approaching the front. Another, surprised in an upper room framebreaking, escaped out of the window, and ran along the roofs of neighbouring houses, climbed down into a garden, and walked calmly through the kitchen past the family there seated at dinner, out into the street and to safety, while the watch was entering the workshop he had just left.

Detection was difficult because witnesses were so unwilling to come forward. Hardly any one would dare to come forward to give evidence against a framebreaker.[2] Even when they did not, as did most of the poorer people, whether framework knitters or no, sympathize with the

[1] See reports of injured hosiers and evidence of witnesses in H.O. 42. 118 et seq.

[2] See reports of Newcastle, Coldham, Sherbrooke, &c., in H.O. 42. 118 et seq.

Luddites, the public usually was afraid of Luddite vengeance if they gave evidence against a framebreaker. Guards placed in charge of frames in threatened warehouses, or on wagons being brought into a place of safety in town, neglected their duty, deserted their posts, and allowed the frames to be broken in their absence, and, as the authorities more than suspected, with their complicity. In another case the guards in one house accused the master stockinger there of leaving the windows open and going out into the town to warn his Luddite friends how they could get in and surprise the little garrison.[1]

There was also the difficulty that the military and the civil power did not get on too well together. Several instances are reported of disagreements between the two. Mr. Becher, an active magistrate of Southwell, objected because the military had been sent into the town against the wishes of the local magistrates, who were satisfied their own forces were sufficient.[2] The officer commanding could only protest that his task was a hard one when one magistrate, like Becher, would censure him for taking a step that another magistrate like Sherbrooke, an influential member of the County Bench, recommended. On other occasions the opposite criticism was made of the military, that they were too dilatory. On one occasion, at the little village of Linton, the officer in charge of the local detachment of troops would not move his men without orders from a magistrate even though the noise of the near-by framebreaking could be distinctly heard.[3]

So serious did matters appear to be getting as January advanced that new and enlarged measures were concerted by the authorities. The town magistrates reorganized their nightly watch,[4] dividing the town into four, frequently changed, areas, in each of which a corporal's guard of five

[1] Conant and Baker.

[2] See letters of Hawker, Coldham, Newcastle, and Becher in H.O. 42. 121.

[3] Hawker to H.O., Jan. 30, 1812, in H.O. 42. 119.

[4] Coldham to Mayor of Leicester, Jan. 27, 1812, in H.O. 42. 119.

men under the charge of a constable were kept moving about. Each guard was frequently relieved and an attempt was made to prevent any one knowing who would compose the piquet, and what its itinerary and even district would be on any particular night or at any specified time. The forces of military at the two guard-rooms in the town, one of them next to the Police Office, were much strengthened. And magistrates were in attendance night and morning to receive reports and to give orders. The Corporation also redoubled the activities of their secret committee, established in December and given free discretion secretly to expend money in acquiring information. The county magistrates found it more difficult to concert adequate measures. There was not a class of trustworthy, middle-class people available as constables.[1] More reliance had to be placed on the military, the civil population being so largely composed of framework knitters and their friends. Constables were, however, enrolled, and in some few areas were of real use. An attempt was made to reorganize the old Watch and Ward, which had fallen into disuse. And recommendations[2] were made to the Government with regard to it, recommendations which were the basis of the Watch and Ward Act presented to Parliament in February. Town and county magistrates also offered liberal rewards, the leading gentry and merchants of the district subscribing to a fund for that purpose.[3]

It was also, at last, possible to get the Government to act. They had been quick to send troops, a great force having been sent to Nottingham in the four weeks following the recommencement of framebreaking on November 4. They had issued a Royal Proclamation[4] in December calling on all officers to discover and apprehend those concerned in the disturbances and offering a reward of £50 for each person arrested and brought to conviction. They had also approved the establishment by the Corpora-

[1] Ibid. [2] See resolutions in H.O. 42. 119.

[3] *Nottingham Journal*, Jan. 28, 1812. [4] Copy in H.O. 42. 119.

tion of Nottingham of a Secret Committee to offer rewards and deal with informers and otherwise seek to discover the authors of the commotion.[1] They had, however, refused[2] requests for Bow Street officers or a Special Commission, and had been unwilling to accept financial and other responsibility for prosecuting offenders and preparing witnesses. Now they were forced by the pressure of local opinion. The county members were calling upon them.[3] The Lord Lieutenant, the Duke of Newcastle,[4] and other local notables, like Lord Middleton,[5] were writing alarmist letters. There was a prospect of the matter being raised in Parliament. The Home Office felt it necessary to act quickly.

Two police magistrates (Mr. Conant from Marlborough Street and Mr. Baker from Hatton Garden) were sent down, together with as many Bow Street officers as could be spared.[6] The General commanding the area was ordered personally to take command in Nottingham.[7] The Cabinet discussed[8] the disturbances and studied a schedule of the letters received by the Home Office. Two Bills were prepared,[9] the Nottingham Peace Bill, which was recommended by the Nottinghamshire magistrates and members,[10] and the Framebreaking Bill, which the Leicester magistrates sought,[11] and the Nottingham authorities opposed.[12]

At the same time the troops in the area were reinforced, two further regiments of regular militia arriving in the area early in February and being cantoned out as needed

[1] *Nottingham Review*, Jan 3, 1812.
[2] Conant to Beckett, Dec. 8, 1811, in H.O. 42. 119.
[3] H.O. to Conant, Jan. 29 and 31, in H.O. 79. 1.
[4] Jan. 10, 1812, in H.O. 42. 119. [5] Jan. 11 in ibid.
[6] H.O. to Conant, Jan. 29 and 31, in H.O. 79. 1.
[7] Conant and Baker's report.
[8] See particulars in letters from H.O. to Conant, Jan. 29 and 31, in H.O. 79. 1.
[9] Debate in Parliament; *Parl. Debates*, xxi. 11. 808 et seq.
[10] Eyre to Ryder, Jan. 23, 1812, in H.O. 42. 119.
[11] Letter to H.O., Jan. 19, 1812, in H.O. 42. 119.
[12] See letters in H.O. 42. 120.

about the district.[1] A new and more energetic commander, General Hawker, took command in place of General Dyott.[2] A constant coming and going of troops created, as *The Times* remarked,[3] an 'appearance of a state of war'. It was indeed an unprecedented situation when more than 3,000 troops,[4] apart from the local militia and yeomanry and police, were needed in one small area for the restoration of public order. Even the smaller force in Nottingham in December had been larger than ever before needed for such a purpose.

The Government was forced by the facts of the situation into further unprecedented measures. It had to agree to pay the expenses of prosecutions and to take measures for protecting witnesses, no one being willing voluntarily to come forward to prosecute or give evidence against a Luddite.[5] It had to make use of spies to try to uncover the secret of the Luddite organization.[6]

The two Bills that were asked for necessitated parliamentary discussion of the matter. There was a brief discussion in the House of Lords on the 4th[7] and in the Commons on the 6th[8] of February. On the 14th the Home Secretary introduced the two Bills.[9] The first, for making framebreaking punishable with death, was a simple measure. The second, the Nottingham Peace Bill, adapting the old provisions of the Watch and Ward to new conditions, was more complicated. It was a Bill to

> 'Enable the Lord Lieutenant of the County, the Sheriff or 5 Justices, when disturbances existed, to call a meeting, and to give immediate notice, in the newspapers and on the church

[1] Conant and Baker. [2] Ibid. [3] *Times*, Feb. 1, 1812.

[4] Berks., Cumberland, South Lincoln, Devon, and Bucks. Militia, each with an average strength of at least 600 (the Bucks. were said to be 800 strong, *Journal*, Feb. 8, 1812; the Berks. and Cumberland 1,000 together, Ryder in House of Commons, Feb. 14, 1812) and 1,000 cavalry (Ryder in House of Commons, Feb. 14, 1812).

[5] Sheriff to H.O., Jan. 11, 1812, in H.O. 42. 119.

[6] H.O. to Conant and Baker, Jan. 31 and Feb. 10, 1812, in H.O. 43. 19.

[7] *Parl. Debates*, xxi. 603 et seq.

[8] Ibid., p. 671. [9] Ibid., p. 812.

doors, in the usual manner, that a special meeting would be held, for the purpose of obtaining lists of all male inhabitants of the county, above the age of 21, in order to select from among them such number of constables as they shall think necessary, and, by that means to establish a watch and ward throughout the county, or such districts as might be considered in a turbulent state, and that the magistrates should be empowered to defray the expenses.'

Both Bills went easily and quickly through all their stages. On the Framebreaking Bill alone was there a real difference of opinion. Some members, and especially Whigs in Parliament, doubted the value, when the lesser penalties of the old law, which made framebreakers liable to transportation, had not been applied, of increasing the penalty.[1] They felt, as did many local authorities in Nottinghamshire,[2] that the penalty of death would make witnesses still more unwilling to come forward, juries still less willing to convict. It had already been difficult enough to get information. Now, so Mr. Coldham of Nottingham suggested,[3] it would be harder still. Many of his former informants would not act a moment longer once their information might cause the death of a fellow creature. The majority of Parliament, however, like the Leicester justices, believed that the penalty of death would have a powerful effect on the general mind.[4] It would be, at the least, an expression of parliamentary opinion as to the enormity of the crime.[5]

Parliament was also little disposed to delay action for the sake of inquiring into the distress, which every one admitted was a prime cause of the disturbances. They doubted whether there was anything material that Parliament could do to relieve distress, which was, as Lord Liverpool expressed it, very much in the natural course of

[1] *Parl. Debates*, xxi. 812 et seq.

[2] Coldham to H.O., Feb. 24, 1812, in H.O. 42. 120. [3] Ibid.

[4] Lamb in House of Commons, *Parl. Debates*, xxi. 818.

[5] Satirical reference of Holland in Lords during debate, *Parl. Debates*, xxi. 965.

things.[1] Penal legislation had been necessary, so he said, for the protection of every successive species of machinery.[2] It had been needed for wool and cotton, it was natural it should be needed for stockings. Whatever the cause of the disputes no one could deny the necessity of putting them down.[3]

As it happened the framebreaking had subsided by the time the Bills became law. There was hardly a single case after the 7th of February.[4] On the one hand the tremendous military garrison,[5] and on the other the prospect of a peaceful settlement, acted to discourage violence. The Luddites had made employers temporarily afraid to manufacture cut-ups or pay low wages.[6] There was also a disposition to look to Parliament for redress. The workmen who had been negotiating with the hosiers back in November and December began in February to prepare a petition to Parliament. A meeting of stockingers was held at the Sir Isaac Newton Inn in Nottingham on the third Monday in February 1812 to collect reports from the different villages and branches of the industry and to prepare a report for submission to Lord Holland, the Recorder of the town, the Members of Parliament for the town and county, and Mr. Whitbread.[7] A committee was formed to manage a petition to Parliament and subscriptions were taken up to finance the project. For the next three months the stockingers were busy with this matter and therefore little disposed, even apart from the danger of it, to resort to framebreaking.

There were apprehensions of trouble, especially during the Assizes in March.[8] There was much talk as to whether the trials should be held for safety's sake outside of Nottingham, or the troops removed, as was customary, from the town during the Assize. Finally, after the troops

[1] Ibid., p. 971. [2] Ibid., p. 810. [3] Ibid.
[4] Conant and Baker. [5] See p. 83, n. 4.
[6] Felkin, op. cit., p. 439. [7] *Nottingham Journal*, Feb. 15, 1812.
[8] See letters in H.O. 42. 121.

had been moved, on the presiding Judge failing to give orders to the contrary, they were moved back on the direct orders of the Government.[1] There was no trouble. Juries, contrary to expectation, did their duty. Out of nine Luddites before the court no less than seven were sentenced, five to terms of fourteen years' transportation, two to terms of five years. The two acquittals were, so the Judge thought, very proper. Juries had been ready on fair cases to convict and the magistrates had behaved with much vigilance. There was little likelihood of the spirit of outrage breaking out again.[2]

There was no trouble also, though some had been expected, on the prisoners being removed to the hulks at Woolwich, or later when their reprieve was refused. The more than 4,000 stockingers who petitioned the Crown for mercy accepted quietly the rejection of their appeal.[3] The civil patrol in the city was changed to a military one.[4] The new Watch and Ward Act was only adopted in principle, names being taken of people who could be called out in case of necessity. No actual constables were enrolled.[5] During April some of the troops were actually removed from Nottingham to the north, where great disturbances were then raging.[6] Not even the attempted murder of Mr. Trentham, a Nottingham hosier, late in April, seriously or for long disturbed the new calm of the midland districts.[7]

Trade seems temporarily to have picked up, probably in the hope of the Orders in Council being repealed and the American market opened.[8] A subscription was also taken up for general charitable relief, the poor of the town of Nottingham were all called upon and no less than 9,000 food tickets were issued.[9] Similar subscriptions in the

[1] See letters in H.O. 42. 121.
[2] Bailey to H.O. March 18, 1812, in H.O. 42. 121.
[3] See letters in H.O. 42. 122.
[4] Coldham to H.O., April 14, in ibid.
[5] Ibid.
[6] *Nottingham Journal*, April 18, 1812.
[7] Ibid., May 2 and *Times*, May 3, 1812.
[8] *Times*, July 17, 1812.
[9] *Nottingham Journal*, May 2 and 16.

county, in such places as Mansfield,[1] served the same purpose, relieving distress and promoting good feeling. Not even the rejection of the Hosiery and Lace Regulation Bill,[2] which had been before Parliament in June, and which had been the chief object and result of the framework knitters' petition, discouraging though it was to those stockingers who believed in peaceful methods, served to interrupt the prevailing calm.

The committee of framework knitters which had been managing the petition to Parliament, and which had relations with all the local groups of stockingers, continued in existence and attempted to organize a Trades Union. The Committee was instructed to

'enquire how the Carpenters, Tailors, Shoe-makers and Cutlers conduct their Union and report to a General Meeting the Plan they consider the most satisfactory, and in future to be adopted by the United Branches of the Framework Knitters'.

A weekly subscription of *2d.* a frame was to be used for this purpose, as was the balance of the money already collected for the purpose of the Petition to Parliament.[3]

The authorities and the hosiers on their side had been active. A great military camp was established in the forest outside Nottingham, with quarters for 3,000 infantry and 500 cavalry, a force amply sufficient to overawe the district.[4] The Corporation Committee for the detection and prosecution of offenders continued to function. In July a permanent committee of hosiers was established, with Messrs. Coldham and Enfield, Town Clerk and Deputy Town Clerk of Nottingham, as Joint Secretaries, to manage a fund, and to look after the interests of the hosiers both by detecting and prosecuting Luddites, by opposing regulations of the manufactory such as those lately proposed in Parliament, and by prosecuting employers who imposed on their workpeople by payment in goods and in other ways.[5]

[1] Ibid. [2] *Parl. Papers*, 1812, ii. 260 et seq.
[3] *Nottingham Journal*, July 18, 1812.
[4] Ibid., May 9, 1812. [5] Ibid., July 24.

The rising price of grain, which reached its zenith towards the end of August, caused very great distress. There were some riots in the markets and guards had to be placed outside some bakers' shops and mills early in September.[1] But apart from that there was no trouble until the winter was well advanced. Conditions by that time had become very serious, America being closed by war even more effectively than it had, until May, by the Non-Intercourse Act, and Europe not yet being open. Wages, temporarily raised by the Luddite commotions, were relapsing again.[2] It was not therefore surprising that on half a dozen Sunday evenings in November and December 1812 and January 1813 there should have been some cases of framebreaking.[3] Most of these attacks were small, a handful of men attacking a house and breaking a few frames and then escaping into the night. There were no large mobs out, as there had been the previous winter, nor were there several attacks upon the same night. It was thought that all the attacks, of which there were only six or seven, and in which some fifty frames were broken, were the work of the same small gang of desperate men, numbering not more than twelve to fourteen, and working for hire.[4]

These attacks did not seriously or for long alarm the authorities. They ceased early in January. For more than a year there was no further trouble. The interest of the stockingers was absorbed in the organization of their Union. Trade had picked up after the French retreat from Moscow and the collapse of the Continental System. Luddism as a widespread campaign in the hosiery districts had come to an end. The severe sentences imposed upon the Yorkshire Luddites at the Special Assizes in January

[1] Stevens to H.O., Sept. 9, 1812, in H.O. 42. 127.

[2] Felkin, op. cit., p. 439.

[3] *Nottingham Journal* and *Review* and *London Times* for Dec. 1812 and Jan. 1813, and H.O. 42. 129–31.

[4] Coldham to H.O., Dec. 29, Newcastle to H.O., Dec. 21, 1812, in H.O. 42. 130.

1813 were widely reported and long remembered. Not for some time, and not then upon the same basis, was Luddism to be renewed.

The main period of Luddism in its main centre had come to an end. It had, for all the alarm it had occasioned, been a restricted movement. Starting in March 1811 and lasting under four weeks, recommencing in November and lasting three months, having one final spurt during November and December 1812, and being almost wholly confined to the town of Nottingham and the country district surrounding it to the north-west, the framebreaking campaign had been a striking episode in the perennial disputes between hosiers and stockingers in the midland framework knitting industries. More than 1,000 stocking frames and upwards of 100 lace machines had been destroyed,[1] more than 200 a month in the months of March, November, and December 1811 and January 1812, and some 50 in the winter of 1812–13. The damage amounted, even at the then depreciated value of the stocking frame, to more than £10,000 (which was the valuation Felkin placed on the broken stocking frames alone).[2] Great forces had been needed to restore order. A striking but temporary success had been achieved by the angry stockingers. But the situation which had provoked the Luddite disturbances remained and the decline of the stockingers' status continued.

[1] Felkin, op. cit., pp. 231 and 239.

[2] Ibid.

V

LANCASHIRE AND CHESHIRE, 1811–13

As the year 1811 drew to a conclusion there was growing anxiety on the part of the magistrates and other officials of the chief towns of Lancashire and Cheshire as to how the labouring classes were to get through the winter.[1] Owing to the highly developed system of spies and secret information which the authorities of this district enjoyed they were privy to the designs of the working classes.[2] They had early and complete information with regard to the small, informal, secret committees of the disaffected which were trying to exploit the general discontent and make a living out of it. They knew almost as soon as the trades themselves of such meetings as that held in Stockport early in November 1811 and attended by delegates from eleven different trades, coming into Stockport to discuss a project for sending a delegate to Ireland to confer with the discontented there.[3] They had frequent reports of meetings to pass resolutions in favour of Peace, of Parliamentary Reform, against the Orders in Council, and against the use of corn, which was needed for food, in distilleries. They knew that the trade societies, which had always been active in and around Manchester, were discussing a general 'turn out'.[4]

While many of these reports, and particularly those referring to large, revolutionary plans and to the possibility of a general rising throughout Great Britain and Ireland, were properly discounted, if only because they were a perennial feature of spies' reports throughout these years, there were several factors to make the authorities really worried. The undoubted and very severe distress of the

[1] e.g. Pilkington to H.O., Nov. 12, 1811, in H.O. 42. 117.
[2] See Chap. XIV.
[3] Agents' report in Fletcher to H.O., Nov. 21, 1811, in ibid.
[4] Depositions of Humphrey Yarwood in H.O. 40. 1.

labouring classes was in itself calculated to provoke disorder. And the example of the Nottinghamshire Luddites, of which full reports were coming through, brought by commercial travellers or delegates of the trade societies, or merely reprinted in the local papers, was a dangerous one, likely to lead to overt acts of disorder. There were rumours of actual delegates from Nottingham. One Williamson, a traveller in stockings from Nottingham, was reported very early in November as having met a committee of the trades in Manchester.[1] At Christmas time it was reported from Stockport that two delegates from Nottingham had met the Stockport weavers at Union Street in that town.[2] During January and February there was talk of 'plenty of Nottingham, Carlisle, and Glasgow Delegates who are holding private meetings every night and instigating ours to riot and confusion'.[3] The spies were sending up frequent tales of a similar kind, though significantly enough their talk was always of Irish or Scottish delegates and never of midland ones, and the interest of their secret committees was always in large-scale plans for revolution rather than in a limited programme of framebreaking. During February there were reports in Manchester and Stockport of subscriptions having been solicited in that part of the country on behalf of the Nottingham rioters.[4]

The grievances of the workers began to be more specific. Threatening letters were received by manufacturers, and particularly by those few employing the new steam looms.[5] Meetings to deliberate on general sources of grievance, low wages, and unemployment and under-employment, and the high price of provisions, and requests on the part of the workers for meetings with their employers continued. But they were accompanied and increasingly overshadowed by

[1] Bent's report in Fletcher to H.O., Nov. 21, 1811, in H.O. 42. 117.

[2] Bulkley to H.O., Dec. 26, 1811, in H.O. 42. 118 and Jan. 1, 1812, in H.O. 42. 110.

[3] J. Meyer to House in London, Feb. 11, 1812, in H.O. 42. 120.

[4] Lloyd to Bulkley, Feb. 11, 1812, in ibid.

[5] Anonymous letter dated April 16, 1812, in H.O. 40. 1.

attempts to intimidate the more unpopular employers, by threatening anonymous letters, and by rumours of an intended attack upon the new machinery. Very early in February Mr. Peter Marsland, one of the earliest and most prominent manufacturers to use the new method of weaving by rotary motion on steam looms, reported that an attempt had been made to fire his factory.[1] At the same time the warehouse of Messrs. Marshall and Sideswell, another Stockport firm, was threatened.[2] Mr. Lloyd, a local attorney and clerk to the Stockport Bench, was reporting at the end of February that a bad spirit had developed amongst the weavers, stirred up by some 'few desperate characters from Ireland'; and that 'they certainly do meditate the destruction of the Looms worked by Steam and employed in factories'.[3]

Precautions were taken. The Stockport magistrates, who had already, as they thought, given the most sympathetic consideration to the general distress, met with a view to increasing the number of special constables.[4] They also made representations to Government that a force of cavalry was needed for the greater security of the district. Such dispositions were, however, too late. On March 20 an attack upon a large scale took place.[5] The warehouse adjoining the residence of Mr. Ratcliffe, 'the original projector of the obnoxious looms', was attacked in the early hours of the morning by a large crowd. The firm and the authorities had received ample warning and very little damage was done. The crowd broke a number of windows and attempted to fire the structure by throwing lighted torches inside. They were, however, unsuccessful in their objects. The authorities immediately arranged for a subscription to defray the cost of a £200 reward which was offered for information leading to conviction of the per-

[1] Feb. 11, 1812, in H.O. 42. 131.

[2] Lloyd to Bulkley, Feb. 11, 1812, in H.O. 42. 120.

[3] Lloyd to H.O., Feb. 26, 1812, in ibid.

[4] Ibid.

[5] Lloyd to H.O., March 21, in H.O. 40. 1.

petrators. The Government was also asked to offer a free pardon to informers.

For some weeks all was quiet. There were rumours of trouble in Manchester and Bolton and elsewhere. But there was no actual trouble. At Bolton there were frequent secret meetings. The active government spies were reporting the existence of a secret committee and also the swearing in, or as it was called 'twisting in', of upwards of 100 disaffected people.[1] Meetings were held on the moor outside the town, some of them being dispersed by the militia, under whose orders the spies were working, and which was privy to all the designs of the disaffected. So early as April 7 there was a rumour that an attack was projected on the neighbouring factory of Wray and Duncroff at Westhoughton.[2] But for some time, despite continued rumours, there was no sign of this project being realized. Both at Bolton and at Stockport, however, there was talk of men with blacked faces wandering about at night, 'twisting in' members of the working class, and soliciting subscriptions. Threatening letters were widely circulated.

The chief cause of anxiety at this time, not merely in this area but throughout the kingdom, was the great scarcity and the famine price of provisions, especially of grain and potatoes. More than once towards the end of March, and in widely separated places, there was angry protest from the crowds which thronged the markets and rumours, happily not realized, of riot. At Manchester, where these rumours had been most insistent, and where distress was very severe, there was an actual riot on April 8, though not directly on account of scarcity of provisions.[3]

It had been intended to hold a meeting to vote an Address to the Prince Regent congratulating him on keep-

[1] See letters from Fletcher to H.O. for various dates in H.O. 40. 1 and H.O. 42. 120–2.

[2] Fletcher to H.O., April 7, 1812, in H.O. 40. 1.

[3] *Manchester Exchange Herald*, April 14, 1812; Prentice, *Historical Sketches of Manchester*, pp. 5–53; and letters in H.O. 40. 1 and 42. 122.

ing his old Ministers in office (it will be remembered that he had at one time been expected to replace them, so soon as he obtained unconditional power as Regent, with his old Whig friends). The Tory administration of the time was bitterly unpopular and it was widely felt that it would be unfair and unwise to allow resolutions so little reflecting the real opinion of Manchester to be passed. Circulars were dispatched throughout the district by Reformers and it was anticipated that a large and by no means unanimous meeting would be the result. Fearing the effects of the large crowd that was expected, the Committee of the Exchange Hall, where the meeting was to have been held, asked the borough reeve and constables to find another room for it. The latter, having failed to secure an alternative room and accepting the excuse that the stairs to the Exchange Dining Hall would not stand a crowd, not perhaps unwillingly cancelled the meeting. Nevertheless, crowds arrived. Meeting in St. Anne's Square a tumultuous gathering passed with acclamation the list of resolutions passed upon a similar occasion by the Livery of London, deploring the maintenance in office of the Perceval administration. Some of them, leaving the main meeting in the Square, gained access to the Exchange. Being left undisturbed they penetrated even into the famous Dining Hall. Gaining confidence they began to get out of hand. Wild words began to give way to violent acts. The crowds pushed and eddied about the Exchange. Some pictures were torn off the walls. The windows were broken. Finally a good deal of damage was done and troops had to be summoned to disperse the mob.

Clearly this occurrence was not a very grave one. It could, as the local officer commanding fully recognized,[1] have been prevented if the magistrates had been more prompt. Though the trouble gained a wide publicity and added greatly to the general alarm, the town of Manchester itself was quite calm again within a day or two. Pre-

[1] Clay to H.O., April 11, 1812, in H.O. 42. 122.

cautions were taken that might well have been taken before. Public-houses were ordered to be closed as early as 7 p.m.[1] Special constables were sworn in. Troops were drafted from other areas and especially from Nottingham,[2] where the disturbances had come to an end.

The centre of interest was, however, very rapidly shifted from Manchester. On the 10th of April there were riots in the market at Bristol.[3] Potatoes were on the rise. Farmers were holding their stocks in the hope of a still greater rise. The mob assembled and losing patience threatened vengeance on the offending merchants and dealers and seized their stocks. At the same time, and for the ensuing few days, there were similar but more serious disturbances in the far north at Carlisle.[4] The Liverpool dealers were said to have bought up all the corn in the market and withheld it from general sale. On this Saturday once again all the corn on the market was quickly bought up by the dealers. A similar move in the case of potatoes was threatened. The crowd, angered beyond endurance at this playing with their distress, seized the carts and sold off the stock at reduced, but still apparently at normal, pre-emergency prices. On the following Monday a supply of corn going to Sandsfield was set upon in the carts *en route* and only saved by the sudden arrival of the magistrates and the military. The authorities pacified the mob by promising the regular market prices. All seemed quiet when a slight fracas developed between the crowd and the returning troops. Apparently the mob jostled the detachment and jeered at it and the latter retaliated by clearing their way by force, a few casualties naturally resulting. In revenge the crowd broke some windows in the mess-room. The Riot Act had to be read and a few volleys fired to disperse the crowd. Disturbances of the kind continued for a number of days.

[1] April 8, 1812; Borough reeve and Constables to H.O. in ibid.
[2] *Nottingham Journal*, April issues.
[3] *Times*, April 11, 1812.
[4] April 21, 1812, Sheriff to H.O., in H.O. 42. 122.

Two hundred and fifty men from the Whitehaven and Penrith Militia had to be dispatched to Carlisle to restore order.[1]

There was similar trouble all over the kingdom.[2] There was a riot at Truro and men went about the country in search of corn. At Barnstaple, Falmouth, and Plymouth a similar disorderly disposition of the people was reported. The authorities tried to secure stocks of grain from vessels in port at Falmouth, while at Plymouth the Mayor ordered the constables to maintain order in the market and prevent regrating. At Leeds, Sheffield, Rochdale, Oldham, Barnsley, Bolton, Manchester, Macclesfield, and Chester there were similar disturbances reported on these and on the ensuing days.

At Macclesfield the disturbances assumed an especially serious aspect.[3] On the morning of April 15, Mr. Daniel Rawson, a factor of the town, received a warning from Stockport that trouble was brewing. Rioters were noticed assembling in the fields outside the town. They entered the market-place. Having inquired how potatoes were selling they disapproved of the price and threw the vegetables into the street. One of the leaders being arrested and lodged in gaol the rest of the mob stormed the building and released him. Returning to the market-place they attacked a number of provision shops, breaking down windows and doors, turning the goods out into the street, rolling the cheeses along the gutter. Proceeding with shouts of triumph down adjoining streets they ransacked a number of shops, completely destroying some and breaking the furniture and overturning the goods in others. A company of the Royal Cumberland Militia, turning out on the first sign of trouble, followed the mob from street to street, keeping discretely in the rear. The magistrates were unwilling to use force and for a time the town was at the

[1] April 21, 1812, Sheriff to H.O., in H.O. 42. 122.

[2] *London Times, Courier, Political Register,* &c., for April 10 et seq.

[3] *Manchester Exchange Herald,* April 21, 1812.

mercy of the crowd. Not until the late afternoon did a detachment of the Macclesfield Volunteer Cavalry arrive and attempt to restore order. By that time the mob, which had left the centre of the town and was threatening a factory upon its outskirts, had split into several portions. In face of the cavalry it divided into two main groups and recrossed the river. The main body took up a defensive position near the town rubbish heap. There the magistrates parleyed with them for upwards of half an hour, the cavalry remaining all the time on the watch. Meanwhile the other body of rioters attacked the house of a Mr. Wood at Beach. On the approach of the cavalry they split and fled. The troops, catching them in the fields adjoining the Manchester road, rode them down. The ground was cleared within ten minutes and a number of men were arrested. Under the guard of a detachment of militia the prisoners were marched to the Town Hall. The rest of the mob, gathering in the market-place, threatened a rescue. But the cavalry had by now assembled in force and had orders to clear the streets. Though this was 'the most perilous part of the service', for the mob clung to the walls and took refuge in the narrow and tortuous alleys from which it was difficult and dangerous to dislodge them, they were at last cornered in the Old Church Yard and dispersed. A nightly patrol of more than 300 was collected and went around the town, calling at the inns and lodging houses and arresting suspicious characters. By eleven the town was quiet. The cavalry remained on duty until two and detachments were kept on the move all night, patrolling the streets. On the following morning a troop of Greys arrived from Stockport and with the assistance of the infantry by then collected it was possible to prevent crowds reassembling. The examination of the prisoners was completed by two o'clock and three men were marched off under guard to Chester. The mob, never allowed to collect in dangerous groups, dispersed, and the town returned to its habitual quiet. The great number of outsiders, colliers or carters from

Hollington and spinners from Stockport, returned weary and disgusted to their homes.

Meanwhile Stockport itself had been the scene of extended disturbances.[1] On Sunday the 14th, the day before the Macclesfield disorders, mobs had collected in the streets of Stockport. They had milled about the town, breaking windows and threatening vengeance on the owners of steam looms. Headed by two men in women's clothes, who were hailed as 'General Ludd's wives', the crowd started by stoning the house of Mr. Grodair, an owner of steam looms, at Edgeley. Moving towards the town they gathered reinforcements as they went and 'carried all before them' at the factories they visited. Returning to Edgeley they burnt Mrs. Grodair's cottage, destroyed the looms in the factory, and cut up the work that had been made upon them. By now almost 3,000 strong they turned from this work of destruction with a great shout of 'Now for Syke's'. Mr. Garside, a respectable gentleman of the place, was injured in trying to turn the mob from their purpose, and only the arrival of the military sufficed to restore order.

On the following nights large mobs moved about the district, terrifying the country people, collecting subscriptions at the houses that they passed. The magistrates and the military were active, Mr. Lloyd, for instance, being always ready to leap into the saddle and ride off into the night with a party of cavalry, to disperse the mobs they might meet in the country lanes or on the moor, and if possible to arrest the ringleaders. By the 18th it could be said that order was restored.[2] The magistrates were working well. They had arrested four prisoners and expected more. They were selecting the most likely cases for prosecution.

Two days later the spirit of disturbance broke out in another place in the same district. The mobs, which were meeting in almost every town in the country, protesting

[1] Lloyd to H.O., April 16, 1812, in H.O. 40. 1.

[2] Lloyd to H.O., April 18, in ibid.

against the high price of provisions and threatening warehouses, were especially vociferous in Oldham.[1] They presented lists of prices to the shops, accompanying with threats of burning the premises. The 'two Methodistic Jacobinical constables not venturing to show themselves'[2] goods were sold at forced prices. Emboldened by this success the mob, which was supported by numbers of people from the surrounding district, and especially from Saddleworth, proceeded to Middleton, where there was a noted steam-loom factory, that of Mr. Burton. The mill, being forewarned of the attack, was heavily guarded and there was a resolute defence. Five men were killed and eighteen wounded and the crowds retreated in disorder and dispersed. The following day further crowds gathered at Oldham, many of them colliers from the surrounding country, and some of them armed. Again there were shouts of 'to the store rooms'. This time, however, the militia was ready for them and the mob left the town, despairing of success there. Once again they proceeded to Middleton. This time, although the military were able to inflict considerable losses upon the attacking party, and particularly upon the colliers from Holmwood, who were in the van, the attack was successful and the mill was destroyed.

Three days later there was another similar attack, this time at Westhoughton near Bolton.[3] The Westhoughton mill of Wray and Duncroff had for some weeks been expecting an attack. On the morning of the 24th it was reported that a mob was moving towards it across the moor. A detachment of troops rode rapidly over from Bolton in response to the manager's call. Upon arrival they found everything peaceful, no sign of rioters, no appearance of danger. Tired of false alarms, which had been frequent during previous weeks, they returned home in disgust. Hardly had they left than the rioters, who had been in hiding near the mill, emerged and proceeded to the attack.

[1] Chippendale to Fletcher, April 23, in H.O. 40. 1. [2] Ibid.
[3] Fletcher to H.O., April 25 and 26, in ibid.

Word was hastily sent to recall the military, but they scented another hoax and insisted upon returning to headquarters. They would not return to the mill without express orders from a magistrate. As a result the mob was able to attack and fire the mill, though the military finally arrived in time to arrest a number of the offenders.

For the next few days, and to a lesser extent for the next few weeks, the local militia harried the district, moving continually about, arresting people on suspicion, knocking up innocent householders at night, creating a veritable reign of terror.[1]

Similar tactics were necessary in the region of Stockport, where the disorder, which had been thought to have been repressed by the 18th, broke out again after an interval of a few days and continued for some little time.[2] Mr. Lloyd and parties of the local militia, together with troops stationed in the town, were out every night, trying to catch up with the marauding parties which were touring the neighbourhood, collecting arms, or forced gifts of money, or indulging in ordinary robberies in lonely country houses.

There had also been further trouble at Manchester, despite the precautions of the authorities. On the 18th of April there was some little disturbance in the market and potatoes were forcibly sold.[3] On the 20th there was great alarm, which was not justified in any actual disorder, because of the presence in the town of numbers of strangers. The state of affairs continued to be very anxious.

The whole area was in a state of fear bordering upon panic. The actual acts of disorder, serious though they had been, were as nothing to the rumours that were circulating. There was talk of a general rising,[4] the disaffected of Manchester and district rising in concert with

[1] See reports in H.O. 40. 1 and H.O. 42. 132.

[2] Prescott to H.O., April 21, 1812, in H.O. 40. 1.

[3] Magistrates to H.O., April 27, 1812, in H.O. 42. 122.

[4] Wright to H.O., April 19, 1812, in ibid. See also letters from Prescott, Lloyd, Chippendale, Fletcher, &c., for April and May 1812, in H.O. 40. 1. and H.O. 42. 120 et seq.

their fellows in the midlands, in London, in Scotland, and in Ireland. So early as the 19th of April reports were reaching the Home Office that such a rising was intended for May 1. It was widely believed that the first few days of May would see a general, national outbreak verging upon revolution.

In the event these fears were not realized. The first week of May passed without any acts of disorder whatever, except for occasional robberies or collections of arms, which were to continue throughout the summer. Officials like General Maitland, officer commanding the troops in the area, doubted whether such a rising had ever been seriously intended.[1] They believed the whole trouble extended no farther than it had actually shown itself in disorder, and was wholly rooted in the prevailing distress.

To begin with it had been very difficult to get the magistrates to act.[2] Again and again, in this as in the other disturbed districts, it was complained that there were too few magistrates willing to act quickly and vigorously. It was feared also to call out the militia, lest that were to put arms in the hands of the most powerfully disaffected.[3] The civil authorities were eager to throw all responsibility for restoring order upon the military.

Gradually, however, adequate precautions were taken. The various Lords Lieutenant, Fitzwilliam (West Riding), Stamford (Cheshire), and Derby (Lancashire) visited their Lieutenancies to stir their subordinates into action.[4] It was determined early in May to initiate the provisions of the Watch and Ward Act in the country south of the Ribble.[5] Here and there, although no general adoption of the Act was possible, a system of watching and warding was established, often by means of a voluntary association of the principal inhabitants of a locality for the defence of property. General Maitland tried to encourage this system

[1] Maitland to Ryder, May 4 and 6, 1812, in H.O. 40. 1.

[2] Maitland to Ryder, June 19, 1812, in ibid.

[3] Prescott to H.O., April 27, 1812, in ibid.

[4] See letters from Maitland, May 4, 6, &c., in H.O. 40. 1 and H.O. 42. 122, 123.

[5] Fletcher to H.O., May 1, 1812, in H.O. 40. 1.

of defence by making his grants of military assistance dependent upon the degree of local and civilian effort that had been shown.[1]

No less than 1,500 special constables were enrolled in the Salford Hundred, a number equal to 10 per cent. of the adult males and 2 per cent. of the entire population.[2] No less than 4,000 were reckoned also to be available in case of need. The militia was so organized as to be available in sufficient force for a period of fifteen weeks without calling on any individual for more than the normal service.[3] Four hundred special constables were enrolled at Bolton and others in the neighbouring disturbed towns.[4] Five hundred members of Colonel Sylvester's regiment of Manchester Militia were on duty at the beginning of May and 20 men from each company of the other two local regiments, Colonels Cook and Kenyon.[5] Colonel Fletcher, commanding the militia at Bolton, had 132 men, together with 71 from his staff and recruiting parties, available to co-operate with Major Pilkington's 41 Yeomanry.[6]

There were besides tremendous regular forces in the district. Eight regiments of regular militia, containing 71 companies of infantry, and 3 cavalry regiments, containing some 27 troops of Horse Guards and Dragoons, were distributed about the district.[7] These troops were stationed about the area, in the various cotton towns, as garrisons in many of the villages, as guards in particular factories, at the area head-quarters at Manchester and Liverpool, or in the garrison camp at Kersal Moor. General Maitland was in supreme command, Generals Dixon (Manchester) and Acland (Liverpool) being under his orders in charge of operations in the two districts into which the area was divided. Maitland was also in close touch with General

[1] Maitland to Ryder, May 4 and 6, 1812, in H.O. 40. 1.

[2] Fletcher to H.O., May 1, 1812, in ibid. [3] Ibid. [4] Ibid.

[5] Report of meeting of Manchester magistrates, April 28, in H.O. 42. 122.

[6] Fletcher to H.O., May 1, 1812, in H.O. 40. 1.

[7] Statement of forces in Maitland to H.O., May 9, 1812, in ibid.

Grey, commanding in Yorkshire, whom he was to supersede in June, thus uniting the entire northern command.

Despite these tremendous forces, disorder continued. There were no further attacks upon machinery, and no further mob riots by day. There were, however, continuously throughout the summer, though to a diminishing extent in and after June, raids for arms, or secret drills, or common robberies by night. Even as late as the middle of June parties of 100 men and upwards were still said to be active around Stockport, touring the countryside by night, terrifying the populace, and collecting arms and money.[1] It was for long extremely difficult to get the civil authorities to act. The major responsibility fell upon the military. And their forces, tremendous though they were, were yet insufficient to give the local towns and villages, and the individual manufacturers and magistrates, the guards they asked for.

The military were indeed unwilling to do so even if they could. They believed that the military should be the last and not the first line of defence, that the only real defence against attacks upon property by the lower orders was associations in defence of property amongst the upper classes.[2] They believed also, if they were not careful, that the manufacturers would use the military as a means of depressing still further the wages of their workpeople, with whom men like Maitland had considerable sympathy.[3]

What really brought disturbances to an end, apart from an improvement of conditions, which followed very rapidly upon the repeal of the Orders in Council in June,[4] was the action of rapidly moving bodies of military. Throughout the summer and early autumn, especially in the neighbourhood of Stockport, Bolton, and Ashton-under-Lyne, which had been amongst the most disturbed of all, small parties

[1] Lloyd to H.O., June 17, 1812, in H.O. 40. 1.

[2] Maitland to H.O., May 4 and 6, 1812, in ibid.

[3] Ibid.

[4] Maitland to H.O., June 19, 1812, in H.O. 42. 124.

of military, together with constables and spies, and where possible a magistrate, were kept moving from place to place, staying in each village just long enough to penetrate if possible into the designs of the disaffected, being on the watch at night to disperse disorderly mobs before they should have time to cause any damage, changing from place to place so quickly and secretly that the Luddites could never know when the coast was clear.[1]

Spies were also a great help in this area. From the very beginning they had been so closely in with the designs of the disaffected as to give the authorities warning of the attacks projected.[2] Mainly owing to their information a number of Luddites and others accused of complicity in the disorders were arrested in April and May. It was found possible to hold Special Commissions of Assize at Lancaster[3] and Chester[4] at the end of the month. At Lancaster there were 58 prisoners, and of these no less than 28 were convicted, 8 to death, 13 to long terms of transportation. At Chester out of 47 prisoners no less than 29 were convicted, 15 to death, 8 to transportation, and 6 to imprisonment. Some of these convicts were sentenced for riots in the market, like the poor Manchester woman who was hanged for stealing potatoes. Others were convicted for administering illegal oaths, an offence resting solely upon the evidence of spies, and, as I shall later seek to show, not directly connected with Luddism. Still others were cases of ordinary robbery, only connected with Luddism in that the terror the Luddites had created gave these robbers their chance. A small minority of the prisoners only were genuine Luddites in the sense of being machine breakers.

These convictions struck great terror into the minds of the people generally. Luddism became as dangerous a business as the use of machinery or dealing in provisions so recently had been. There were occasional disorders,

[1] See reports of Captain Raynes, the local officer in command, in H.O. 40. 1 and 2. [2] See reports in letters of Fletcher to H.O.

[3] See reports from Mr. Park in H.O., in H.O. 42. 123 and 124. [4] Ibid.

great numbers of threatening letters, two or three murders,[1] especially in Manchester, which may have been related to Luddism, and the continued nocturnal drills and raids for arms. But increasingly the countryside gained confidence. By August there were in this area hardly any further acts of disorder. Around Stockport men were coming in and taking the oath of allegiance, confessing[2] to their previous connexion with Luddism in order to win the free pardon that Parliament[3] had accorded to those who should freely confess their offences. Early in October more men came in to take the Oath of Allegiance near Bolton, the region where the spies had been most active, and where stories of illegal oaths seem to have originated.[4] The magistrates and military were free to turn their whole attention to the north, to the West Riding, where alone actual overt acts of disorder continued. Even there, where, since June, the centre of the disturbances had been situated, confidence was returning fast.

There were rumours of trouble in the winter, and the magistrates, especially of Stockport, were again scared at the popular distress and at the prospect of it leading to disorder.[5] These fears were never realized, this winter, nor in the succeeding, and often very troubled winters.

Luddism in Lancashire and Cheshire, attacks upon steam looms, provision riots, raids for arms, nightly drills and robberies, which had been a source of terrible anxiety in April, and which had alarmed the counties from February to July, were by the end of 1812 completely at an end.

[1] e.g. assault upon a sergeant of militia and his girl, and upon Mr. Antrobus, a manufacturer, the former being fatal, May 11, 1812, Manchester, reported in Hay to H.O. in H.O. 40. 1.

[2] Lloyd and Prescott to H.O., letters for August and September 1812, in H.O. 40. 2 and H.O. 42. 126 and 127.

[3] Illegal Oaths Act, May 1812, and Act of Indemnity, July 1812. See Journals of Parliament and Hansard.

[4] Clayton to H.O., Oct. 18, 1812, in H.O. 42. 128.

[5] Prescott to H.O., Nov. 8, 1812, in H.O. 42. 129.

VI

YORKSHIRE LUDDISM

THE news of the Nottinghamshire framebreaking was eagerly studied by the Yorkshire croppers. They, as we have seen, even more than other classes of the great industrial population of that part of the country, were bitterly discontented with existing conditions. They shared with the more than 250,000 other inhabitants of the region, as they did with the inhabitants of Lancashire and Cheshire, of the midlands, and indeed of every industrial district, woollen, cotton, iron, coal, in the country, the pressure of high prices and deficient employment.[1] But they had also an added grievance of their own, the introduction of new shearing frames, throwing the old hand croppers out of work, and of gig mills, competing with the small, semi-domestic workshops in which the trade had been previously concentrated. They hardly needed the example of the Nottinghamshire Luddites, of which travellers[2] as well as the newspapers were bringing them news, to be provoked into disturbance. They had always been a mutinous class, always, in good times as well as bad, apt to oppose any new expedients threatening their status.[3] They had been temporarily worsted during the years immediately preceding 1812. The new machines and factories, which they had so long and so successfully fought, were being widely introduced. The angry croppers were being turned off in handfuls and were forced to subside on to the Poor Law

[1] *Leeds Mercury*, Dec. 7, 1811.

[2] The only actual report of a delegate from Nottingham coming to Yorkshire at this time, as distinct from general rumours, is given by Peel (*Risings of the Luddites*, p. 56) who refers to the visit of a man named Weightman. Cf. the visit of Williamson to Bolton (Fletcher to H.O., Dec. 1811) and of other delegates to Stockport (Bulkley to H.O., Dec. and Jan. 1811–12).

[3] *Manchester Exchange Herald*, April 21, 1812: the croppers were 'notoriously the least manageable of any persons employed in this important manufacture'.

or else, if they were lucky, to seek work in a new mill. They heard of disorders elsewhere with a sense of added irritation. It was provoking indeed to the renowned, independent croppers of York that they should be slipping helplessly into the depression while a pack of Nottinghamshire stockingers were making an apparently successful fight against their fate.

During January 1812 rumours of impending trouble became so definite that precautions were taken by the authorities. Here and there a manufacturer would set guards over his mill. Here and there, as at Wakefield and Skipton, a small nightly watch was established.[1] One Wednesday night in mid-January a witness came before the magistrates of the Borough of Leeds to give evidence upon oath 'of a conspiracy to destroy the Machinery of certain Mills' in the town and neighbourhood 'employed in the dressing of cloth'. Precautions were quickly taken and the authorities were able to disperse a party of men, disguised and with blacked faces, on a bridge outside the town. One of the mob, a man named Shaw, was arrested and committed to York Castle for trial.[2]

On the following Sunday morning, at 2 a.m., a more serious occurrence was reported. An attack was made upon the mill of Messrs. Oates, Wood, and Smithson at Oatlands, near Leeds, and it was set on fire.[3] Although it was widely reported that this attack was the work of a 'conspiracy against machinery obnoxious to shearmen' that had recently been formed in the district, and that some of the numerous unemployed had had a hand in it, no definite information could be obtained, despite the reward that was offered.

Precautions were redoubled throughout the district, more manufacturers setting guards upon their property, more towns and villages establishing a small nightly

[1] *Leeds Intelligencer*, Jan 20, 1812.
[2] *Leeds Mercury*, Jan. 10, 1812.
[3] Oates, Wood, and Smithson to H.O., Jan. 22, 1812, in H.O. 42. 119.

watch. The neighbourhood became greatly alarmed at the reports which began to come in of parties of men secretly traversing the moors by night. Again and again a frightened countryman would come into town of a morning to report that he had heard the sound of marching feet, or the echo of gun-shots, during the dead of the previous night.

Early in February the purpose of all this mysterious marching became apparent. Bands of men, disguised and armed, had been knocking up terrified master craftsmen and manufacturers in the cold, early morning, compelling them to come down and open the doors of their adjoining workshops, into which the angry mob would pour in order to break any new shearing frames or dressing machines that they might find therein. These marauding parties,[1] meeting secretly, moving quickly from place to place, taking a scanty twenty minutes to commence, complete their attacks, and to make a clean getaway, and seldom if ever meeting with any resistance, were very difficult to deal with. The inadequate guard which the district possessed was mislead by the false rumours that reached them, the Luddites firing shots in different parts of the country, and allowing the noise of their marching to be heard, in order to lead the military off upon a false scent.

Attacks were frequent, there being no less than nine separate cases of machine breaking reported in the area of Huddersfield between February 23 and March 11.[2] The magistrates, who were not very numerous in this area, were mostly somewhat slow to act, though one of their number, Mr. Joseph Radcliffe of Milnesbridge House near Huddersfield,[3] was a notable exception. They were eager

[1] For descriptions, see Peel, op. cit., and depositions of victims in H.O. 40. 1 and H.O. 42. 119 et seq.

[2] See letters from Radcliffe, Scott, &c., to H.O. for Feb. and March 1812, in ibid.

[3] Mr. Radcliffe was one of the very few magistrates to take an outstanding part in sending up reports about and in trying to suppress the Luddite disturbances. His letters are a major source of information with regard to disturbances in the Huddersfield area.

for Government help, for spies to penetrate the designs of the disaffected, for further troops, for extraordinary powers, so that they might search for the arms which the Luddites were already beginning to demand of their victims, in addition to the keys of the workshops in which the obnoxious machines were housed. But they were slow to organize local defence arrangements, the local population being unwilling to act, either from fear of or sympathy with the Luddites. Only ample military reinforcements would, it was felt, sufficiently restore public confidence as to allow local police arrangements to be made. Huddersfield, for example, wished for at least 100 infantry in addition to the two troops of cavalry already stationed there.[1]

Various extra precautions were taken. Further troops were sent across from Hull, and divided between Leeds and Huddersfield.[2] The Regular Militia and Dragoons in that district, in so far as they could be spared from garrison duty in those towns, where the two local commanders, Colonel Campbell and Major Gordon had their headquarters, were distributed about the various villages, being either billeted in the local inns or stationed in twos and threes as guards in particular factories. The leading manufacturers and other residents of Huddersfield formed a Committee for Suppressing the Outrages, of which Mr. John Horsfall, an outstanding pioneer in the use of the new machinery, was Chairman.[3] Through Mr. Radcliffe this Committee requested the Home Office to send them further reinforcements and also Bow Street officers, so that they might be able to institute a regular, adequate nightly watch.[4] They wished also to be able to offer a free pardon to accomplices who would give information leading to convictions. The manufacturers of Leeds were similarly active, meeting to discuss disturbances and offering a

[1] Radcliffe to H.O., Feb. 29, 1812, in H.O. 40. 1.
[2] Grey to H.O., March 16, 1812, in H.O. 42. 121.
[3] Radcliffe to H.O., March 17, 1812, in ibid.
[4] Same to the same, March 1, in ibid.

reward for information with regard to the firing of Messrs. Oates, Wood and Smithson's factory.[1] The local members, including the venerable Mr. William Wilberforce, went to see the Home Secretary to beg for his redoubled efforts.[2]

The Government, while it had to refuse requests for Bow Street officers, and while it was unable to offer all the extra troops the local magistrates demanded (as General Grey later remarked, to grant all the requests for troops which came in would have required the use of the entire British Army),[3] did what it could. It agreed to help in the matter both of rewards and pardons provided it was given in each case specific information as to what was required.[4] It issued a Proclamation on March 17 offering a reward of 200 guineas for information with regard to the disturbances in the Huddersfield area.[5] It enjoined upon the local authorities that they should make greater use of special constables and, if possible, of the Watch and Ward.

A Special General Sessions of the Peace was actually summoned for April 1 in order to institute the provisions of the Watch and Ward Act.[6] Additional rewards for information were offered both in Leeds and Huddersfield. The movement of troops in the area was continual, further reinforcements being brought up from Sheffield, and there being a continual interchange between Leeds and Huddersfield, and between each of those centres and the surrounding villages.[7]

Despite all these efforts disorders continued, not merely in the country, where the hilly, open moorland made detection very difficult, but even in the city, where one would have thought adequate defence arrangements would have been possible. On March 24 the mill of Messrs. William Thompson and Brothers at Rawdon near Leeds

[1] *Leeds Intelligencer*, March 16, 1812.
[2] H.O. to Radcliffe, in H.O. 43. 20.
[3] Grey to H.O., May 23, 1812, in H.O. 42. 123.
[4] H.O. to Radcliffe, in H.O. 43. 20.
[5] *Leeds Intelligencer*, March 23 and 30, 1812.
[6] Ibid. [7] Ibid.

was attacked and the shears and other machinery were destroyed.[1] On the following night some men broke into the press shops of Messrs. Dickinson, Carr and Company, in Waters Lane, Leeds, and destroyed a considerable amount of cloth.[2] Generous rewards for information were unsuccessful in uncovering particulars of either of these attacks.

The receipt of anonymous, threatening letters by manufacturers using the new machinery was continual. Many of these men, especially the smaller ones, with modest, rural workshops, were terrified into discontinuing the use of the unpopular frames. Most of these letters were specific, warning particular manufacturers that their machinery would be broken unless they voluntarily put it down and reverted to the old methods. Some were more grandiloquent, like that received by Mr. Smith, a resident of Huddersfield and a prominent user of the new frames. This letter,[3] endorsed 'Redressers for ever', and signed 'By the General of the Army of Redressers, Ned Ludd, Clerk', started off like many of the others.

'Sir,

Information has just been given in that you are a holder of those detestable Shearing Frames, and I was desired by my men to write to you and give you fair warning to pull them down, and for that purpose I desire that you will understand I am now writing to you. You will take notice that if they are not taken down by the end of next week I shall attach one of my Lieutenants with at least 300 men to destroy them, and furthermore take notice that if you give us the trouble of coming so far we will increase your misfortunes by burning your Buildings down to ashes, and if you have the impudence to fire at any of my Men they have orders to Murder you and burn all your Housing. . . .'

The letter then proceeded, however, to speak of larger matters. Vast numbers of men were enrolled for the

[1] Ibid., *Leeds Mercury*, March 30, and letters in H.O. 42. 119.
[2] Ibid.
[3] In H.O. 40. 11.

purpose of breaking obnoxious machinery, not merely at Leeds and Huddersfield but in other places. They had news that the workers were preparing to rise in most of the large towns of the West Riding and in 'all the cotton country'. Disappointed with the Prince Regent's letter to Lord Grey, which showed that he was intending to keep in power, 'that damned set of rogues, Perceval and Co., to whom we attribute all the miseries of our Country', they were determined to seek redress by force. They would have help from the Papists in Ireland and from the French. They were tired of petitioning. 'We petition no more—that won't do—fighting must.' They would never be content until 'the House of Commons passes an Act to put down all the Machinery hurtful to the Commonwealth' and repealed that with regard to framebreaking.

Such letters created great alarm, and they lent colour to the reports of the spies, with their talk of delegates from Ireland, of bands of disaffected in London, Glasgow, and Dublin, as well as the provinces of England, and of plans for a general rising. They seemed to be substantiated by the raids for arms, and by the nightly drills, which began to accompany and were soon to take the place of machine breaking. For what purpose could the Luddites want arms (and by the end of the summer they had almost denuded the north of England of privately owned arms) if not for a general rising?

Apart from these vague threats and rumours disorder was, however, still limited chiefly to the breaking of machinery. A typical attack was that reported by William Hinchcliffe,[1] cloth dresser of Golcar. He put in a deposition swearing:

'That about the hour of One in the Morning of the 27th. of February Instant himself and family were alarmed by a Gun being fired through his window, when he saw a large number of people about his house—that soon afterwards the Door of his Shop was broken open and he heard a number of People

[1] Deposition in Radcliffe to H.O., Feb. 29, 1812, in H.O. 40. 1.

rush in, and a great Noise of Hammers striking the frames and Shears there—some People broke open his House and came in; a voice said "Where is he—bring him out". . . . "Lets kill him". A man attempted to break open the parlour door, but another prevented him and said "Let him alone for this time." Another voice said, "If you cause us to come again upon this Subject, We'll take your life." Someone called of them to come out and bid them fall in—that this Examinant saw upwards of fifty people about his house and heard a great many more, that their faces were disguised being marked black and white—That as soon as they were gone, this Examinant went out to see what they had done and found Five Dressing or Shearing frames and about Thirty pairs of Shears broke to pieces.'

A Mr. Roberts, cloth dresser of South Crofton, who had taken down his new shearing frames, begged the mob which came to his house not to break his shears.[1] They promised they would not, if he really had taken down his frames. They threatened him, however, with a pistol, and made him sit on the floor while they searched his house and workshop. Having broken two dressing frames in the shop, which was situated in an adjoining barn, they returned to warn him, 'If you set the frames up again we'll blow your brains out.' They also warned his wife to tell her father that if he did not take his frames down they would go to Marsden next week with 400 men to break them. But they kept their promise and did not damage anything but the machinery, and of that only the two obnoxious dressing machines. It was indeed, despite all the talk of burning buildings, very exceptional for anything to be taken from a house which was attacked except arms, or for anything to be injured except the new machinery.

So frequent and successful had such attacks been, and so great was the alarm that they had occasioned, that by the beginning of April almost all the smaller establishments had discontinued the use of the new frames, either because they had been broken or because their owners had

[1] In Radcliffe to H.O., March 14, in ibid.

voluntarily put them away to prevent their being broken.[1] Only in the larger establishments, which were usually guarded, were the new methods still employed. There was bitter dissension between the masters; men like Horsfall and Cartwright, the owner of a great mill at Rawfolds, being very scornful of their timid colleagues, like Brook of Longroyd Bridge, who put down their machines rather than face a Luddite attack.[2] But even in the face of their colleagues' scorn, and on pain of being branded as cowards, most of the smaller masters, many of whom sympathized with the Luddites and had only taken up the new methods because their competitors were doing so, preferred not to run the risk of Luddite vengeance.

The Luddites were, therefore, compelled to turn their attention in April to the larger establishments, of which a few, notably in Leeds, had, as we have seen, already been attacked. On the 9th a large body of men, some hundreds strong, disguised and armed, was reported to be marching in military array across the country near Wakefield.[3] Gathered, as it was reported, from a number of different places, Heckmondwike, Birstall, Dewsbury, Mirfield, Huddersfield, this body attacked the house and workshops of Mr. Foster, a manufacturer of Horbury near Wakefield. They dragged the three sons of Mr. Foster out of bed and rushed them, still in their nightshirts, shivering with fear and cold, across the space between the house and the work-sheds. They compelled the young Fosters at the point of the pistol to open the doors. Rushing through the first shed they came to that in which the cropping machinery was set up. The men in front, armed with great hammers, called in derision 'Enoch', after Enoch Taylor, a noted maker of the new machines, immediately set in to smash the dressing machines and shearing frames that were there.

[1] Memorial of Huddersfield Committee to H.O., in H.O. 40. 1.

[2] Peel, op. cit., p. 135.

[3] *Leeds Intelligencer*, April 13; *Leeds Mercury*, April 18; Fitzwilliam to Ryder, April 22, 1812, in H.O. 42. 122.

The shears, the gig mill, and the cloth made in and upon them were all destroyed. Finally the shop in which the offending machinery had been situated was set on fire. All other machinery, and all goods other than those made upon the offending frames, together with the house and other outbuildings, were, however, spared. And no harm was done to any of the family or employees.

Two nights later the Luddites proceeded to the greatest of the offending establishments, belonging to a noted defender of the new methods, upon which an attack had long been expected. This mill, that of William Cartwright of Rawfolds, had especially attracted the attention of the distressed and discontented croppers, belonging as it did to so outstanding a supporter of the new machines, and being situated in the centre of a district in which many small, hand shops still survived. Earlier in the disturbances some frames of Mr. Cartwright's had been taken from the wagons in which they were being brought to the mill, the convoy having been caught by a band of Luddites at a lonely spot upon Hightown Moor. The mob had held up the drivers, thrown the frames on to the moor, and beaten the machinery to pieces where it lay.[1] Nothing deterred by this foretaste of what the angry Luddites had in store for him Mr. Cartwright continued to use the new methods, merely taking the precaution of sleeping above the mill, together with some guards whom he had brought from Huddersfield.

The Luddites, whose ringleaders, at least on this occasion, it was later discovered, came from the nearby little workshop of John Wood at Liversedge,[2] had taken great pains to plan this attack, the climax of their local movement. They had hoped that at least 200 men would turn out and come to the meeting place in the fields near Cooper Bridge

[1] For details of this and the subsequent attack, see Peel, op. cit.; Hansard, *Proceedings of York Special Commission*; and correspondence of H.O. for April, especially Bull to Ryder and Greenwood to Ryder, April 15, 1812, in H.O. 42. 122.

[2] Peel, op. cit., pp. 30 et seq.

at the appointed hour, 11 p.m., on the night of Saturday, April 11. In fact only about 150 men turned up, and many of these were by no means eager or happy in their enterprise, having been intimidated by their fellows into coming. It was found necessary to post guards before and behind, to keep stragglers from deserting, and also to make fiery speeches to revive the flagging spirits of the men, waiting fearfully in the cold, dark night for the hour of midnight, when the attack was timed to commence, and marching half-heartedly through the night towards the mill. The surprise upon which the Luddites had counted was not realized, the watch dog in the mill having been aroused by the sound of the advancing force, and having woken the tiny garrison with his furious barking. He was only just in time, however. Hardly had the alarm been given before a rain of blows upon the great doors of the mill showed that the attack had been commenced. A brisk fire was opened by the little garrison of four employees and five soldiers and was continued for twenty minutes. The assailants tried to return this fire but they were unable to reach the garrison, which was barricaded in upon the second floor, and their bullets spent themselves upon the walls, or were buried in the woodwork of the massive doors. Attacking in front and behind the Luddites found that they could make no impression either way. The doors and the walls defied their efforts, blunting the hammers and axes which were pounding upon them. The mob was dismayed at such an unexpected resistance. They were afraid that at any moment the military might arrive, many of the latter being billeted in public-houses within a narrow radius and within earshot of the great alarm bell which was booming out above the mill. After several vain attempts to effect an entry even the fiercest of the Luddites were compelled to admit that success was impossible, and the mob beat a disorderly retreat.

Soon after they had gone people began to appear upon the scene. First of all was a local *bon vivant*, returning home late from an evening out. He made it his business to attend to the two wounded whom the Luddites had left behind. Cartwright's party then coming out found a scene of great disorder, the remains of hammers and hatchets, bits of torn clothing, the footsteps of many people, and traces of blood, which indicated that the casualties had exceeded the two wounded who had been left behind. The windows upon the ground floor of the mill were all broken and there were marks of a furious onslaught upon the door.

The two wounded men were carried off to a neighbouring inn. They were too seriously injured for recovery to be possible. Great attempts were made, however, to extract confessions from them before they died.[1] It was even rumoured that they were tortured, the traces of *aqua fortis* upon the bedding upon which they had been sleeping convincing Luddites that this was so, in spite of the official explanation that this acid had been used in an attempt to causterize the wounds. Amongst other eager amateur detectives who tried to worm out of these men some of the secrets of the Luddites was the Rev. Hammond Robertson, a fiery Anglican parson immortalized in the pages of *Shirley*. It is said that just before the end John Booth, one of the victims, a tinner's apprentice and the son of a local preacher from Huddersfield, making a last effort to rise, beckoned to Robertson. 'Can you keep a secret?' he said. 'I can', eagerly replied the hopeful cleric. 'So can I', flashed back the Luddite, turning over to die.

Great crowds turned out for the funerals of these two men in the following week. On the Wednesday at Halifax a great concourse of people, with mourning bands of white crêpe about their arms, followed William Hartley's body to the grave. The next day a similar crowd turned out to pay its last respects to Booth, who was to be buried at Huddersfield, only to find that the authorities fearing disorder had hurried through the funeral a scanty hour ahead of the expected time.

[1] Peel, op. cit., pp. 100–4.

The failure of this attack did a great deal to restore confidence to the neighbourhood and to discourage the Luddites. It had proved to the district that defence was possible, at least in the case of the larger establishments. The military and police arrangements were, besides, much strengthened. It was reported by the local papers that 'Leeds and Huddersfield have, with their piquets, military patroles, etc. assumed the appearance rather of garrison towns than of the peaceable abodes of Trade and Industry'.[1] After the 11th further troops were drafted into the area, the Denbigh Militia from York being stationed partly at Leeds and partly at Huddersfield and elsewhere in the Spen valley.[2] Although there had been some fear that the militia would sympathize with the rioters, it being even rumoured 'That part of the Local form part of this Lawless Banditti',[3] part of the local militia and yeomanry was called out, and proved perfectly loyal. In Huddersfield also the Watch and Ward Act was put into operation so far as local conditions allowed.[4] A number of special constables were enrolled. A semi-military patrol was instituted. At the same time throughout the district the military, instead of waiting for definite news of disorder, patrolled the countryside every night, keeping the roads clear, preventing mobs assembling, and dispersing any suspicious groups they found. As a result there were no further cases of machine breaking, though nightly drills, or raids for arms, and occasional robberies continued to be reported. These, like the earlier and successful machine-breaking raids, were conducted in the open country, upon isolated farmsteads and workshops, which could not possibly be defended. It was difficult to prevent them in the way that further machine breaking, which would now have to be directed against large, well-guarded

[1] *Leeds Mercury*, April 4, 1812.

[2] Fitzwilliam to Ryder, April 22, 1812, in H.O. 42. 122.

[3] Enclosure from J. Carr in ibid.

[4] Ibid. and letters from Radcliffe, Scott, &c., in H.O. 42. 122 and H.O. 40. 1.

establishments, could be prevented. They continued, with increasing force during May and the early part of June, throughout the summer, and created very great alarm.

Almost every night during this distressing summer there were nocturnal alarms, villages and lonely houses on the moor being frightened by the noise of marching men, or by the echo of signals, shots, and words of command. The district was denuded of arms, first by the Luddites and then by the constables and military, who tried, often without success and in the face of the jeering of the bystanders, to induce people voluntarily to surrender their arms to the authorities in order that they might not fall into the hands of the Luddites. Gradually the rapidly moving bodies of military broke down the confidence of the rioters and made it unsafe to be abroad, marching, drilling, and raiding by night. Gradually the confidence of the people returned so that they were willing to oppose, and give evidence against, the Luddites. Gradually the disorder came to an end for a similar reason to that which had brought machine breaking to an end, because all the arms in the small houses, which alone could safely be attacked, had been collected either by the Luddites or by the authorities. Although there were some cases of disorder late in the summer, and some robberies, and even an occasional case of machine breaking in the autumn and early winter, substantial order was restored by the beginning of July. Thereafter disorders, though they persisted longer in the West Riding than in Lancashire and Cheshire, were exceptional. They were also thought to be the work not of the Luddites who had been out in the early summer but of ordinary robbers, of whom several gangs were active, taking advantage of the Luddite name, which terrorized the inhabitants and prevented defence.[1]

In the late spring and early summer there was, however, very great alarm. Even as late as the end of June the

[1] Maitland to H.O., Sept. 13, 1812, in H.O. 42. 127.

Vice-Lieutenant of the Riding was talking[1] of the 'total Insecurity' (doubly underlined) of the well affected and of the 'rapid and extending Organization and drilling of the rebellious'. 'Except', he reported, 'the very spots which were occupied by Soldiers, the country was virtually in the possession of the Lawless—the disaffected out-numbering by many degrees the peaceable inhabitants.' Various factors, besides the continued raids for arms and nightly drills of the disaffected, contributed to this state of semi-panic.

Amongst other things the attempted murder of Mr. Cartwright[2] on April 18, and the actual murder of Mr. Horsfall[3] on April 27, greatly alarmed the district. They made manufacturers afraid to use the new machines (even a year later the authorities were having to beg them to do so and to assure them that they were safe)[4] and they made magistrates afraid to act (even the active Mr. Radcliffe was continually begging for a more effective personal bodyguard).[5] Other similar outrages, though really few in number, were enough to create the feeling that no one who opposed the Luddites was safe. Two members of the local militia and a special constable were said to have been shot at in the neighbourhood of Huddersfield.[6] A woman, suspected of giving information to the authorities, was assaulted in the streets.[7] At Leeds, Colonel Campbell, local officer commanding, was shot at as he was entering his house.[8]

It was impossible at this time, despite the use of spies and the offering of very great rewards for information, and despite an offer of a free pardon to any accomplice who would confess, to obtain any inkling of who was responsible

[1] Wood to Fitzwilliam, June 17, 1812, in H.O. 40. 1.
[2] Peel, op. cit., pp. 110 et seq.
[3] Ibid. and Hansard, *Proceedings of the York Special Commission.*
[4] Hobhouse to H.O., Jan. 11, 1813, in H.O. 42. 132.
[5] See letters in May 1812 and Jan. 1813, in H.O. 43. 21.
[6] See local papers for April and May 1812.
[7] Ibid. [8] Ibid.

for these outrages. While there were no further murders or assaults there were very frequent raids for arms. Gangs of twenty or more, acting with the same secrecy and dispatch that had characterized the frame-breaking parties, called on all the houses in the district where arms were suspected of being kept. Such was the general terror that they rarely met with any opposition.

There were now (at the beginning of May) very considerable forces in the area. The West Kent Militia was operating in the Leeds-Huddersfield area.[1] There were squadrons of dragoons at Leeds, Huddersfield, and Wakefield, troops of dragoons at Burnley, Halifax, and Bradford; companies of infantry at Barnsley and Penistone, besides three troops of dragoons and about 300 infantry remaining at Sheffield. All these towns had been the scene of trouble in April, during which month there had been, as we have seen, provision and other riots in every part of the country. Sheffield[2] had been the scene of a sharp disturbance, including an attack upon the armoury of the local militia, from which upwards of a 100 stand of arms had been stolen. Only in Huddersfield and its immediate environs, however, were the disturbances to be continued in the following months. But it took some time for it to be apparent, and generally appreciated, that future disorders were to be so strictly localized, and it was thought necessary for some time to keep the troops in the area thus widely distributed.

Great though this force was it was not regarded by the local authorities as sufficient. Not merely were the manufacturers appealing for guards and the magistrates for reinforcements, so that the officer commanding, General Grey, was driven almost crazy by demands he could not possibly meet, but even the junior military officers, men like Major Gordon, who had 200 infantry under his

[1] Grey to H.O., May 8, 1812, in H.O. 42. 123.

[2] Wortley to H.O., April 16 and 18; Wood to H.O., April 17, 1812, in H.O. 43. 20.

command at Huddersfield, were appealing for a larger force.[1]

There was too great a tendency to depend on the military. The population was disinclined to stir itself and the magistrates were not eager to gain an unenviable notoriety by over-exertion in the matter. It was found extremely difficult to apply the Watch and Ward Act, both because the inhabitants were afraid of the danger, and the authorities of the expense, of the system, and because it was feared that many of the men who might be called upon were themselves too sympathetic to the Luddites.[2] It was reported that many villages had held meetings, attended by almost the whole population, to petition the magistrates not to enforce the Watch and Ward Act.[3]

General Maitland, officer commanding the combined Manchester-Liverpool area, and Lord Fitzwilliam, Lord Lieutenant of the West Riding, both came into the area in May in order to promote local defence arrangements. They attended a meeting of the Lieutenancy at Wakefield on May 14.[4] The militia was divided into four sections and the order of calling it out was determined. By this means a force of 3,000 men was made available for a period of two months. Balloting for this purpose was commenced without delay, so that the force might be ready as needed. Steps were also taken to increase the number of local special constables and to encourage the local authorities either to institute the Watch and Ward or to improvise a substitute, voluntary defence association. Though the response as a whole was disappointing in some places it was immediate. Halifax wrote up on the 16th to declare that they had formed a Voluntary Association and wanted an Order declaring the town subject to the provisions of the Watch and Ward Act, 'as was the case at Huddersfield'.[5] Only

[1] In Grey to H.O., May 8, 1812, in H.O. 42. 123.
[2] J. Carr in Fitzwilliam to Ryder, April 22, 1812, in H.O. 42. 122.
[3] Memorial from Huddersfield Committee in H.O. 40. 1.
[4] Maitland to H.O., May 16, 1812, in H.O. 42. 123.
[5] Coulhurst to Fitzwilliam, May 16, in ibid.

such an order from above, so they said, would serve to bring the Act into operation, local opinion being what it was.

Two further meetings of the Lieutenancy were held in June, the Vice-Lieutenant, Sir Francis Wood, presiding, the second on the 22nd, a joint meeting of deputy lieutenants and magistrates. A new military law was urged to give power to the authorities compulsorily to collect arms, it being found impossible to induce the populace to surrender them voluntarily.[1] It was also asked at the second meeting that power should be granted to disperse nocturnal meetings without reading the Riot Act.[2] A stimulus was given to the formation of voluntary associations by adopting General Maitland's suggestion and making the dispatch of military assistance to any place dependent upon a local association of sufficient strength having been formed voluntarily. The magistrates and deputy lieutenants within ten miles of Wakefield were formed into a committee for carrying these resolutions into effect, and they were charged with seeing that full reports of local defence arrangements, associations formed, special constables enrolled, &c., be sent to the Clerk of the Peace, Thomas Bolland.[3]

During June the disorders took a surprising turn. Common robberies, which to begin with had been exceptional, Luddites rigidly confining themselves to their specific offences, machine breaking and the collection of arms, became very frequent. At first a tendency was noticed for the marauding gangs to collect lead, presumably for use in the form of bullets.[4] Now they collected money, provisions, &c. Sometimes they were lucky. A gang who visited the cottage of John Taylor at Haslegrove on June 18 managed to get away with a bill of exchange for £45 4*s*.,

[1] See reports in H.O. 40. 1.

[2] See various letters from Wood to H.O., especially during June 1812, in H.O. 42. 12 et seq. and in H.O. 40. 1.

[3] *Leeds Intelligencer*, June 29, 1812.

[4] See depositions sent up by local magistrates.

two pound notes, and about thirty shillings in silver and copper.[1] Another haul, however, consisted merely of a dozen pounds of butter.[2] Usually the yield of such robberies would be small, but the risk being small also, in the then existing state of general terror, there was a great inducement to ordinary criminals to profit by the prevailing conditions.

Three things, other than the exhaustion of the movement due to its (within its limited field) complete success, seem to have brought it to an end. In the first place the rapidly moving bodies of military, co-operating with local police officers and spies, who were kept on the move, patrolling the whole area, in a similar manner to those under Captain Raynes's command in the Stockport area[3] (which had so largely been responsible for restoring order there) were successful in alarming the Luddites and in making it unsafe for them to be out at night. They made the echo of their horses' hooves pounding the roads as common a sound in the late summer as that of Luddite footsteps and signals had been a month or so before. The increasing concentration of troops was also a reassuring feature to the local population. By September 1 there were said to be no less than 1,000 troops billeted in the thirty public-houses of Huddersfield.[4] There was no longer anywhere for the Luddites to hatch their plans over a mug of ale. Every little village had its guard. No terrified householder was by then far from help. No Luddite band could know that the coast was clear or whether a little band of galloping troops might not come suddenly into sight.

A second cause of the break-down of Yorkshire Luddism was the use of spies. At the very beginning of the disturbances the suggestion had been made that spies should be used.[5] The idea was taken up more than once. In the

[1] Deposition in H.O. 42. 124.

[2] Evidence of Swallow and others at York Special Commission, Hansard, op. cit.

[3] See reports in H.O. 40. 1 and 2.

[4] *London Times*, Sept. 1, 1812.

[5] Radcliffe to Ryder, Feb. 4, 1812, in H.O. 42. 120.

early summer great attempts were made, in which the Home Secretary himself and General Maitland were both directly concerned, to find some suitable men from the west country, clothiers and croppers themselves, who might come north and worm their way into the designs of the Yorkshire Luddites.[1] It was found, however, impossible to get men sharp enough to outwit the canny northern folk, or bold enough to come on so dangerous an errand. Help was found from nearer home. The Rev. Mr. Hay, Chairman of the Manchester Bench, and Mr. Lloyd, Clerk to the Stockport Chairman, both of whom had been employing spies, and had been otherwise active in their own districts, were now, in June and July, and in the autumn, free to turn their attention to the West Riding, and they were quick to offer their assistance. They sent at least four of their spies to Yorkshire in June.[2] Two of these men, MacDonald and Gosling, who had been sent up by Nadin, Deputy Constable of Manchester, to Halifax, succeeded almost as soon as they had arrived, in penetrating the Luddite plans.[3] They got into conversation with a cropper named Milnes. Pretending to be Luddites themselves and plying Milnes with ale MacDonald and Gosling wormed their way into his confidence. They asked to be 'twisted in' or admitted as members of the Luddite confederacy. Milnes agreed to do this and took MacDonald to the house of Baines, an old cropper living near by, where a little gathering, Baines, his three sons, and two friends, was sitting talking. MacDonald was introduced and after a little talk it was decided to swear him in then and there, old Mr. Baines administering the oath and little Zachary

[1] See correspondence between Maitland and Sidmouth during May and June 1812 in H.O. 40. 1 and 2, and H.O. 42. 123 et seq.

[2] Taylor, Whitehead, MacDonald, and Gosling, see letters and depositions in Lloyd and Hay to H.O. in H.O. 40. 1 and 2, and H.O. 42. 123–6.

[3] York Special Commission, evidence of Baines and others; *Leeds Mercury*, issues for July 1812; Peel, op. cit.; Prentice, *Historical Sketches of Manchester*.

Baines watching the door. Gosling, who was not there, later swore to have overheard MacDonald talking with Milnes the next day and boasting of having been 'twisted in', the others cautioning him to keep quiet about it.

Various arrests were possible as a result of this information. By the end of the summer there was quite a little group of prisoners awaiting trial, men accused of complicity in the attack on Rawfolds Mill and these prisoners accused of administering unlawful oaths. The major authors of the disturbances were still at large. Very few arrests had yet been possible, and there were no convictions. But the Luddites were getting frightened. They knew that there were spies about and they were therefore getting afraid to talk, or to trust any one. They were afraid also that their colleagues might break down and confess, or come in secretly to give evidence, in order to win a pardon for themselves. In this way in the autumn the whole conspiracy was discovered, Benjamin Walker, one of the four murderers of Mr. Horsfall, who had already been questioned several times upon suspicion, breaking down and confessing everything, his mother having pressed him to do so to save his own neck, and lest one of his colleagues might do so first.[1] Very many arrests were possible, one confession leading to another, and one discovery to many others. Once the Luddites lost confidence in their security, and began to fear detection, as they did soon after spies began to be employed, the movement came rapidly to an end.

A third encouraging feature was the improvement in conditions which followed the repeal of the Orders in Council. There was also prospect of a good harvest. By July Lord Sidmouth could talk of high hopes of 'an abundant harvest and of general and continued employment'.[2] Although the American market was closed by war almost as soon as it was opened by repeal of the

[1] Lloyd to H.O., especially Oct. 18, 1812, in H.O. 42. 128.

[2] Sidmouth to Fitzwilliam, July 16, 1812, in H.O. 43. 21.

Orders in Council, so that a few shipments only got sent out, the European market opened sufficiently to make up for this loss. By December it could be said that 'everything [was] up . . . and in the Cotton Parts of the Country they [were] even working long days'.[1] The period of intense trade depression and of closed markets, which dated from February 1811, was, by June 1812, for the time being, at an end.

During the autumn, although common robberies continued, Luddism as such was thought to be entirely ceased. There were, so the Treasury Solicitor thought, signs that many of the robberies were committed by a gang who availed themselves of the popular prejudices of the country to commit general plunder, and not by the Luddites.[2] The Lord Lieutenant distinguished[3] between:

1. Murderers and Terrorists.
2. Destroyers of Machinery.
3. Housebreakers for arms or mere plunder.
4. Twisters-in or the administrators of oaths.

While these classes overlapped it is more than probable that all but a very few Luddites confined themselves to offences 2 or 4 or to the collection of arms, which was a subsidiary of 2. By the autumn these Luddites were again orderly. The only continued trouble was caused by the various robber gangs who were using the Luddite name, and profiting by the general terror, which was kept up long after valid reason for it had ceased.

It is doubtful whether the parliamentary inquiries into Luddism in June,[4] and the Acts of Parliament which followed them in July, had really contributed very much towards the suppression of the disorder, which had, indeed, really long passed its zenith, though the Committees did

[1] Maitland to H.O., Dec. 21, 1812, in H.O. 42. 130.
[2] Hobhouse to H.O., Nov. 29, 1812, in H.O. 42. 129.
[3] Letter to H.O., Nov. 4, in ibid.
[4] *Parl. Debates*, xxiii. 951 et seq. and 1028 et seq.

not realize that[1] before they had reported. Indeed the Committees' reports, and the alarmist speeches of Ministers in Parliament, may be said to have prolonged rather than allayed the general terror and anxiety. Speeches like that of Castlereigh,[2] who said that the proceedings of the rioters were such 'that all the army of the Empire could not afford protection to the King's faithful subjects against the depredations, as the law at present stood', were frankly exaggerated and only served to perpetuate the general terror. The Whigs, who were the chief critics of the Government, were right when they said[3] that the reports of the Committees were hardly warranted by the evidence, that there was no proof of an extensive combination, of armies of rioters and dumps of arms, of extended revolutionary plans, or, indeed, of anything but isolated attacks and a persistent campaign against machinery. They, had they but known it, could have got ample evidence from the reports of the Government's own servants, and notably General Maitland, to show that the disorder was limited to the forms and places in which it had shown itself,[4] and could have been suppressed had the existing law been promptly, generally, and vigorously applied.[5]

The Committees reported in June. The Acts of Parliament, *The Preservation of the Public Peace Bill* and the *Act of Indemnity,* were passed in July. They had been preceded in May by the *Unlawful Oaths Bill,* making the administration of a secret oath a criminal offence, a measure directed particularly to the Lancashire and Cheshire situation, whence most of the evidence of unlawful oaths is to be drawn. The Peace Bill gave enlarged

[1] So early as May 9 Colonel Campbell, local officer commanding at Leeds, after a tour of the district, felt able to say 'I cannot help thinking that this alarm is kept up more from the past outrages than from any real cause of immediate danger'.

[2] *Parl. Debates,* xxiii. 1028 et seq.

[3] Ibid., pp. 962 et seq.

[4] Maitland to H.O., especially June 18, 1812, in H.O. 40. 1.

[5] Ibid. and statements of various members in Commons debates, *Parl. Debates,* xxiii. 962 et seq.

powers to the magistracy in districts where disturbances were feared. It was based upon weaknesses in the existing system as experienced in Yorkshire as well as Lancashire, and as reported by Maitland and other officials. It was restricted to the disturbed districts (with power to the Government to extend by Proclamation its provisions to other areas) and was to be temporary. It provided:

1. That the magistrates should have power to search for arms upon suspicion and to call on the public to surrender them.
2. That they should have power upon an emergency immediately and without reading the Riot Act to disperse tumultuous assemblies and arrest suspected persons.
3. That, because of a shortage of magistrates in the disturbed districts, magistrates from adjoining areas should have a concurrent jurisdiction.

The Act of Indemnity, granting a free pardon to people who should confess their offences, particularly with regard to the administration of illegal oaths, was intended to encourage moderate Luddites to give up their illegal course. Very few arrests were made under, and little use was made of, these various Acts. They did, however, serve to express the interest of Parliament in the situation.

During November and December plans were made for the trial of the prisoners who had been arrested during the summer and autumn, of whom about 100 were said by then to have been lodged in York Castle.[1] It was decided to hold a Special Commission, though the ordinary Assize Judge, Mr. Justice Bailey, had kept his commission open and was ready to serve. He was regarded as too lenient, and two more impressive judges were chosen, Baron Thomson and Justice Le Blanc.[2] Robberies continued and alarm was general, even on the part of the

[1] Leeds papers for November.

[2] See letters on this subject in H.O. 42. 129.

magistrates.[1] It was thought necessary to take special precautions (even to the extent of carrying witnesses away to secret places of safety),[2] for the protection of people concerned in the prosecutions, which were under the direct supervision of the Treasury Solicitor.

A great concourse of people gathered in York for the trials,[3] which opened on Monday, January 3, 1813. Mr. Park, Attorney for the Duchy of Lancaster, was Counsel for the Prosecution.[4] Mr. Brougham had been retained for the defence. Some of the most prominent gentlemen of Yorkshire formed the Grand Jury. A great body of troops was massed in the Castle, where the trials were held, and in the town, for the protection of the court.

Nearly half the prisoners indicted, or 30 out of 64, were discharged without trial, nominally as an act of clemency and after capital and other heavy convictions had been obtained against the ringleaders, but really from lack of adequate evidence.[5] Of the 34 cases tried, 7, or more than one-fifth, were acquitted. Of the remaining cases 1 was transferred to the next assizes, 1 discharged as King's evidence, 1 sentenced to death but pardoned on condition of transportation for life, 7 transported for 7 years (for taking illegal oaths), and no less than 17 were hanged.[6]

It was in these capital cases that the Court and the public was most interested and these were taken first. The most dramatic was that of the Crown versus Mellor, Thorpe, and Smith, croppers of Liversedge, near Huddersfield, charged with the murder of John Horsfall. These three men were convicted mainly on the evidence of their accomplice, Benjamin Walker, who had turned King's Evidence. It was proved that they had not merely planned this

[1] See Fitzwilliam to H.O., Nov. 4, 1812, in H.O. 42. 129, and H.O. to Radcliffe, Dec. 4, in H.O. 79. 2.

[2] Lloyd to H.O., Oct. 18, 1812, in H.O. 42. 128.

[3] See reports in press, in Hansard, op. cit. (of which several editions are extant), and in Peel, op. cit.

[4] See reports from Hobhouse, Park, Allison, &c., in H.O. 42. 131–2.

[5] Hansard, op. cit.

[6] Ibid.

murder, waylaying Horsfall on his return from market one evening in April and shooting him as he rode by the coppice where they were hiding, but also had been ringleaders in many cases of framebreaking, including the attack on Rawfolds Mill. They could have been convicted on a number of counts. There was no doubt of their guilt, though they tried to create flimsy alibis, and the cases took all day to try.[1] They were sentenced to death and executed in the castle yard at York within two days of their trial.

The other capital cases were as follows, five for machine breaking[2] (the attack on Rawfolds Mill), three for stealing arms (in the latter part of August),[3] seven for ordinary robberies.[4] There were therefore at the end of the trials no less than fifteen persons lying under sentence of death. Of these all but one were actually executed, being hanged, like their three predecessors, the murderers of Horsfall, in the castle yard in the presence of the great crowds who had come to York for these notorious trials.

The remaining cases were less serious, being chiefly for the administration of illegal oaths. The Crown was successful in obtaining seven convictions, five out of the six men charged with administering an oath to the spy MacDonald at Halifax,[5] and two out of the three men charged with swearing in another spy at Barnsley,[6] being convicted and sentenced to seven years' transportation apiece. The Prosecuting Attorney was pleased and surprised with these convictions, he had anticipated trouble in getting the juries to believe the informers' evidence, more especially since MacDonald was only able to attend under writ of habeas corpus, being himself under arrest on a charge of assault at Manchester. The Defence Attorneys, however, instead of trying to break down the Crown witnesses by cross examination, relied upon alibis, which the

[1] For a graphic account, see Peel, op. cit., also Hansard, op. cit., pp. 32–73.

[2] Hansard.

[3] Hobhouse to H.O., Jan. 9, 1813, in H.O. 42. 132.

[4] Ibid. and Hansard, op. cit., pp. 5 et seq.

[5] Ibid.

[6] Hansard, op. cit., pp. 104–14.

Court, having heard so many false alibis during the trials, was by then unwilling to accept.[1]

This tremendous toll of life, seventeen hangings being exceptional even in those times, struck terror into the hearts of the Luddites. The authorities gave wide publicity to these trials, which had, in any case, been reported in the press in every city in the kingdom. Special reports in pamphlet form were issued and widely and freely circulated.[2] At the same time a Proclamation was issued offering a free pardon to any who should still come in and confess their offences and purge them by taking the Oath of Allegiance.[3] It was desired to enforce the effect of the policy of severe punishment of the guilty by an example of mercy to the merely misguided. To win over the latter other methods were also resorted to. Pamphlets extolling the virtues of machinery,[4] showing that it was as silly to break frames as it would be to break simpler machines, spades or ploughs, and pointing out to the populace that the only effects of such violence would be to drive the trades to other, safer regions, were issued, and received more attention now than they had in the previous year, when the Luddites were still undetected and confident.

Unfortunately the terror of the loyal, and of the manufacturers, did not abate as fast as the confidence of the Luddites. More than one official appeal had to be made to manufacturers to persevere in the use of machinery.[5] Pamphlets had to be issued showing that its use was necessary if the country's industries were to be able to withstand the pressure of foreign competition.[6] For some time it was necessary to maintain an unusually large military garrison in the districts which had been the scene

[1] Hobhouse to H.O., Jan. 9, 1813, in H.O. 42. 132.

[2] Copy in H.O. 42. 132.

[3] Feb. 9, 1813, in H.O. 42. 132.

[4] See examples in letters from Manchester in H.O. 42. 123 and H.O. 40. 1.

[5] Hobhouse to H.O., Jan. 11, 1813, in H.O. 42. 132.

[6] Ibid.

of Luddism, although the bulk of the force was withdrawn during March 1813.[1]

The Government was occupied for some little time after the disturbances had come in fact to an end with liquidating its obligations. Messrs. Lloyd and Allison, who had been active in ferreting out the Luddite conspiracy, were given, after some delay, small rewards. They had also to be explicitly enjoined not to continue their work, it not being the desire of Government to advance any further prosecutions.[2] Mr. Radcliffe, who had been recommended by the Lord Lieutenant for a Baronetcy, and who deserved some expression of the authorities' thanks, was ultimately given this (for such an occasion) unprecedented honour.[3] Mr. William Cartwright also, who had apparently lost heavily because of the prominent part he had taken in opposing the Luddites, and who was sending in pitiful petitions stating that his loyalty had brought him near to bankruptcy, was ultimately given some small compensation by the Government.[4] Both Radcliffe and Cartwright also were the recipients of votes of thanks from the local manufacturers and authorities, the latter receiving also a public subscription by way of further reward.[5]

Captain Raynes and other officers who had been active received rewards in the form of seniority and promotions.[6] Their subordinates, the spies engaged upon this business, were also rewarded, with money, some £70 being distributed for this purpose by Mr. Hobhouse, the Treasury Solicitor, before he left York.[7] The Luddite informers, and

[1] See Sidmouth to Maitland, March 29, 1813, in H.O. 43. 21.

[2] Hobhouse to H.O., Jan. 13, 1813, in H.O. 42. 132.

[3] Maitland to H.O., Dec. 23, 1812, in H.O. 42. 131, and H.O. to Fitzwilliam, Dec. 25, in H.O. 43. 21.

[4] See letters from Cartwright to H.O. in H.O. 42. 130 and 147. In the latter letter (Dec. 12, 1815) C. mentions that he has received £300 through General Wynyard.

[5] Resolutions of meeting in Halifax in H.O. 42. 133.

[6] Maitland to H.O., March 20, 1813, in H.O. 42. 133, and H.O. to Montrose, April 8, and Grafton, May 23, 1813, in H.O. 43. 22.

[7] Acland to H.O., Jan. 24, 1813, in H.O. 40. 2.

especially Walker, were, however, less fortunate. Their requests for reward were turned down. They were shunned alike by their fellows, the former Luddites whom they had incriminated, and by the authorities who had used their evidence but resented their importunity. Walker, particularly, though he had in fact a good legal claim against the Huddersfield Committee for the reward that they had offered for information leading to the conviction of Horsfall's murderers, was never told so, and was never able to collect any reward or to make other than a poor, mendicant existence.[1]

The district relapsed, if not into its normal calm, at any rate into submission. The interest of the working classes, here as elsewhere, was turned to the matters of peace and parliamentary reform, which seemed, with the collapse of Napoleon's power, to be less academic than they had been, and more worthy of a cropper's attention.[2] The writings of Cobbett and other propagandists also, which were winning the attention of the working classes, seem to have had an enormous influence in turning them from violent courses.[3] Yorkshire Luddism was, after the York trials in January 1813, at an end.

[1] Occasional letters from Walker or about him crop up in later correspondence of the Home Office between 1813 and 1817.

[2] Maitland to H.O.

[3] Peel, op. cit., p. 281 says 'Beyond all question' the decline of Luddism 'was hastened materially by the writings of the famous William Cobbett'.

VII

DISTURBANCES, 1813–17

LUDDISM collapsed after the York trials and did not show itself again for more than a year. Prices had fallen from their distressing height and trade was better.[1] There was not the same motive of extreme distress to drive the workers into riot. It had been proved also, by the use of spies and soldiers, quite possible to bring the rioters to conviction. The tremendous toll of executions (no less than forty Luddites or robbers and other rioters classified as Luddites, having been hanged at Chester, Lancaster, and York, after the Special Commission Proceedings in those towns in the year 1812–13) had struck terror into the rioters, who had previously been so confident. Although the public anxiety continued long after there was any real need for it, and though special precautions were continued well on into the summer of 1813, there were no overt acts of disorder to disturb the public peace. Gradually, beginning in the early spring, it was thought safe to move some of the great body of troops away from the last of the three disturbed areas to return to order, the West Riding, and by the end of the year little more than the normal garrison was left in this district, or in any other of the previous scenes of Luddism, with the exception of Nottingham, which had a special extra garrison of dragoons as late as April of the following year, 1814.[2] The other emergency measures of the authorities, special nightly patrols, the maintenance of secret prosecuting committees, the enrolling of special constables and persons liable to serve under the Watch and Ward, the employment of more than the normal number of spies, were also gradually discontinued, the Nottingham patrol, for example, being dismissed in the

[1] Maitland to H.O., Dec. 21, 1812, in H.O. 42. 130, and *Nottingham Gazette*, Feb. 12, 1813.

[2] H.O. to Coldham, April 13, 1814, in H.O. 43. 22.

summer of 1813, there having been no disturbances of any kind for so long a time.[1]

The interest of the working classes was turned to other matters. It was generally reported by the authorities, and the evidence of spies seems to confirm the fact, that petitions for peace and parliamentary reform, and the formation of Spencean Societies and Hampden Clubs, began to absorb the energies of the people.[2] The political, radical movement, the work of Cartwright, Cobbett, and Place, upon the one hand, and the more disjointed, ineffective revolutionary, seditious movement, the work of agitators like Benbow, Thistlewood, and the Watsons, on the other, which had been factors in many of the events of 1811–13, and had unnecessarily confused the spies and some of the authorities of those days, because they seemed to be, though in fact they were not, connected with Luddism, now replaced Luddism as the centre of interest. To study and to understand all their ramifications is an almost impossible task, and one which is not our present concern. It is sufficient to note that they provided an outlet for the energies, despairs, and hopes of many erstwhile Luddites, who had, in those difficult years, to have some way of letting off steam, whether it took the form of breaking machines or of passing resolutions for reform.

It is apparent also that the more normal activities of distressed workers, the organization of Trades Unions, the attempts to raise wages and otherwise improve conditions of work by petitions, by negotiations with the employers, and by strikes, which had temporarily, so far as the Luddites were concerned, been discontinued in favour of more direct action, were now coming into their own again. Reports from each of the previously disturbed districts indicated that in 1813–14, after the collapse of Luddism,

[1] Coldham to H.O., April 13, 1814, in H.O. 42. 138.

[2] Maitland to H.O., Aug. 5, 1812, in H.O. 42. 126, and Peel, op. cit., p. 281.

as in 1810–12, before its irruption, negotiations about wages, and proposals for a 'general turn out', absorbed the attention of the workers.[1]

Various activities of this kind, in particular, drew upon the energy of former Luddites. Various others, which probably had no connexion with Luddism, alarmed the authorities, whom memories of the Luddite risings had made fearful. Mr. Hay, for instance, from Manchester, was in 1813 proposing to the Home Office a Bill to regulate Friendly Societies, of whom a great number were in existence.[2] He felt that they often formed a cover, and a safe and easy way of collecting funds for more dangerous activities, and he thought they ought to be regulated closely, lest they be perverted from their real objects. The next year he was worried about the policy of 'The Union Society of Printers, Cutters and Drawers in Lancashire, Cheshire, Derbyshire, etc'.[3] This Union had, apparently, as one of its chief objects, that of preventing the masters from using machinery. Its methods were, however, widely different from those of the Luddites, being merely agreements among the workpeople not to accept employment from any masters who should make use of the obnoxious machinery. Even so Mr. Hay thought that the combination was illegal and should be suppressed. It was, however, impossible to find sufficient evidence to justify a prosecution. The next year Lancashire was troubled by yet another similar matter,[4] by a conspiracy of the calico printers of Lancashire to prevent their employers using machinery. The master printers were making an effort to resist 'the long continued combination of the men'. It was feared that disorder might result. That it did not is a sign

[1] Fletcher to H.O., Dec. 13, 1813, in H.O. 42. 136.

[2] Hay to Sidmouth, Feb. 4, 1813, in H.O. 42. 132.

[3] See H.O. to Hay, March 1, 1814, in H.O. 43. 22; Swainson to H.O., Jan. 31, 1815, in H.O. 42. 142; and Wright and Evans to H.O., Dec. 29, 1815, in H.O. 42. 147, &c.

[4] See various letters to and from the Lancashire magistrates in, especially, H.O. 42. 142 and 147.

of the extent to which popular feelings had turned away from violent methods.

The only one of these unions which seemed to have any definite connexion with Luddism was that of the framework knitters, 'The Nottingham Union',[1] as it was popularly called, which was the major focus of the interest of the midland workers from the summer of 1812, when it was formed, to that of 1814, when prosecutions and a recrudescence of framebreaking precipitated its collapse. This union was a definite outcome of the framework knitters' petition to Parliament in the spring of 1812,[2] which in its turn was an outcome of previous movements amongst the stockingers in favour of negotiation,[3] movements which the framebreaking of 1811–12 had temporarily discredited, but which came into their own again as soon as framebreaking began to get dangerous towards the end of 1812.[4] As early as February 1812 some of the leading stockingers, amongst whom Gravener Henson was a moving spirit, advertised that a meeting[5] of delegates from the various hosiery villages would be held at the sign of Sir Isaac Newton, Glasshouse Lane, Nottingham, to consider the state of trade and make reports to Whitbread and other members of Parliament. This meeting led to the formation of a committee to supervise the business of a petition to Parliament, a committee[6] which was active throughout the summer, and which was financed by weekly contributions from the stockingers.

[1] For particulars of the Society's organization, see (*a*) *Nottingham Gazette*, June 24, 1814. (*b*) Opinions of Attorney and Solicitor-General in Home Office Papers for Feb. 1814, H.O. 42. 137. (*c*) The following letters: Woodcock to Hobhouse, Nov. 16, 1813, in H.O. 42. 135; Coldham to H.O., Feb. 20, and Litchfield to Beckett (and enclosures) Feb. 16, 1814, both in H.O. 42. 137; Sculthorpe to H.O., April 12, 1814, in H.O. 42. 138.

[2] See Chap. IV, p. 85.

[3] Chap. II, pp. 43, 44, 47, and *Parl. Papers*, 1812, ii. 259.

[4] Chap. IV, p. 85, and issues of *Nottingham Journal* and *Review* and *London Times* for Nov. and Dec. 1812.

[5] Ibid., and *Nottingham Journal*, Feb. 15, 1813.

[6] Ibid., p. 87, and issues of *Nottingham Journal* and *Review* for May, June, and July, 1812.

The failure of the Bill, the hosiery clauses being struck out in Committee and even the emasculated Bill being defeated in the Lords, caused great disappointment and almost bought about a break up of the committee.[1] It led in the end, however, not to its collapse but to its expansion. A General Meeting[2] of the Trade on July 15, 1812, decided to print and circulate throughout the hosiery districts a copy of the evidence against the recent Bill and also to instruct the committee to:

'enquire how the Carpenters, Tailors, Shoe-makers, and Cutlers conduct their Union and report to a General Meeting the Plan they consider the most satisfactory, and in future to be adopted by the United Branches of Framework Knitters'.

The weekly subscription of *2d.* per week per member, and the balance of all funds in hand, which amounted to at least £200, were to be devoted to this purpose. A plan of campaign was agreed upon, the interest of each branch of the trade, plain or skilled, silk, cotton, or worsted, being considered equally important, but to be advanced in succession.

Later in the same year a constitution[3] was drawn up. The Union was to be known as 'The Society for Obtaining Parliamentary Relief, and for the Encouragement of Mechanics in Mechanism', or, as it was sometimes put, '... for the Encouragement of Improvements in Mechanics and Manufactures'. Its members, who paid a weekly subscription of *2d.* or *3d.*, besides being liable to fines for infraction of rules, and who were entitled to certain Friendly Society benefits during sickness, unemployment, &c., were organized in local branches, of which there were said[4] in 1814 to be at least 20, with a total membership of some 2,000, in the immediate neighbourhood of Nottingham alone. Each branch was governed by a local committee

[1] Chap. IV, p. 87, and *Nottingham Journal*, July 18, 1812.
[2] Ibid.
[3] *Nottingham Gazette*, June 24, 1814.
[4] Woodcock to H.O., Nov. 16, 1813, in H.O. 42. 135.

having a free discretion on local matters. Groups of branches having more than 30 members each and more than 200 in all, could form central committees. These central committees were united in their turn into general central committees, at Nottingham, Derby, Leicester, Glasgow, and Dublin. From amongst the Nottingham General Central Committee was chosen a small central executive committee of five members having the supreme ruling of the combination. Central committees might draw on the funds of local societies, up to £10 on their own discretion, and as regards further amounts with the consent of the General Central Committee. The latter committees, and the Central Executive Committee, could draw on any or all local funds at will.

The combination thus organized was to hold an annual conference of representatives of the central committees of the three midland counties, while every three years there was to be a conference of delegates from all the central committees in the 'Empire'. The first such conference seems to have been held in May 1813[1] while the official date of the annual conference was the first Monday in August.

This combination was said[2] to have three main objects. It wanted to put an end to the evil of inexperienced workmen owning frames, and breaking all the regulations of the trade, doing fraudulent work and driving regular workmen out of employ. It wanted to end the evil of speculation in frames leading to over-production and exorbitant rents. Finally it wished to reward inventors, 'who were usually robbed', and to make sure that new inventions should be exploited only by, and new methods taught only to, members of the Union.

In pursuit of these objects a number of activities[3] were undertaken. Offices or 'houses of call' were established in Nottingham and other towns. These offices kept a record

[1] Woodcock to Holtoms, Nov. 16, 1813, in H.O. 42. 135.
[2] *Nottingham Gazette*, June 24, 1814.
[3] See references on p. 138, n. 1.

of all frames unemployed and waiting to be hired, of all work open to be done, and of all framework knitters needing work. Members registered with the 'houses of call' all particulars, of the frames on which they were working, the gauge, the rent, the work, the owner, the employer, and the price. Members who had no work, or who were not satisfied with the terms of the work they had, were supported until they should get, either from the Society or from some other employer, work at a fair rate. In order to provide work for some unemployed members and to keep wages up by making it unnecessary for any member to accept work at less than a fair rate of wages, the Society itself bought up material, giving it out to members to be made up into hose. The resulting finished product, of which it was later said a great amount had been manufactured, was sold in Nottingham and London by agents of the Society. The Society also paid benefits to members who were sick or old, or even, sometimes, on strike or in prison, this latter practice, of contributing towards the legal expenses of indicted members,[1] being, however, exceptional and strongly criticized by most of the branches. Rewards were also paid to inventors of new machines and new methods, on condition that they were sold or taught only to members.

The Union was also, of course, occupied with the normal business of a trades union, with negotiations with the hosiers and with attempts to keep up, or force up, wages. An order of work was drawn up,[2] the plain silk branch being dealt with first, and the interests of the other branches of the trade being put next in order, the Lace Committee, for example, agreeing not to put forward its claims until those of the plain silk trade had been met, and the plain three needle branch of the silk trade deferring its claims to those of the two needle branch. Apparently

[1] Woodcock to H.O., Nov. 16, 1813, in H.O. 42. 135.

[2] Enfield to H.O., Aug. 11, 1814, together with enclosures, all in H.O. 42. 140.

progress was slow, and little success was achieved in this direction, for we find in 1814 the plain silk branch still monopolizing most of the Society's attention.[1]

In order to forward all these objects the Society was in need of considerable funds. Towards them it could look to several sources of income. The weekly subscription of 2*d.* or 3*d.* per member, together with extra subscriptions or donations from more prosperous stockingers, and friends of the trade, who could afford more, were the major standby. In addition there was an income from fines, for breaches of the Society's by-laws, and, sometimes and to a limited extent, a profit from sales. It was also said[2] that some hosiers contributed, more probably from fear than from real sympathy, and during the disturbances in May 1814 one hosier put in a paper said to have been received from the Union:

> 'Masters pay their Subscriptions the same as the Journeymen and it is hoped that you will not be so remiss as to do as the rest of the masters in the branch.
>
> William Freeman, Secretary.'

There are signs that the total income from all sources was large, particularly at times of difficulty when the Union had a fight on its hands. Mr. Coldham said[3] in May 1814 that the Nottingham branches alone had been able to collect as much as £115 in one week that month. Mr. Sculthorpe had estimated[4] the previous month that the total weekly income of the Nottingham district branches together was probably as much as £150. Some later accounts[5] of the combination which were confiscated, show a total income for the period April 25 to July 4, 1814, of £1,302 10*s.* 7½*d.*, or an average of just over £130 a week. While these amounts are probably larger than usual because of the interest aroused by the strike and the

[1] *Nottingham Gazette*, June 17, 1814.
[2] Coldham to H.O., May 10, 1814, in H.O. 42. 139.
[3] Ibid. [4] April 12, 1814, in H.O. 42. 138.
[5] Coldham to H.O., July 11, 1814, in H.O. 42. 140.

framebreaking which took place that spring and summer, and while other areas almost certainly were not as rich as the Nottingham district, it is still certain, after making all reasonable allowances, that the Union was, if not a wealthy, at least not a poor organization.

It was not popular with conservative people or with the authorities, who made several attempts to get at it and suppress it.[1] Its statutes had, however, been very cunningly devised. It was said that Sir Samuel Romilly and Mr. Samuel Marryat had been consulted in connexion with the original plan.[2] Mr. Coldham had to report[3] that the Nottingham magistrates, who would willingly have seized its papers, did not see their way clear to doing so:

'. . . not being political or connected with any political purposes, I cannot see that they come under the 39th Geo. III, or that we have any evidence to proceed against them under the Combination Acts.'

So long as it avoided formally associating itself with definite plans for a strike or of framebreaking, as it did for nearly two years, it was safe from interference.

Throughout 1813 and part of 1814 therefore, even in the midlands, where the danger of another outbreak was greatest, the working classes were quiet, expending their energies, and working off their discontent, in purely industrial and legal activities, in the sort of attempts to better their condition that had occupied them before they had descended to Luddism. Unions such as those that we have mentioned, and a host of others, absorbed such of their attention as the pressure of work, for industry was active, and the interest of the reform movement, left free. The younger and more restless spirits also, who were always the ringleaders of Luddism, and who would have little sympathy for permanent, peaceful activities,

[1] See correspondence with Law Officers of the Crown in Home Office Domestic Letter Books for 1813 and 1814.

[2] Coldham to H.O., May 10, 1814, in H.O. 42. 138.

[3] Coldham to H.O., April 13, 1814, in H.O. 42. 138.

political or industrial, found an outlet for their energy in poaching and in petty crime, 'robbing orchards and hen roosts'.[1]

This quiescence of Luddism, and indeed of all serious, open popular disturbance, continued, except in the midlands, throughout 1814, and with isolated exceptions, throughout 1815. Not until the post-war depression began to settle heavily upon the country during 1816 was it seriously threatened.

In Nottinghamshire there was, however, a fourth period of Luddite activity in the spring and summer of 1814 (the previous three periods were, it will be remembered, March 1811, November 1811 to February 1812, and November 1812 to January 1813, the second being the worst). This fourth attack of the Luddites was said[2] to have grown definitely out of the activities of the Nottingham Union. The efforts and propaganda of the Society had made the men discontented with wages which they would otherwise have cheerfully accepted. This seems too simple an explanation of the disorder, which was, probably, more due to the shortage of work, and the depression of trade,[3] from which the district was suffering more than was normal, though not so severely as in 1811 and 1812.

The immediate cause of the outbreak was clearly a dispute between the combination and some of the hosiers over an advance in wages that the workers were demanding.[4] A strike was threatened. Threatening letters, some of them signed 'Edward Ludd', began to be received by hosiers who stood out against the advance. Several hosiers, notably Messrs. C. and J. Ray, were won over by such tactics, and

[1] See reports of secret agent in correspondence of Coldham and Enfield with H.O., 1814-17.

[2] *Nottingham Gazette*, issues from April to Sept. 1814.

[3] Ibid., see especially August issues. The *Gazette* believed the trade would have to content itself with smaller wages and smaller profits if it was to withstand the pressure of foreign competition.

[4] See correspondence of the H.O. with the midlands' authorities for March-August 1814, H.O. 42. 137-41.

by the arguments of the Union officials, to agree to pay the desired advance. The body of the hosiers' meeting in London on April 21, 1814, decided, however, to resist the proposal, and they and Mr. Coldham (who had just become Secretary to a newly formed committee of hosiers, which had taken over the duties of the original committee for prosecuting framebreakers, which by then had closed its books) with difficulty induced the minority firms, which were paying the advance, to fall into line and resist it. The disappointment of the framework knitters issued in wrath against, particularly, the firms which had changed their minds and were now refusing an advance they had previously agreed to grant. Messrs. Ray's hands, being assured of the support of the rest of the trade, declared a strike on April 26. The hands of other firms, and notably that of Beardmore and Parker, joined in the strike. The lines closed on both sides, the hosiers all agreeing to oppose the combination and refuse employment to the strikers and to all hands who should help them, the Union and the workers in firms other than those first striking, supporting the strikers and trying to sustain the advance.

While this strike, and the fight between the framework knitters' union and the hosiers' committee, of which it was an incident, were going on, framebreaking had been recommenced,[1] whether with the goodwill of the strikers and the union it is impossible to say. On April 7 it was reported[2] that three frames, the property of Messrs. Needham and Nixon, a firm noted for their opposition to the disputed advance, had been broken at Kimberley. One or two other similar cases were reported during the next few days, in and out of Nottingham.

Precautions[3] were quickly taken, much more rapidly than in previous outbreaks of Luddism. Arrangements

[1] For particulars see ibid. and local papers, and also Felkin, op. cit., and Blackner, *History of Nottingham*.

[2] Coldham to H.O., April 7, 1814, in H.O. 42. 138.

[3] H.O. to Coldham, April 13, in H.O. 43. 22, and Coldham to H.O., of same date, in H.O. 42. 138.

were made for an enlarged and paid constabulary to co-operate with the military guard, which was fortunately still available, and a patrol of special constables was immediately organized (on the model of the old patrol, used in 1812, but finally discontinued in the summer of 1813). Such measures were quickly successful in bringing what was in any case a sporadic outbreak of framebreaking to an end.

There were one or two isolated attacks in May but on the whole the district was quiet, although the strike continued, from the middle of April till the middle of July. Then, and with greater frequency during August and the first part of September, further Luddite attacks were reported.[1] Once again the authorities had to deprecate the apathy shown by the general populace, their failure properly to criticize or oppose the Luddites' actions, their unwillingness to come forward as witnesses. The local authorities began to get alarmed and to appeal to the Government for troops.[2]

In September, however, rather significantly just after the arrest of a young stockinger called James Towle, the attacks came to an end. Towle was arrested[3] on the evidence of Mr. Garton, a formerly prosperous stockinger of Basford. On the night of September 5, in the early morning, long after Garton had gone to bed, he was woken up by shouts of 'Who's there? . . . It's Ned . . . Neds to your duty'. Amongst various voices he thought he distinguished that of Towle, a young stockinger who lived not more than 100 yards away. The assailants took about half an hour to complete their work of destruction, Garton keeping meanwhile closely to his room and making no attempt to oppose them. As soon as they had gone, however, he came out and surveyed the damage, finding six

[1] See H.O. 42. 140–4 for reports of Nottinghamshire magistrates, and also local papers.

[2] See Coldham to H.O., and H.O. to Coldham in H.O. 42. 140.

[3] Coldham to H.O., Oct. 15, 1814, in H.O. 42. 141 and Sutton, *Date Book of Events . . . connected with Nottingham*, p. 313.

out of eleven frames to have been broken. Knocking up one of the neighbours he then went around to Towle's house, suspecting him of the crime both because of the voice, resembling Towle's, which he had overheard during the attack, and because Towle had previously been reported to have criticized Garton for 'bating', or paying reduced wages, and had threatened to break his frames. Towle was not to be found either at his home or at Papplewick, where it had been suggested he might be discovered. It was not until six the next morning, returning after a fruitless night's search, that the searching party found him at Basford at the house where he was employed. Despite his defence, that he had been sleeping all night at his master's house so as to be ready to start early in the morning on some work needing to be finished, and that Garton was a prejudiced witness, having previously threatened Towle and said, if his frames were broken he would know whom to look for, meaning Towle, the latter was arrested and lodged in gaol.

Towle's arrest seemed to have broken up the conspiracy, of which, it appears from later evidence,[1] he had indeed been a ringleader. Framebreaking came to an end. It was, however, some time before the district returned to its normal calm. Garton, particularly, was the victim of many threats and went in terror of his life. A guard was placed about his house. Even so an attack was made at about 9.30 p.m. on the night of October 14.[2] Three men broke in first and they were followed by a large crowd crying 'Damn him. Where is he?' They milled around the house, seeking for Garton, shouting and firing wildly into the air. The little guard, at first too surprised and frightened to make any defence, was stirred to action. It began to fire and succeeded in driving the Luddites back, one of the latter, a man of the name of Samuel Bamford, being killed. As the attacking party was retreating

[1] See letters from Nottinghamshire magistrates and reports of their secret agents in H.O. 42. 153–8. [2] See p. 146, n. 3.

in some disorder they were frightened by the appearance of a man at a neighbouring door. Thinking him to be a constable they shot at him, as he stood in the light of his open door, and killed him instantly. He turned out to be not a constable but an innocent bystander, one William Kirby, on whom Mrs. Garton had been calling, and who had come out at her request to see what was the meaning of the shots that they had overheard. The Coroner's Jury naturally brought in a verdict of murder against persons unknown, meaning the Luddites, for Kirby's death, and of justifiable homicide for that of the Luddite Bamford. A Royal Proclamation, an offer of free pardon and reward to accomplices, and a reward of £200, were all unsuccessful in eliciting information.

The general terror continued, though there were no open disturbances to justify it. Garton retreated in terror from Basford and was maintained in hiding at the expense of the Government.[1] So profound was the general obloquy in which he was held that no bids were advanced at an auction of his effects. The alarm was continued right up to the Assizes of 1815 at which Towle came up for trial. It was freely rumoured[2] that the latter's friends would mob the court if he were condemned. The judge, the Mr. Justice Bailey against whom so many criticisms had been made for clemency in dealing with the Luddites, was said to have been extremely agitated and to have looked 'as pale and anxious as the prisoner'. The court was crowded so that it was difficult for the ample guards to clear a passage as they brought the prisoner in to stand his trial. Both judge and jury were said by the local authorities to have been affected by this terror; the former summing up in favour of the prisoner, and holding Garton prejudiced, and his evidence of an overheard voice inadequate, and Towle's alibi good; and the latter following his recommendations and returning a verdict of 'Not

[1] *Nottingham Gazette*, Jan. 6, 1815.

[2] Coldham to H.O., March 21 and 27, 1815, in H.O. 42. 143.

Guilty' The acquittal, concession to fear though it might be thought, had apparently the best effects, and real calm was at last restored.

The actual framebreaking had, of course, ceased long since, in the preceding September. The strike had also collapsed, and with it, to some extent, the Union. In July, acting upon evidence[1] received from one of Messrs. Ray's hands, two officials of the Union were arrested and charged with the offence of giving and receiving money for the restraint of trade. They were convicted and sentenced. Although the sentences were light they were sufficient. They alarmed the members of the Society and precipitated a break-up of the combination, which the failure of the workers to secure the desired and bitterly fought for advance had in any case rendered likely. A combination of this kind, like a strike and like framebreaking, was dependent for continued support upon its capacity to achieve, at least in reasonable measure, its objects. The hosiers had stood firm throughout this summer against the combination and against the advance. They had, as they had not been able to do in previous outbreaks, succeeded in coercing the minority and forcing the whole trade into line, against the workers. The authorities too had been active, much more so than in 1811–12.[2] The decline of the combination set in. It may be measured by such facts as this: that in the following November the Mansfield Framework Knitters Society had ceased to exist and that of its bank balance £10 had been handed over to the Nottingham Society, which continued to hang on, and the rest distributed amongst the members.[3] The decline of the combination, though not complete, began immediately.

1815 was, on the whole, a quiet year in the midlands,

[1] Coldham to H.O., July 7, 1814, in H.O. 42. 140.

[2] This was also true of the next period of Luddism, in the summer and autumn of 1816.

[3] Woodcoke to H.O., Nov. 11, 1814, in H.O. 42. 141.

as in the rest of the Kingdom. There was alarm at the time of the Spring Assizes,[1] when Towle was up for trial, but it did not lead to anything. There was talk by the secret agent now employed by Mr. Coldham and the hosiers' committee, of secret and seditious meetings and plans for revolution, which were a new thing in Nottinghamshire, though common enough elsewhere in the country.[2] In April it was thought well to issue a Proclamation warning people against a meeting proposed to be held in the forest.[3] In May one Peter Green was arrested[4] on a charge of being concerned in a seditious meeting of unemployed, held to consider their distresses and to petition the Prince against the recently passed Corn Bill, a measure for the protection of the farmer, hard hit by the collapse of the exaggerated war demand. The passage of this Bill caused continued muttering, especially in Nottingham, though it did not there produce any disorder.[5] The agent continued throughout the summer to talk of secret meetings in ale-houses and in the forest, meetings which, if they were 'small and rather aimless', were able, according to his report, to indulge in large plans, for the assassination of Messrs. Coldham, Becher and Stevens, to send delegates to London and Yorkshire, to raise large funds, to concert plans for a general rising.[6] Gravener Henson, who was privy to all the framework knitters' combinations in these years, and who had been a moving spirit in the Nottingham Union, was charged with being concerned in these seditious plans also.[7] It was said that he had been to London and Yorkshire and had also talked of being able to raise 25,000 men at two hours' notice. Similar meetings were reported[8] from

1 Coldham to H.O., March 21 and 27, 1815, in H.O. 42. 143.

2 The regular Domestic Letter Books of the Home Office, series 42 and 43, together with series 70, Private and Secret Papers, throughout this period, from 1810–20, are full of spies reports from every area.

3 Coldham to H.O., April 24, 1815, in H.O. 42. 144.

4 Ibid., May 30.

5 Blackner and Sutton, op. cit.

6 Coldham to H.O., and enclosures, June 17 and 24, 1815, in H.O. 42. 144.

7 Ibid., June 3, July 8.

8 Ibid., and Mayor of Leicester to H.O., July 1.

Leicester, and a request was made for Bow Street officers to spy them out.

The authorities were properly suspicious with regard to many of these rumours, and they noted that in fact the little meetings proved to be too poor to maintain the delegate system about which they talked. They realized how easy it was for the spies to confuse one thing with another, the Nottingham Union, or an innocent visit of Gravener Henson to London, with really revolutionary plans. They realized also that one area was keeping up the spirits of another, each, though its own resources were small, being led to believe that the resources of the discontented in other places were tremendous. It was heartening also that, in spite of all these rumours, and similar ones were coming from other districts and from every spy, there was little actual disorder.

The only overt disorders that there were during the year were quite unconnected with one another and with Luddism. In London in March there was almost a week's rioting[1] on the occasion of the passage of the Corn Bill. It was quite serious while it lasted. The approaches to the Houses of Parliament, the streets of Westminster, and the houses of ministers and members noted for their support of the Bill, were the scene of riotous assemblages. Members were mobbed going to and from the House. It was for a short time feared that a really serious situation might develop. Actually, however, the riots, like most London disturbances, died down almost as suddenly as they had arisen, there being no disposition on the part of the authorities to give way and the number of troops on hand being very adequate.

At Norwich, on the occasion of the Agricultural Show, there was a demonstration against the Bill,[2] though it did not lead to anything. At Nottingham, as we have seen, there was muttering. Otherwise there was only an undercurrent of discontent.

[1] London press for March 1815, and H.O. 42. 143.
[2] Letters from magistrates, March 17, 1815, in H.O. 42. 143.

Later in the year there were two isolated centres of disturbance. For a month in September and October there were serious disputes in Hull,[1] Newcastle, and South Shields. Arising out of a dispute between the seamen and the shipowners, these disorders left the docks for some time in the hands of the rioters. Troops and indeed ships had to be sent to the area before it was quieted. Only after a considerable show of force were the magistrates able to patch up a settlement.

Later still, in November, a danger of riot was reported[2] from Staffordshire, where some of the workpeople had recently been discharged. Yeomanry and militia were held in readiness. Extra military forces were moved to the area. Within a week it could be said that the trouble, a mere local and temporary industrial dispute, was at an end.

It was not till 1816, four full years after the suppression of Luddism as a widespread movement of disorder, that there was again general disturbance. In that year, and almost continuously thereafter for several years, there was trouble in the industrial districts. That confused and apparently dangerous internal situation which drove the Liverpool Government into its repressive policy, and to the hated invasions of popular liberty known as the 'Six Acts', had its origins in the events of 1816. That year was, in a measure, that of the birth of Chartism and of the death of Luddism. That is to say that in that year the last Luddite outbreak properly so called took place. And in that year also the profound post-war popular discontents, which were to issue, amongst other things, in Chartism, first began to show themselves.

There was a sudden and extreme slump in trade following the final conclusion of more than a quarter-century of war. Industries which had been adjusted to an inflated, artificial war demand had suddenly to find a normal level. British industries, which had enjoyed a long start during

[1] See Letters in H.O. 43. 24 and 42. 146. [2] Ibid.

the years that the world was at war, and which had had a virtual monopoly of such trade as there was during the war, had now to stand up to normal competition. They found competing national industries growing up in many countries, industries, like the infant ones of America, which were now strong enough to obtain tariff protection from their governments. The great body of men employed at war, in the army and navy, or sailing under letters of marque or running contraband of war, and the still larger body employed at home on war-time tasks, making munitions, weaving uniforms, producing war supplies, found themselves out of a job. The world, and especially Britain, which had borne an unusually heavy share of the war's burdens, was impoverished by long fighting, loaded down with debt, faced with tremendous difficulties in the always complicated, lengthy, painful task of reconstruction. It was some time before the development of new industries and methods, and of new sources of wealth, and the necessary readjustments of industry, society, and politics, were carried far enough to relieve the tremendous social strains to which every class of the people, but particularly the working class, was then subjected. During this long time, and particularly during the immediate post-war years, during the bitterly unpopular administration of Liverpool, Castlereagh, and Sidmouth, there were, in the sufferings of the people, in the country as well as in the towns, seeds of every kind of discontent and disorder.

In the early summer of 1816 the files of the Home Office once again, for the first time for four years, knew the ominous heading 'DISTURBANCES'. There were reports in the bundles of papers so entitled from many areas, north, south, east, and west. Cardigan,[1] Shields,[2] Sunderland,[3] Hull,[4] Staffordshire,[5] Suffolk,[6] Norfolk,[7] Birmingham,[8] and Bridport,[9] districts of very different types, agricultural as

[1] Letters and reports in H.O. 43. 24 and 42. 151–2.
[2] Ibid. [3] Ibid. [4] Ibid. [5] Ibid.
[6] Ibid. [7] Ibid. [8] Ibid. [9] Ibid.

well as industrial, were on this list. In most places the disorders which were reported were very temporary. In some places, notably in Birmingham, they hardly extended beyond rather tumultuous meetings. The really serious centre of disturbance was East Anglia.

Centred in the Isle of Ely, but extending into Suffolk, and involving also the towns of Wisbech and Norwich, there was in May 1816 a widespread agricultural disturbance.[1] Tumultuous meetings gave way to rick firings and other signs of disorder. On the 24th of May it was reported[2] that the Isle of Ely was in an alarming state. Mobs at Littleport and Downham had mobbed the magistrates, demanding better wages and more modest prices. Another letter[3] referred to the 'present unsettled, disturbed, and dissatisfied state of the lower orders of the Town and Vicinity of Wisbech'. Major-General Sir John Byng was immediately sent into the area to take command and fresh troops were drafted for service there. The disturbances, an expression of the prevailing intense and general agricultural distress, which lay behind other disorders, as, for instance, those at Bridport, were quickly suppressed. The Crown agreed to defray the expenses of prosecutions and by the 18th of July a Special Commission was sitting at Ely to try the offenders. The sentences were heavy, more so than local opinion thought necessary. A meeting of inhabitants protested[4] against the sentence of seven years' transportation on the nine men convicted, especially since the district was again orderly and the men had been lead to expect sentences only of one year. The Government was, however, proof against all appeals for mercy.

Later in the year reports came in from places as distant and widely separated as Frome,[5] Stockport,[6] Bolton,[7]

[1] Letters and reports in H.O. 43. 24 and 42. 151–2.
[2] Ward to H.O., ack. in H.O. 43. 24.
[3] Jobson and others to H.O., ack., in ibid.
[4] In H.O. 42. 152.
[5] Ibid.
[6] Lloyd to H.O., July 1, 1816, in ibid.
[7] Fletcher to H.O., and Magistrates to H.O., Aug. 22, in ibid.

Coventry,[1] Hinkley,[2] and Birmingham,[3] of distress and disturbance. Mostly these disorders did not extend farther than angry meetings, but they were symptomatic of the uneasy state of the country, a sign of the pressure of conditions. Even more alarming was the isolated case of machine breaking reported[4] from Huddersfield. On February 24 at night, in the approved Luddite manner, an attack was made on the workshops of John Roberts, cloth-dresser of Quarnley, near Huddersfield, and 4 frames, 4 pairs of shears, and 39 panes of glass, to a total value of £25 17*s.* 6*d.*, were broken. It was feared that a recrudescence of Yorkshire Luddism was in sight. The manufacturers, and especially the redoubtable William Cartwright of Rawfolds, assured the authorities that they would repell attacks, placing guards and defending their property, 'as they ought to do' but too generally had not done in 1812. Whether because of this spirit of opposition and the precautions that were taken or no, the attack was not repeated, though it served to keep up for some time a general spirit of alarm.

Only in the midlands was there at this time continued disorder. Thence once again, for the fifth time, reports began to come in of disorderly assemblages and nightly attacks. Early in June some point net lace machines were broken at New Radford.[5] A few days later seven men broke into another house and destroyed twelve point net machines, creating a bad precedent because, as it was reported, 'Ned Ludd turned thief' and stole some lace.[6] Further, similar attacks continued. Finally, as a climax to the month's disturbances, on the night of June 28 the factory of Heathcote and Boden at Loughborough, one of the largest in the district, and belonging to a noted, wealthy hosier, a leading pioneer in the use of the recently

[1] Podmore to H.O., July 1, in ibid.

[2] Ibid.

[3] Ibid.

[4] Allison to H.O., Feb. 26, 1816, in H.O. 42. 148.

[5] Felkin, op. cit., p. 237, and Sutton, op. cit., p. 322.

[6] Ibid.

constructed and much improved lace machines now coming into use, was assaulted.[1] A number of men, mostly from the neighbourhood of Nottingham, many of them disguised and armed, entered the casting shop at the rear of the factory at about midnight. Overpowering the three guards in this room, one of whom, Jacob Asher, was rendered insensible by a shot from a blunderbuss, they passed through the setting-up room. Securing the guards here and on the first floor, most of whom were overcome with fear, the Luddites demolished most of the 25 machines standing on the three sections of this level of the building. The five men on guard above, being terrified by all this noise, were secured without resistance. The shouts of 'advance with the blunderbusses', 'more blunderbusses here', were too much for them. Hardly, however, had the Luddites commenced their attack upon the machinery upon this third and top floor before they were alarmed by noises from below. Not until they had satisfied themselves again that the coast was clear did they return to the attack, setting upon the remaining frames with a great shout of 'Ludds, do your duty well. It's a Waterloo job, by God.' Completing their work in a further quarter of an hour, the Luddites then retired. They shook hands with Jacob Asher, who had now returned to consciousness, and whom it had not been intended to hurt, and retreated into the night, collecting their own guards, whom they had posted about the factory to give an alarm, as they did so. The factory guards, though free to do so, were far too terrified to give chase.

So considerable an attack, made, unlike most Luddite escapades, against a factory and not merely against the small house or workshop of a working stockinger, and involving damage of between six and eight thousand pounds worth of property,[2] created great alarm. Very energetic attempts were made to discover and apprehend

[1] Local press; Sutton, op. cit., p. 324; and various letters in H.O. 42. 152.
[2] Felkin, op. cit., p. 238.

the offenders, of whom there were said to be seventeen. James Towle, the stockinger acquitted in the previous year of an attack on Garton's frames at Basford, was arrested,[1] tried at the summer assizes at Leicester, and, in spite of renewed rumours of the court being mobbed, convicted and sentenced to death. Kept in gaol for some time in the hope that he might make a confession, in the end, apparently, he did so.[2] He was then promptly (in the middle of November) executed. A tremendous crowd followed him to his grave, coming from Hucknall, Bulwell, Arnold, and other places, to see one who was regarded, even by men who would not themselves break frames, as a martyr to his fellows' cause, go to his, to them, honoured grave.

His trial,[3] and even his execution,[4] were not followed, as it had been hoped they would be, by a cessation of framebreaking. There was indeed almost an intensification of it, his friends, lead by his brother Bill, being, as it was later reported,[5] eager to show 'Jem that they could do something without him'. Reports came up to London of a 'great number of frames having been destroyed'.[6] Thirty more were broken in one night in October at Linby before a crowd of 100.[7] The Duke of Newcastle even thought that conditions were worse than they had been in 1811–12 and '13.[8]

The real difference, and the factor which made the situation much less serious than then, was the greater activity of the magistrates and gentry.[9] Though complaints were made now, as they had been before, that 'magistrates were asleep',[10] and that the military was too strict in requiring

[1] Enfield to H.O., Aug. 10, Lockett to H.O., Aug. 11, 1816, in H.O. 42. 152. [2] Enfield to H.O., Nov. 2, 1816, in H.O. 42. 155.
[3] See Reports in H.O. 42. 155 and n. 6. [4] Ibid.
[5] Confession of Burton in Rolleston to H.O., Feb. 9, 1817, in H.O. 42. 159. [6] Allsopp to H.O., Oct. 16, 1816, in H.O. 42. 153.
[7] For account of attacks see local papers and letters of local magistrates in H.O. 42. 153–4.
[8] Letter to H.O., Nov. 6, 1816, in H.O. 42. 155. [9] Ibid.
[10] Gill to H.O., Oct. 14, 1816, in H.O. 42. 153.

written orders to move,[1] even when the noise of the Luddites' attacks could be heard, upon the whole adequate precautions were promptly taken. Informers were busy, and were soon able, as they had not been in 1812, to penetrate the designs of the Luddites.[2] The Watch and Ward was instituted[3] and civil and military patrols were set on foot, adequate guards being posted, as they had been at Heathcote and Boden's, at the various factories and in the villages, and being willing, as the Loughborough guards were not, to act.

The authorities were quick to note the real characteristics of this outbreak. It was the work of a small body of men,[4] though sympathized with, and perhaps financially supported by,[5] the rank and file of the stockinger and lace workers, and by their committees and unions. It was directed not against 'any particular description of Loom, but against all Looms let for work below certain fixed rates of wages',[6] its object being the power of dictation in respect to wages and conditions of work, and its motive the unusual distresses from which the workers were suffering. It collapsed very rapidly once the confessions of Towle and of one or two other prisoners, and the activities of the government informers, enabled the ringleaders to be arrested.

During the winter a number of men were arrested.[7] By the beginning of 1817 the leading Luddites, who turned out mostly to be young men like Towle, and associated with his gang, who had been so boastful the previous summer, were either in gaol or in hiding and in terror of their lives. When the prisoners were brought to trial all

1 Sherbrooke to H.O., Nov. 16, 1816, in H.O. 42. 155.

2 See reports in H.O. 42. 153–9.

3 Enfield to H.O., Oct. 21 and 23, 1816, in H.O. 42. 154.

4 See depositions of arrested men, e.g. in Rolleston to H.O., Feb. 9, 1817, in H.O. 42. 159.

5 See confession in Enfield to H.O., March 26, in H.O. 42. 158.

6 Fane to H.O., Oct. 24, 1816, in H.O. 42. 154.

7 Accounts in H.O. 42. 159.

expectations of disorder were belied.[1] No less than eight men were condemned to death. While two of these were respited and transported the remaining six were publicly hanged. The executions, on April 17, 1817, like the trials, passed off without any 'semblance of disorder'.[2]

During the winter of 1816–17 therefore Nottinghamshire Luddism again, and finally, collapsed. Trade was improving slightly in the spring of 1817.[3] The stockingers were becoming interested in the idea of peaceful negotiations with the hosiers and petitions to Parliament. Frame-breaking being discredited, the hosiery and lace workers were once again, as they had been in 1812, thinking of trying to realize by propaganda what they could not get by violence. The Petitions from, and the Committee of Parliament upon, the Framework Knitting Industry, though features of the year 1819,[4] were being prepared in the previous years. They, and the Committee of Parliament for inquiry into the industry in 1845,[5] together with the strikes, the combinations of stockingers and hosiers, the public subscriptions for relief, and other expedients which were reported,[6] especially between 1819 and 1822, were the channels into which, for the next half-century, the framework knitters, in their despair, poured their discontent and their hopes for better times. Luddism, shown in long experience to be an ineffective way of securing redress, except occasionally and for a short while, was finally crushed by the weight of authority. The Luddites who were swung off midland gallows in 1816–17, like the 40 Luddites who were hanged in the north in 1812–13, were a grim and effective warning to their colleagues and successors not again to attempt to solve industrial disputes by machine wrecking.

The collapse of Luddism did not, however, lead to a

[1] Sherbrooke to H.O., March 1, 1817, in H.O. 42. 161, and Fane to H.O., April 17, in H.O. 42. 165.

[2] Ibid.

[3] Ibid.

[4] See *Parl. Papers*, 1819, for reports and minutes of evidence.

[5] See *Parl. Papers*, 1845.

[6] Felkin, op. cit., pp. 243–53.

restoration of general order. Machine breaking, which had been the major feature of popular disturbances in the years 1811 and '12, was a minor feature in those of the years 1816 and '17. We have noted the widespread, though temporary, disturbances of the summer of 1816. As the winter of 1816–17 developed, the situation, so far from improving, grew worse. Alarming reports came into the Home Office from every district. Bolton,[1] Manchester,[2] Stockport,[3] Carlisle,[4] Huddersfield,[5] Oldham,[6] Sheffield,[7] were all reporting dangerous and seditious meetings, issuing in the latter four places either into actual, though temporary riots, or such serious danger of them as to lead the local authorites to request immediate military reinforcements. At the same time, meetings[8] in the Spa Fields at London were becoming particularly large and stormy. In the light of the spies' reports[9] of secret, seditious meetings attended by Benbow, the Watsons, and Thistlewood, and of plans for a general rising, these events were thought to be a sign of greater pending dangers still.

The public alarm, which was natural in days of such distress, so soon after the excesses of the French Revolution, was excessive and uncritical. The public, like the spies and the authorites who relied upon the latters' information, was little able to distinguish between tub-thumpers letting off steam and real revolutionaries trying to promote riot. Innocent, though radical, political meetings,[10] to consider petitions and pass resolutions, and the

[1] Fletcher to H.O., esp. Aug. 30, 1816, in H.O. 79. 2, and Nov. 5, in H.O. 42. 155.

[2] Magistrates to H.O., esp. Nield to H.O., Nov. 4, in ibid.

[3] Lloyd to H.O., letters in ibid.

[4] Byng to H.O., Nov. 4, in ibid.

[5] Ibid.

[6] Nield to H.O., Nov. 4, in ibid.

[7] Fitzwilliam to H.O., Dec. 7, Wortley to H.O., Dec. 12, in H.O. 42. 156.

[8] See, especially, various bundles of papers usually endorsed 'Thistlewood Papers' in Home Office Letter Books, 1815–17.

[9] Ibid.

[10] Cf. the case of the Manchester men acquitted of taking illegal oaths in 1812, when Nadin, the deputy constable, and the spies on whose

normal activites of Friendly Societies, Hampden Clubs, Spencean Societies and Trades Unions, and the passage of the quite legal delegates of such groups about the country, became dangerous in the light of actual, though limited disorders, and of the alarmist rumours which were freely circulating. The continual talk of the spies of plans for an armed rising and of contact between the disaffected in different areas, though never substantiated in fact, was believed because of the definite evidence of sedition, treason or lesser crime that could be proved against a very few, not very powerful men like the Watsons. Because a few impractical revolutionaries talked of seizing the Tower of London,[1] and because an actual mob at Spa Fields once attacked some gunsmiths' shops,[2] the Government and the public were lead to think it necessary to prepare for a general rising.

In January 1817 special secret committees of Parliament[3] were appointed once again to consider the internal state of the country and the necessity for emergency measures. Again, as in 1812, they were fed with the reports of the government's army of informers. The reports they received, especially at a time when the Prince Regent had been insulted by having stones thrown at his coach as he went to open Parliament,[4] seemed sufficient to justify extreme measures. A suspension of the Habeas Corpus Act was considered, for the last time in British history, and the repressive policy of Sidmouth and Castlereigh, which was to issue a year or so later in the notorious 'Six Acts', was set in motion. Spies were sent down from London, headed by 'Oliver', dean of the corps.[5] Others were employed in great numbers by the local authorities.[6] The latter were

information he worked, confused an innocent reform meeting with a Luddite assemblage.

[1] See letters submitted to the Cabinet in Jan. 1817, in H.O. 42. 158.

[2] See London papers, Nov. 1816–Feb. 1817.

[3] See H.O. 42. 158 and also *Parl. Papers, Journals, Debates*, for Jan. and Feb. 1817.

[4] London papers, Jan. 1817.

[5] See Chap. XIV.

[6] Ibid.

warned, through the agency of the Lord Lieutenant, and were ordered[1] to perfect arrangements for calling out militia and yeomanry and the Watch and Ward rapidly in case of need.

Three limited outbreaks alone occurred to lend the colour of necessity to all these precautions.

At Manchester[2] the meetings for reform, which were continual, and the general discontent, which was extreme, being played upon by agitators and by the spies, issued in a plan for following up petitions by sending representatives to London to present petitions in person. There was a proposal that 'leaders of tens' should go, a rough and ready method of selecting delegates which seemed to imply some sort of organization on the part of the workers from whom these delegates were drawn. A small, poor group of men and women actually set out, inadequately equipped with supplies for their long journey, and carrying their blankets on their backs. They did not get far. Many fell by the way. They were harried by the authorities. Few reached the midlands, none, so far as can be traced, reached London.

This pitiful little march was followed by a number of arrests, the Manchester authorities claiming[3] that they could prove it was intended as a prelude to a much more serious venture, a general rising. No evidence to substantiate this, or other alarmist tales, came out, however, despite the arrests and the examination of prisoners, some of whom were even taken before the Secretary of State and other members of the Government.[4] The prisoners being ultimately discharged without trial it is a fair assumption that the rumours were exaggerated and that the 'March of the Blanketeers', which hardly deserves the slight notoriety it has attained, was what it appeared to be, a vain idea on the part of a few poor, discontented workers,

[1] Circular in H.O. 42. 158.

[2] See H.O. 42. 159 et seq., and Prentice, op. cit.

[3] Hay and other Manchester magistrates to H.O., Jan. to June, 1817, and Prentice, op. cit., pp. 95 et seq.

[4] In H.O. 42. 159–60.

that Parliament would pay more attention to their personal pleas than to their petitions.

The two other outbreaks were hardly greater. The best known, to which the impressive name of 'The Pentridge Revolution' has been given, was a march of Derbyshire peasants and stockingers upon Nottingham.[1] On June 8, 1817, during the night, a mob of about fifty men collected from the villages of Ripley, Pentridge, Alfreton, and South Wingfield, at the last-named place. They proceeded together towards Nottingham, stopping at a few houses to recruit more men and to collect money and arms. Passing Swanwick and Langley Mill they entered Nottinghamshire between two and three in the morning at Eastwood, amounting now to a force of about 300. Getting no word of the concerted rising in other places which they had been lead to expect, the little army began to lose confidence. Men slank away one by one. A detachment of hussars from Nottingham, warned by a messenger from Eastwood, who had ridden to Nottingham and found the town awake, having expected the attack, rode out to meet the rioters. Coming over the hill towards Eastwood as the sun was coming up over the horizon, this body of troops saw before them only a frightened little mob of less than fifty men. The rioters scattered at once on sight of the military, but some thirty of them were ridden down and arrested. Others, including the leader, Jeremiah Brandreth, were arrested during the course of the next few days. They were promptly tried by Special Commission, the leaders being sentenced to death, and hanged as traitors.[2]

Actually they were clearly poor, misguided countryfolk, deluded by their leaders, amongst whom were Government spies, into thinking that a general rising would do good, and was possible. They would never have risen in their locality had they not been lead to think that their fellow

[1] See letters from Nottinghamshire and Derbyshire magistrates in H.O. 42. 166; local papers; and Sutton, op. cit.

[2] Report of trial in Arnold, *Life of Thomas, 1st Lord Denman*.

countrymen in hundreds and thousands would rise elsewhere. They were, to use an American term, just 'suckers', who were silly enough to think that an armed rising could relieve their very great distress. Like the Luddites they were driven by distress into violence that was foredoomed to failure. The execution of so many of their leaders, coming on top of the Luddite executions, did much to cow the midlands into quiet.

The 'Huddersfield Rising'[1] was very similar, though it has attracted less attention. A few hundred men gathered on the night of June 8, at Engine Bridge outside Huddersfield. Other little groups collected at Henley and Holmfirth. Shots were fired at the yeomanry and at one or two constables who came out to investigate. Retreating to gather strength the military found upon their return that the rioters, losing confidence because they were not reinforced, had scattered of themselves. The ringleaders absconded. An attempt to proceed against a few of the rank and file on a charge of burglary, which was deemed more convenient than that of treason, failed. Because there were no convictions, and no leaders as picturesque as Brandreth, whose counsel, Denman,[2] had won his client a great deal of enviable publicity, the rising was more quickly forgotten than the Derbyshire one. It was, however, almost exactly comparable, similar in size, in object, in abject failure.

These two 'risings' were all the overt evidence that emerged as to the danger of a general rising. They were obviously so small, so ineffective, so disconnected, so much the work of a few spies[3] and agitators playing upon the feelings of poor, ignorant men, that they did not create much alarm. They served indeed more to provoke a reaction against the Government's repressive policy, and especially the spy system, which was then so largely un-

[1] See *Leeds Mercury* for July 1817 and H.O. correspondence for May, June, and July, H.O. 42. 166–7.

[2] Arnold, op. cit.

[3] See Chap. XIV.

covered,[1] than to strengthen the elements in favour of repression. They were also, obviously, quite unconnected with Luddism, except in so far as the same population provided the personnel for them and for Luddism. They, and similar vain protests against depression and distress, were, with the reform movement and with trades union activity, the resource of a working class which had tried Luddism and found it wanting.

[1] By the *Leeds Mercury* and by Whitbread in Parliament.

VIII

THE AIMS AND OBJECTS OF THE LUDDITES

It has been generally thought that the object of the Luddites was to prevent the introduction of new machinery economizing labour.[1] To some extent it was. The new shearing frames and gig mills in the West Riding of Yorkshire and the steam looms in Lancashire and Cheshire in 1812, and the improved lace machines in Nottinghamshire and Leicestershire in 1816, which were attacked by the Luddites, were the object of their vengeance because they economized labour, created unemployment amongst hand-workers, and tended to lower the average rate of the latter's wages. These machines, though they were not absolutely new, having been in existence, coming gradually into use, over a period of five or ten years, were recent enough to be blamed for many of the evils from which the workers of those districts were suffering in the years 1811–17, for which they were in fact, in a measure, responsible.

It was clearly recognized by contemporary authorities that this was so. The Parliamentary Committees say so.[2] Papers like the *Manchester Exchange Herald* talk of the new power looms as being in 1812 'as decided an object of vengeance with the cotton weavers as the shearing machines with the croppers'.[3] The threatening letters which northern manufacturers received specifically warned them to discontinue using the new machinery on pain of a Luddite attack. Manufacturers who did so, even if they paid low wages or were otherwise unpopular, were, in the

[1] Note Lord Liverpool's statement in Parliament, that legislation had been needed for the protection of new machinery in every manufacture in which it had previously been introduced, and was therefore, in 1812, now needed for the same reason in the hosiery and lace trades. *Parl. Debates*, 1812, xxi. 1167.

[2] *Parl. Debates*, xxiii. 951 et seq. and 1028 et seq.

[3] April 21, 1812, quoting from the London evening paper *Alfred*.

north of England, free from danger. The Luddites proper rigidly confined themselves to attacks upon shearing frames, gig mills, steam looms, and factories using power-driven machinery. Other machinery and the goods made upon them, as well as the persons and other property of the manufacturers, were safe.

Antipathy to new machinery was not, however, a motive of the midland Luddites, except in 1816, and even then it was only a minor object. There was, in fact, no new machinery in the midlands in 1811–12. It is true that the Parliamentary Committees, and upon one occasion the Duke of Newcastle,[1] talk of antipathy to machinery of a new construction allowing women to do the work previously done by men. These statements, however, are general. And they seem to be unfounded. There is no trace of such machinery being in existence, fewer women and children being, in fact, employed in 1812 than was normal in the industries. There is conclusive evidence to prove that the Committees' reports were false. The *Nottingham Review* of December 6, 1811, was at pains to point out 'that there [was] no new machinery in Nottingham or its neighbourhood against which the workmen direct their vengeance'. Mr. Hayne, a well-known local manufacturer, corroborates this statement, so far as the lace trade is concerned. The objections of the workmen were 'not against any particular Machine but to the sorts of work produced'.[2] General Fane makes a similar statement[3] with regard to the Luddites' objects in the disturbances of 1816, when there was a new machine in the midlands, saying the riots were 'not a war against any particular description of Loom, but against all Looms, let for work below certain fixed rates of wages'.

The object of the midland Luddites in breaking frames

[1] To Ryder, Nov. 16, 1811, in H.O. 42. 119.

[2] 'Observations on the Nottingham Disturbances' in letter to H.O., Feb. 12, 1812, in H.O. 42. 131.

[3] Fane to H.O., Oct. 24, 1816, in H.O. 42. 154.

and lace machines was not to prevent their introduction but coerce their owners. What they prized was, as General Fane remarked,[1] 'the power of dictation in respect to wages'. Mr. Coldham refers[2] to the 1811–12 framebreaking as being 'upheld by a considerable number of mechanics for coercing the Hosiers in the price of their labour and mode of conducting their manufacture'. Mr. Becher takes a similar view of it;[3] in his opinion the object of the Luddites was to destroy the frames 'of every person by whom they conceived themselves to be aggrieved or oppressed'. It was very seldom, and then only unintentionally and in error, that they injured the frames of the better employers; the general tendency of the system was 'a proscription against persons and work of a specific description'.

The actual records of the riots bear out these facts. Time and again the Luddites would visit a house and break some frames and spare others of the same make, because some were making 'cut-ups', or were owned by hosiers paying low prices or in goods, while others were employed on good work at fair wages. The tone of injured innocence used by some hosiers protesting against the destruction of their frames and saying that they had always done fair work and paid good wages, shows that it was generally believed that to do so was sufficient protection.[4] Frames were seldom if ever injured unless they were employed on 'cut-ups', which was the most prolific cause of frame-breaking, or on other fraudulent work, or belonged to hosiers paying low wages or in kind, or to stockingers taking too many apprentices. It was not particular machinery but particular practices and particular employers against which the Luddites' vengeance was directed in the midlands.

[1] Fane to H.O., Oct. 24, 1816, in H.O. 42, 154,

[2] Letter to H.O., Jan. 14, 1812, in H.O. 42. 119.

[3] Letter to H.O., Feb. 11, 1812, in H.O. 42. 120.

[4] See advertisements in Nottingham papers.

This is true even though there were certain 'wide' frames, said to be of new construction, in the midlands in 1811–13, and some new lace machines in 1816, against which the Luddites' vengeance was particularly directed. These machines were broken because they were used chiefly, if not solely, for fraudulent work, or by undercutting employers. They were spared when, if ever, they were used on standard work at standard wages. The 'wide' frames, which had originally been used only for making pantaloons and other knitted goods by the piece, were during the first decade of the nineteenth century very frequently turned to the manufacture of 'cut-up' hosiery. In this way one workman could do the work hitherto done by several men, albeit the finished product was a poor article, likely to bring the trade into disrepute. By 1811 the 'wide' frame had largely superseded the narrow frames previously employed, thus increasing output and economizing labour, and seriously aggravating existing over-production. Even so it was only at a time of great depression, some years after 'wide' frames had been generally introduced, that Luddite vengeance was directed against them. And even then it was only wide frames used for the manufacture of 'cut-ups' or other cheap work which were attacked.

Similarly with the new lace machines, or 'Loughborough improved', which were coming in between 1810 and 1816, and which were drawing the workers into factories. Although they economized labour they were not attacked until a period of acute depression and trade disputes arrived, as it did in 1816, nor were the machines of fair employers, paying fair wages, even then in danger. The attack upon Heathcote and Boden's factory, which employed the new machines in 1816, was provoked by the firm's competitors more because it had lately reduced wages than because it, like other firms, which were not attacked, used new labour-saving machinery.[1]

[1] Sutton, op. cit., pp. 324–5.

The objects of the Nottinghamshire Luddites were more complicated than those of their Yorkshire colleagues, whose simple aim it was to prevent the introduction of new machinery. The midland Luddites hoped to obtain, by attacks upon machinery, a series of concessions from their employers, and certain arrangements within the trade that they had previously been seeking by other means. They have left behind certain evidence of their own upon this point. There is an interesting document[1] in the Home Office files purporting to be a Proclamation of the Framework Knitters issued from 'Ned Lud's Office, Sherwood Forest'. This declaration, after stating that the Charter of the old Framework Knitters Company gave the men the right to break frames, and declaring that the Act of 28 Geo. III making framebreaking a felony had been obtained in the 'most fraudulent, interested, and electioneering manner' and was therefore null and void, warned all hosiers, lace manufacturers, and proprietors of frames that the Luddites would:

'break and destroy all manner of frames whatsoever that make the following spurious articles and all frames whatsoever that do not pay the regular price heretofore agreed to by the Masters and Workmen. All point Net frames making Single press and frames not working by the rack and rent and not paying the price regulated in 1810. Warp Frames working Single yarn or two course hole not working by the rack not paying the rent and prices as regulated in 1809 Whereas all plain Silk Frames not making work according to the Gage Frames not marking the work according to quality. Whereas all Frames of whatsoever description the Workmen of whom are not paid in the Current Coin of the Realm . . . will invariably be destroyed.'

A similar statement of objects appears in a series of verses, called 'General Ludd's triumph', that are also to be found in the Home Office Papers.[2]

[1] In Coldham to H.O., Jan. 14, 1812, in H.O. 42. 119.

[2] Copy in H.O. 42. 119.

The Guilty may fear but no vengeance he aims
At the honest man's life or Estate,
His wrath is entirely confined to wide frames
And those that old prices abate.
These Engines of mischief were sentenced to die
By unanimous vote of the Trade
And Ludd who can all opposition defy
Was the Grand Executioner made.

Let the wise and the great lend their aid and advice
Nor e'er their assistance withdraw
Till full fashioned work at the old fashioned price
Is established by custom and law.
Then the trade when this arduous contest is o'er
Shall raise in full splendour its head
And colting and cutting and squaring no more
Shall deprive honest workmen of bread.

Every evidence that is available goes to indicate that these were indeed the objects that the midland Luddites were seeking. They were, it should be noticed, the same objects that midland hosiers and stockingers had so long been seeking to achieve by negotiation. They were also the objects that the framework knitters themselves sought to achieve by petitions to Parliament and by the formation of the Nottingham 'Union' and by strikes.

This motive of coercing employers into granting higher wages and better conditions of work, the main one of the midland Luddites, was also a minor one of some at any rate of the northern machine breakers. Low wages were a prime cause of the Stockport riots. There, as in Nottingham, machine breaking followed a period of more peaceful attempts on the part of the workers, and even of some of the employers and magistrates, to secure higher wages and more regular employment. Few of the rioters at Stockport, or Middleton, or Westhoughton, or Macclesfield, can have seriously hoped to prevent steam looms being employed. They did hope, by attacks upon steam looms, to coerce the employers and the authorities into relieving their distress, to which unemployment, under-employment, low wages, and high prices were, as we have seen, all contributing factors, and which it was natural for the workers to think was due to the new machines and their owners.

A third object of the rioters of 1811–13, to all of whom, as well as to machine breakers, the name Luddite was given, was to reduce the famine price of provisions. Riots in the markets, and attacks upon bakery and provision shops, were a feature of disturbance everywhere, outside as well as inside the specifically Luddite areas. The high price of provisions was widely noted as a universal and important cause of Luddism, as of other disorder. The sole object of many of the poor men and women who were hanged as Luddites at Lancaster in 1812, and a minor object of many of the Stockport, Oldham, Middleton, Macclesfield, and other rioters, as well as a serious contributing factor in every disturbance of that year, was a reduction in the terrible price of every necessity of life.

Not all the Luddites were as clear as to their objects as the Yorkshire croppers who wished to get rid of the shearing frames, and the Nottingham framework knitters who wished to raise wages and to prevent frauds, or even as the Lancashire rioters who wanted to prevent speculation and profiteering in foodstuffs. Particularly in the cotton country many people must have joined in the disturbances without any very clear idea of why they did so. Especially must this have been true of the crowds concerned in the Macclesfield, Middleton, and Stockport disturbances, in each of which it was reported that people from outside the town, colliers, navvies, and other workers, had been prominently concerned in the disorder.[1] It was a matter of surprise and distress to the authorities that such workers, not directly or personally affected by the new machinery, should have joined in the riots. Observers

[1] See accounts of various northern riots in Manchester papers for March, April, and May 1812.

might well ask, as did the author of one tract[1] in defence of machinery, why the colliers and navvies should join the cotton weavers in breaking steam looms. Did not the looms burn coal, and consist of iron, which created a further demand for coal? Did not coal mines and steam engines and factories all create traffic for the canals, and therefore work for the navvies? That the weavers should be breaking looms, though it might be regretted, could be understood; their hostility to machinery, even if shortsighted, was intelligible. But for colliers, navvies, and other workers, gaining rather than losing by the changes which were following the slow penetration of the steam engine and the factory, was astonishing and irrational. It goes to show, what other evidence would suggest, that many people were willing to join in the Luddite disturbances, without any clear idea of what their objects were, because, like the Irishman of fiction, they wanted to be in the fight, just because it was a fight, or because they were so dissatisfied with conditions generally as to be willing to join any movement of protest. A major object of the Luddites, particularly in the cotton country, but to some extent in every disturbed district, was to protest dramatically and effectively against existing conditions, with only a vague indefinite hope of improving them.

It was widely said at the time that the Luddites had a further and more fundamental object, to which the other four objects we have discussed were only a cover, the object of overthrowing the existing system of government. The raids for arms, the system of delegates from district to district, the drilling of the disaffected on the northern moors by night, the oath-bound conspiracy, the projects for a general rising, in all of which many contemporaries believed, were taken as proof that something much more fundamental than a mere protest against industrial conditions was intended. Twice at least, in May 1812 and in March 1817, it was seriously believed by some of the

[1] Copy in Hay to H.O., May 10, 1812, in H.O. 40. 1.

Manchester authorities that a general rising was intended. The 'Pentridge Revolution' and the 'Huddersfield Rising', small and abortive attempts though they were, were intended by their sponsors, according to the informers' reports, to be parts of a national movement which was to overthrow the Government and to establish a provisional one with Sir Francis Burdett at its head. The spies were, indeed, talking continually of the danger of such a general rising, of the great numbers of disaffected enrolled in every area, of the likelihood of help from Ireland and France once the English industrial districts should start the revolution. Even the Parliamentary Committees of Secrecy in 1812, though they would not go so far as to believe all these rumours, or to conclude that there was in fact real danger of such a political movement, felt constrained to hold that the disaffected had political motives, and were a source of great danger to the public order, and not merely to machinery.

This view is, however, to be discounted. There is no evidence whatever of any political motives on the part of the Luddites. There is not one single instance in which it can be proved that a Luddite attack was directed towards anything deeper than disputes between masters and men, between workmen and their employers. There was not a single Luddite, and hardly a single rioter of any kind, with the exception of the unfortunate Brandreth and his colleagues of the 'Pentridge Revolution', against whom a charge of treason was advanced, or could lie. There is no sign, despite the great efforts of the spies to prove such motives, that the Luddites, or indeed any but a few unimportant, unrepresentative, irresponsible agitators, had any large or political designs.

This fact was clearly recognized by the best informed contemporary witnesses. Mr. Ryder in February 1811 talked[1] of the midland disturbances as having originated in disputes between the masters and the journeymen and

[1] *Parl. Debates*, xxi. 11, 671 and 812.

as being a purely local industrial matter. General Maitland, on the very morrow of the date upon which the Manchester rising was rumoured to have been timed to commence, felt able to say[1] that he was 'a total disbeliever that either such rising was seriously intended or that they [the Luddites] were in such state of organization as to admit of it'. A month or so later he felt able to say[2] that all his experience and information convinced him:

'that at present the whole of these Revolutionary Movements are limited to the lowest orders of the people generally; to the places where they show themselves; and that no concert exists, nor no plan is laid, further than is manifested in the open acts of violence that are daily committed.'

The officers commanding in the midlands and the north in 1817, Generals Fane and Byng, came to precisely the same conclusion. So did the local authorities in their reports to the Home Secretary, and the local members of Parliament, with unimportant exceptions, in their speeches in the House.

Whatever danger of Revolution there might have been in Regency England, and I shall return to that point later, there was no such danger from the Luddites who, in so far as they had definite objects at all, wished only to prevent the introduction of new machinery, to coerce their employers into improving their wages and conditions of work, to prevent speculation in foodstuffs, and, by creating a state of public alarm, to secure local, immediate, economic advantages.

[1] May 4, 1812, in H.O. 40. 1. [2] June 10, in ibid.

IX

THE ORGANIZATION OF THE LUDDITES

It was frequently suggested at the time[1] that the Luddites were enrolled in a numerous, oath-bound conspiracy, the different districts being connected with one another by a system of delegates, and the whole organization being directed by a series of committees. It was believed that this organization had control of ample funds, some of which were expended in payment of the actual machine breakers. It was further rumoured that large bands of men belonging to this confederacy were drilling by night upon the northern moors, preparing for a general rising,[2] for which they were well equipped with arms and plans. It was an integral part of this theory that the English Luddites, with their machine breaking and other objects, were only one unit in a much larger band of disaffected, organized in all the manufacturing districts of the kingdom, and in Ireland,[3] from which, and from France,[4] support was to be expected in the event of a rising. To alarmists believing in such tales, to which the spies' reports all tended, it was obvious that Luddism was only a cover to much larger and more dangerous designs.

There were, however, very few people who believed so much. The midland authorities, and the Home Secretary and other members of the Government, with regard to the

[1] See report of Parliamentary Secret Committees, *Parl. Debates*, xxiii. 951 et seq. and 1028 et seq.; and report of debates on Public Peace Bill, ibid., pp. 1056 et seq., 1099 et seq., 1195, and 1256.

[2] For reports with regard to a general rising, see particularly Manchester correspondence with the H.O. for April and May 1812, in H.O. 40. 1 and H.O. 42. 122 and 123, and March, April, and May 1817, in H.O. 42. 164, 5 and 6.

[3] See informers' reports, particularly from Lancashire and Cheshire, enclosed in magistrates' letters to be found in series H.O. 117–67 and H.O. 40. 1 and 2.

[4] Ibid. and threatening letters such as that received by Smith of Huddersfield in March 1812 (copy in memorial from Huddersfield Committee to H.O. in H.O. 40. 1).

midland disturbances, discounted this idea of political motives behind Luddism.[1] General Maitland and his successors in the northern command were equally certain that there was no elaborate organization, and, except on the part of a few irresponsible people, no serious, seditious motives, in northern Luddism. Despite the most careful search no large dumps of arms, such as the spies talked about, were found. No connexion could be traced between the disaffected in one district and those in others, except in so far as the regular informers' tales of itinerant delegates from London to Dublin, via the north of England and Glasgow, are to be believed. Despite every effort on the part of the authorities and spies no system of committees and no plan of revolution could be uncovered. All the evidence goes to prove, what General Maitland and others suggested,[2] that the disaffection was limited to the forms and places in which it showed itself.

One of the reasons why these alarming rumours of national organization and of political motives on the part of the Luddites were believed was because of the difficulty of distinguishing between Luddism and other popular movements. There were contemporaneously with the Luddite disturbances other movements amongst the workers, regular trades union movements involving large bodies of men, smaller, more secret political agitations, and bands of men united for purposes of common robbery. It was easy for the spies, and for the rather poorly informed authorities, to confuse one thing with another, and to attribute to the Luddites the organization, the objects, or the acts of other, really quite different and independent groups of men.

It was particularly easy to do this because the objects of the Luddites and of the ordinary working class and trades union organizations were in fact so similar. The

[1] See speeches in House of Commons in Feb. 1812; *Parl. Debates*, xxi. 11, 671 et seq. and 812 et seq.

[2] See letters from northern authorities for May, June, and July 1812, and for Nov. 1812 to Feb. 1813, in H.O. 40. 1 and 2, and H.O. 42. 122–32, especially Maitland to H.O., June 19, 1812, in H.O. 40. 1.

Nottinghamshire Luddites, for example, were trying to secure by framebreaking exactly the same things that their fellows were trying to secure, before, during, and after the riots, by means of negotiations with employers, petitions to the Framework Knitters Company and to Parliament, and such movements of their own as the Nottingham Union or 'Society for the Improvement of Mechanics and Mechanism'. Framebreaking was the expedient of the Luddites while a strike or 'turn out' was the limit of direct action to which the more peaceful framework knitters would go in pursuit of the same objects.

Similarly in the north of England machine breaking, or Luddism, was the expedient to which one group of workers, or the body of workers at one time, resorted, in order to achieve objects, the raising of wages, the securing of more regular employment and better conditions of work, which they sought at other times, and which their fellows continued to seek at the same time, through the medium of trade associations, by petition, or threat, or 'turn out'.

These normal, non-political activities and organizations of the workers in the industries and districts from which the Luddites were recruited were often elaborately developed. They were sometimes, like the organization of shearmen in the West Riding of Yorkshire, very powerful organizations, having contact, by means of delegates and otherwise, with workers in other areas, the west country and Scotland particularly, and able for some time to prevent practices, such as the introduction of new machinery, to which they objected. They were frequently, like the Nottingham Union, and like the *ad hoc* committees of the stockingers in the hosiery and lace trades, which have been described, possessed of a complicated organization, spreading widely throughout the industry, and of ample funds. They were, as General Maitland remarked[1] with regard to the situation in Lancashire and Cheshire, accustomed constantly, for many years before the commencement of Luddism, to

[1] Maitland to H.O., June 19, 1812, in H.O. 40. 1.

make every sort of effort to 'keep up the price of manufacturing wages'. They were undoubtedly often in touch with one another, creating mutual committees, sending fraternal delegates to one another's meetings. It was to such organizations and such activities that many of the spies' reports undoubtedly referred.

The Combination Acts and others laws prohibiting associations 'in restraint of trade' tended to drive such working class movements underground. Committees of spinners and weavers were frequently compelled to meet in secrecy and to wear an appearance of mystery and illegality even when their objects and activities were perfectly normal, the protection and advancement by means merely of negotiation or strike of their standard of life and conditions of work.[1] It was clearly a situation of this kind which was existing in the cotton towns during the years 1810, '11, and '12, and which was being reported to the Government by its spies and informers in the period immediately preceding the commencement of riots and machine breaking. It was out of such a situation, by the conversion of some workers and workers' groups from the idea of peaceful and legal to that of violent and illegal methods of obtaining redress of grievances, that Lancashire and Cheshire Luddism developed. It was to such organizations and practices that the workers reverted when Luddism had been suppressed. It was solely with such things that many, probably the great majority of them, were concerned even during the period of machine breaking, since it was clearly shown that, at any rate in the Manchester-Stockport area, all but a very small minority of the men had retired from the workers' committees before the latter reached the point of considering anything approximating to Luddism.[2]

[1] See depositions of Whitehead (in Maitland to H.O., July 5, 1812, in H.O. 42. 125), Yarwood (in Lloyd to Beckett, June 21, in H.O. 40. 1), Whittaker (dated July 4, copy in H.O. 42. 121), and Taylor (dated May 7, in H.O. 42. 123).

[2] Ibid.

There was, however, at any rate at some places and times, actual if informal connexion between these normal trade committees and the machine breakers. It was not merely that the great majority of the workers sympathized with, even when they did not take part in, actual acts of Luddism. It was not even that they were often willing to subscribe to the funds of the Luddite gangs, as they clearly were, especially in the midlands, from fear as well as sympathy. It was that some cases can be proved of actual workers' committees formally subsidizing the frame-breakers.

There are at least two major instances of this happening. The first in point of time, although the least significant, comes from the north. It appears from the evidence of various spies and informers[1] that there were formed in the latter part of 1811 and in the beginning of 1812, at Manchester, Bolton, and Stockport, and perhaps in other neighbouring towns, small secret committees of representatives from the various trades. These committees had clearly grown out of the regular attempts of the weavers and others to secure an advance of wages and other purely industrial objects. They were a result of continual failure of such peaceful attempts, of desperation making a small minority of the men willing to consider violent expedients. These committees had some informal contact with one another by a system of delegates from town to town. They employed various permanent officials, the chief member of the Manchester Committee, John Buckley, receiving, for instance, 30*s*. a week. They were supported by contributions from the various trades. They held meetings at various public-houses in the district and talked of all sorts of wild ways of securing redress of grievances, including the old idea of a 'general turn out' and the new one of an attack upon steam looms.

[1] References cited on p. 179, note 1, and reports of the two Stones's, of Bent, 'L. F. B.', &c., in letters from Bolton, Oldham, and Manchester, in H.O. 40. 1 and H.O. 42. 117 et seq.

There seems, however, to be little evidence that the committees, except at Bolton, had any direct or formal connexion with the actual attacks which took place, whether upon factories or provision shops. It was obviously difficult for the committee members to collect the subscriptions of the associated trades. Little more seems to have been received than was enough to pay for the costs of food and ale at the little secret committee meetings, and for the small expenses of the delegates who wandered from town to town, with indented tally cards to prove their identity, and with little purpose, apparently, except to swear one another in, and to talk in each centre, to the few poor committee-men they met there, of the great numbers and large confident plans of the disaffected in the other centres. The system that is exposed was indeed a poor and ineffective one, that of little knots of poor, unemployed weavers and spinners and representatives of other trades, wandering about the cotton towns, trying to stir up discontent, but able only with great difficulty to collect a few shillings a week for their own expenses, and having to keep one another's spirits up by a series of lies as to the great hopes and numbers of the disaffected elsewhere. Even this poor system, which was not responsible for more than a few nightly meetings and for 'twisting in' at most a few hundred men, came to a rapid end, it being, for instance, found necessary to disband the Manchester Committee after a few months, nothing having been done, the tailors, spinners, and others having fallen behind in their contributions, and Buckley and other leaders having fallen into disfavour and being suspected of being spies.

This suspicion of the leaders as spies was, at any rate in some cases, well founded. Bent, a Manchester cotton spinner, the treasurer of the Manchester Committee and a frequent delegate from Manchester to the neighbouring towns, was, for instance, no other than 'B', most regular and useful of government spies in the cotton country in

1812.[1] Some of the funds expended by this committee, to which its treasurer was willing to lend money,[2] were being paid in fact by the Government, through the expense account of its agent, who was so clever in avoiding detection by his fellows as on one occasion narrowly to escape being arrested with them and charged with sedition.[3]

Spies were equally in evidence at Bolton, where alone, so far as it can be proved, one of these small committees was responsible for an actual open riot.[4] A little committee was formed here in February or March 1812, at the instigation of two delegates from Stockport. Three men, Garrett, Hurst, and Radcliffe, agreed to appoint one Richard Charlton as its first member. Charlton chose Radcliffe, Radcliffe Hurst, Hurst Waddington (later very useful as a government agent), and Waddington Garrett. These few men, assisted and directed by two other men, Simeon and John Stones, both spies, the 'Old S ' and 'Young S ' of numberless reports,[5] went around 'twisting people in' and compelling them on pain of various penalties to contribute funds towards, and otherwise support, the purposes of the secret committee. Various meetings were held in local public-houses and on Dean Moor outside the town. One such nightly meeting, attended by perhaps 20–30 people, many of them spies and members of the militia, was alarmed by a rumour that the military were approaching and broke up in disorder, 'Old S' falling into a pool of water in a disused quarry in his haste to get away. On another occasion[6] a similar but slightly larger group, numbering about fifty, many of whom were disguised, came across one Holland Bowden, a sergeant of the local militia, and, according to his and

[1] Reports chiefly in letters from Bolton.

[2] Taylor's deposition, May 7, 1812, in H.O. 42. 123.

[3] Lloyd to H.O., Aug. 31, 1812, in H.O. 42. 126, and H.O. to Fletcher, Sept. 2, and to Lloyd, in H.O. 79. 2.

[4] Full reports in letters from Fletcher to H.O. in H.O. 40. 1 and 2, H.O. 79. 1 and 2, and H.O. 42. 117 et seq.

[5] Ibid.

[6] Fletcher to H.O., April 22, 1812, in H.O. 40. 1.

the spies' stories, forcibly compelled him to take the Luddite oath. Still later, on April 24, after repeated warnings and false alarms, a larger mob, including and being encouraged by, members of this group and various government spies, attacked and destroyed the steam loom factory at Westhoughton.

These northern committees, therefore, though growing out of and being financially supported by the members of ordinary trade associations, were poor unrepresentative things. Largely directed by spies, controlled by a little group of men who made this petty sedition their source of income, playing at nightly meetings and at the administration of fearsome oaths as a means of creating alarm and assuring this income, these secret committees in the cotton towns, though probably in a measure responsible for inflaming popular opinion, and therefore contributory agents in the disorders and in Luddism, which were contemporaneous with their activity, were not the actual effective agents of Luddism. They were a fungoid growth, growing out of a confused situation, and standing between the ordinary trade associations which sought wage advances by peaceful means and the Luddite gangs and mobs who sought them by violence. They exploited the situation and provoked the Luddites in order to gain an income and importance for themselves.

In the midlands it was different. Here there was, at any rate in 1816, direct connexion between the trade associations and the Luddites, though here also, as the government informers grew active, foolish little secret committees were formed, as they had been in the north, by professional agitators and by government agents who saw a chance of making a living by playing upon the popular distress and discontent, and by pretending to other workers that their secret meetings and the coming and going of their delegates, were contributing to a redress of grievances.[1]

[1] A very complete picture of the way these secret committees worked can be obtained by comparing the spies' reports enclosed in letters from

These secret committees, whose wild talk, as reported by the spies, who formed a large part of their membership, so alarmed the authorities, were really, like the robber gangs, by-products of Luddism. In the midlands and the north it was clearly recognized by the local authorities that there were criminals in the district taking advantage of the situation to commit ordinary crime under cover of the Luddite name. The *Nottingham Journal* of December 10, 1811, distinguished between genuine Luddites and 'the yet more numerous class who adopted the nom de guerre "Ned Ludd's men" as a cloak for the commission of almost every crime'. It was similarly discovered in Yorkshire in the winter of 1812 that there were several gangs at work 'who availed themselves of the Popular Prejudices of the Country to commit general plunder'.[1] The Luddites proper rigidly confined themselves to their specific offences, breaking machinery and (in the north) collecting arms. Time and again instances are recorded of their resisting the temptation to steal money or to damage anything but the machinery to which they objected. Their restraint rather than their violence was an occasion for wonder. They were not to be held responsible for ordinary robberies which were clearly the work of different groups of men, gangs of common thieves using the Luddite name, knowing that it saved them from all danger of resistance or pursuit.

Some at any rate of the forced subscriptions which were widely reported from each of the disturbed districts, though said to be for the support of the Luddites and contributed as such, were really for such robber gangs, or secret committees, as those we have described. It was an easy way

Fletcher, Coldham, Enfield, and other magistrates and clerks, to be found in series H.O. 40, 42, and 79, with the workers' cases, to be found in such sources as the following: Confessions of Bolton weavers in Clayton to H.O., Oct. 18, 1812, in H.O. 42. 128; reports from Nottingham for May, June, and July 1817, in H.O. 42. 165–7; and trials of Brandreth, &c., in Arnold, *Life of Thomas, 1st Lord Denman.*

[1] Hobhouse to H.O., Nov. 29, 1812, in H.O. 42. 129.

of making money in those days to pretend to be a Luddite. It was not to be expected that the temptation would be resisted. It is necessary to remember that many nominal Luddites were frauds, like the robber gangs and the secret committees.

There were, however, some genuine Luddite gangs, and some genuine trade committees supporting them. Felkin talks[1] of evidence 'shewing that in both trades, hosiery and lace, when it was a question of breaking frames the work was done for hire'. Mr. Coldham, while the disturbances were still raging, said[2] that the men actively engaged in breaking frames were 'supported by pecuniary contributions from those engaged in productive labour'. Mr. Becher makes a similar charge:[3]

'It may be asked, how are the Framebreakers or Luddites supported—to this I reply that they are not numerous, that they receive contributions from the people in work and that there is scarcely a stockinger who will not give half his victuals to these "friends of the poor man" as they are styled who beg in the evening from house to house, exposing for sale the Framework Knitters' Act as a protection against the vagrant laws.'

Sutton, another important contemporary authority, says:[4] 'Had there been no funds raised to encourage the "practical Ned Ludds" it is evident there would have been little destruction of machinery, for the actual perpetrators were animated as much by the hope of reward as by the mistaken notion that they were benefiting trade'.

These funds upon which the actual professional Luddites relied were collected partly by the framebreakers themselves, going around peaceably by day[5] or violently and secretly by night.[6] They were collected also, however,

[1] Felkin, op. cit., pp. 238–40.
[2] Coldham to H.O., Jan. 14, 1812, in H.O. 42. 119.
[3] Becher to H.O., Feb. 11, 1812, in H.O. 42. 120.
[4] Sutton, op. cit., p. 334.
[5] As in Leicestershire in Dec. 1811 (depositions in Rutland to H.O., Jan. 5, 1812, in H.O. 42. 119).
[6] As in the environs of Stockport in April 1812 (reports in Lloyd and Prescott to H.O., in H.O. 40. 1).

by the trade committees, which were not themselves directly concerned in Luddism. There is no evidence to show that a great trade organization like the Nottingham Union, though it supported strikers and was a party in the dispute in 1814 which precipitated the renewed framebreaking of that year, supported or even, as an organization, condoned framebreaking. There is, however, evidence that smaller trade committees did so. The 'Twist Lace Committee', for example, was said[1] by various informers in 1816 who came in to confess their offences and who exposed the basis of the framebreaking of that year, to have paid out money to the perpetrators of various outrages. It had discussed the employment of men to intimidate, and if necessary kill, workmen who refused to come out on strike. It was said to have even paid varying amounts from 4*s*. to 43*s*. for such purposes. It was even reported that it had paid ten men 10*s*. apiece on account to go to Leicester to kill the judge presiding at the Assizes there over the trial of the Luddite Towle.

The 'Warp Lace Committee' is similarly reported[2] to have advanced £40 to the framebreaking gang which carried through the attack on Heathcote and Boden's factory at Loughborough, besides raising money for the defence of the Luddites later placed on trial on account of the attack. The 'Loughborough Committee' is said to have given this 'Warp Lace Committee' a joint note to repay this £40, which was apparently its responsibility, within three months.

We get in the case of this Loughborough attack a clear picture of how Luddism, at this time and place, was organized. The suggestion that Heathcote and Boden's machines should be broken came from the firm's own employees, whose wages had recently been greatly reduced,

[1] See evidence of Badder, Slater, Blackburn, Mitchell, the various anonymous secret agents and others, and letters from Mr. Enfield, in Home Office files for 1816 and 1817, H.O. 42. 152–67.

[2] Ibid. and Felkin, op. cit., pp. 238 et seq. and Sutton, op. cit., p. 334.

and from those of the rival firm of Lacey.[1] These men, who were all either suffering from or fearing a reduction of wages, subscribed money for the payment of the framebreakers. The idea was taken up by the 'Loughborough Committee' and by the 'Warp Lace Committee'. Through the agency of the treasurer of the latter committee,[2] a man named Ward, an arrangement was made with the Luddite gang, seventeen strong and apparently well known within the trade.[3] The latter, who had been concerned in many Luddite attacks, were to receive from £100–120 for this attack, payable upon its completion. They actually received some £40, it not being possible to raise the balance, but it had been hoped until the last to get more. One of the men concerned in this attack later testified that he personally had received £5 as his share of the proceeds.[4]

Similar evidence is available with regard to a few other attacks. Ward, the treasurer of the Warp Lace Committee, is reported to have paid £10 on one occasion for an attack upon some frames in Woolpack Lane, Nottingham.[5] Another Luddite testified that he and his friends had carried through a framebreaking venture at Lambley at the request of the local stockingers, who had promised to help later on at Bulwell.[6] He and his gang had been rewarded with '17*d.* for drink for doing the job'.

This professionalizing of Luddism in the midlands was obviously largely responsible for the long continuance of the system. It was proved that the gang which had carried through the Loughborough attack, and which had been so active in the following autumn, from July to November 1816, had also been concerned in almost every attack in the preceding years. They were young stockingers, accustomed to the exciting pastime of poaching. And they

[1] Sutton, op. cit., p. 334.

[2] See evidence of Joseph Mitchell in Enfield to H.O., March 26, 1817, in H.O. 42. 168.

[3] See p. 186, n. 1.

[4] Burton's evidence in Rolleston to H.O., Feb. 9, 1817, in H.O. 42. 159.

[5] See p. 186, n. 1.

[6] See p. 186, n. 1.

had made Luddism a profitable side-line to framework knitting. It was a potent cause of framebreaking that there should be in existence a gang of reckless young men willing for a consideration to break the frames of any firm or master who was for any reason, on any occasion, unpopular. It meant that any body of stockingers, or committee, which was tired of negotiations and even of strikes, and had command of a few pounds, could easily and safely hire a few Luddites to break the machinery of the masters against whom they had any grievance.

This, or other similar gangs, had obviously been active at any rate since the winter of 1812–13. It will be remembered that at that time the local authorites had said that the framebreaking of November and December 1812 was the work of a gang of 12 or 14 desperate men well known to hang together and intent upon committing some sort of outrage.[1] Felkin had earlier remarked[2] with regard to the framebreaking of the winter of 1811–12 that it was largely the work of four gangs or companies, one each for the districts of Sutton-in-Ashfield, Arnold, Nottingham, and Swanwick. It was believed, he said, that the number of those actually engaged in the work of destruction was small and that most of them were young. The core of midland framebreaking was clearly the work of a small number of permanent, organized gangs, engaging regularly in Luddism, and making an income out of it.

This does not seem to have been the case in the West Riding of Yorkshire, though there again there were clearly one or two small bands of men engaged very frequently in the business of machine breaking. There is no trace in the north, except in regard to the secret committees which we have noticed, of bodies of men making a profit out of Luddism. It is not wise also to assume even in the case of midland Luddism that it was the work only of small professional gangs supported by the trade at large. Over-

[1] Newcastle to H.O., Dec. 21, 1812, in H.O. 42. 130.

[2] Felkin, op. cit., p. 231.

whelmingly at the beginning, and occasionally even at the end, it was the work of large mobs. The first Nottinghamshire attacks were said to be the work of large crowds, 100 or more in number. Even in the winter of 1816, when most of the framebreaking was the work of a small professional gang, on at least one occasion a mob of upwards of 100 was out.[1] When such large numbers were involved, as they were in many of the midland, some of the Yorkshire, and all of the Lancashire and Cheshire attacks, there could be no question of payment. Luddism in such cases, and this was the way in which machine breaking started, was the work not of small organized professional gangs, but of great crowds come together merely from sympathy with the objects of Luddism.

There might be, indeed there often was, considerable *ad hoc* organization on the part of these large mobs of Luddites. Great care was taken in the selection as victims of persons for some reason particularly the objects of popular antipathy.[2] The news of which frames were to be attacked was passed about with great efficiency and secrecy. Bands of Luddites were gathered from many different villages, meeting at a prearranged spot and a prearranged time.[3] There was some discipline in the mobs thus called together, 'General Ludd', who was not one but many, acting in that capacity on different occasions, drawing the body of rioters up in some rough order, and arranging them in sections, under different names and commanders. The men were numbered off, and addressed by number rather than by name. Guards were posted both in order to give an alarm and to prevent faint-hearted men from deserting. The men with hammers and muskets were sent ahead to break down the doors and each man was given some special task. The bands of Luddites approached

[1] *Nottingham Journal*, Oct. 1816.

[2] Coldham to H.O., Jan. 14, 1812, in H.O. 42. 119.

[3] e.g. on the occasion of the attack on Foster's, April 9, and Cartwright's, April 11, 1812, in Yorkshire, and on Bett's and Hollingworth's in Bulwell and Sutton-in-Ashfield, Notts., in Nov. 1811.

their destination, commenced and concluded their attacks, and retreated into the night, quickly, quietly, and in order. Whether the number of attackers were three or four or upwards of 100, and it varied all the way between the two, tending as police arrangements were developed to approximate to the smaller rather than the larger figure, and though they might be watched and applauded by almost the entire population of the village, the Luddite mobs acted with secrecy, with order, and with dispatch. It does not, however, appear that there was any more organization in these large mobs than there is in the crowd which carries through a spontaneous college 'rag'. There was necessarily amongst the Luddites, as in a college crowd, a little group of ringleaders who had made their plans, and whose authority was respected, but there was no need of a permanent formal organization.

There cannot in fact have been such an organization or it would have been discovered by the spies, and through them by the authorities. The only permanent features of Luddism, other than the permanent grievances which the Luddites shared with the ordinary trade associations, were the few, small, youthful, professional gangs. The fact that, in Nottinghamshire in 1816–17, as in the West Riding in 1812, Luddism should have broken up so rapidly once the organization of these gangs should have been penetrated, shows how large a share of responsibility these irresponsible young men must carry for the continuance of the movement. They did not start it. They could not have carried it on without the support of the body of workers, from whom they recruited the large mobs which carried through the early attacks, from whom they drew their financial support, and by whom they were concealed and protected. But they were largely responsible for carrying it on after the body of workers had learnt that it was a reckless, desperate expedient.

It was said that there was connexion between the different bands of Luddites, not merely within each disturbed area but between one area and another.[1] It does not seem to be the case that either of these charges was true. So far as connexion between different Luddite bands in each particular disturbed area is concerned the question is of little importance. News would clearly pass easily within a single manufacturing district, the workers of which were united in a common distress and in common grievances. While some of the tales of delegates are obviously far-fetched, the Mayor of Leicester, for instance, in 1812, confusing representatives of the Nottingham Union with Luddites,[2] and the Lancashire and Cheshire authorities making a similar mistake with regard to the spies and members of secret committees,[3] others are probably true. The mobs from many different villages, which met for machine breaking and riot in each area, and the financial arrangements between the midland frame-breakers and such bodies as the Warp Lace Committee, obviously called for some method of distributing information of intended attacks, and for collecting the frame-breakers who were to take part. They did not call, however, for more than a rudimentary organization, for the dispatch of a few runners to hurry around the local public-houses to recruit volunteers for an attack planned by the ringleaders meeting at any one centre. A few small professional gangs, collecting funds and recruiting frame-breaking parties as needed, was all that was required, and all that seems to have existed in the midlands and in the West Riding. A few hot heads and agitators stirring the mobs of unemployed to riot was all that was needed, and can be proved to have existed, in the cotton country. The state of the public mind was such that support would be

[1] See report of Parliamentary Secret Committees, June 1812.

[2] In Maitland to H.O., June 16, 1812, in H.O. 40. 1.

[3] Stories of Stones, Bent, Whitehead, &c., in letters from Fletcher, Chippendale, Lloyd, Hay, &c., in H.O. 40. 1 and 2, and H.O. 42. 117 et seq. give a picture of the real Lancashire and Cheshire situation, with secret committees largely unconnected with either the regular trade societies or with the Luddites.

readily forthcoming as soon as the news of an intended attack was passed around.

The stories of delegates from district to district are more important. If true they would go far to prove Luddism a more serious matter than has been suggested. There was much talk of such delegates. A report from Bolton in November 1811 talks[1] of a man Williamson, a traveller in stockings from Nottingham, having met a committee of the trades at Manchester. A month later there was a report[2] from Stockport of two delegates from Nottingham having met a group of local weavers. In February 1812 there was talk[3] of subscriptions having been solicited in the cotton country for the support of the Nottingham Luddites. At the same time Manchester people were reporting[4] 'plenty of Nottingham, Carlisle and Glasgow delegates' inciting the local workers to riot and confusion. If Peel is to be believed a Nottingham delegate was at the same time inciting the Yorkshire croppers to disorder.[5]

Similar rumours appeared again later, there being stories from Nottingham in 1815 and 1816 of delegates from thence to Yorkshire and London.[6] It was again suggested in 1817 that there was communication between the different disaffected districts.

All these stories are to be discounted. Some of them are true; there were, no doubt, Nottingham men in the north and vice versa. But there is nothing to show that they were not either travellers like Williamson, ordinary legal trade delegates like Gravener Henson, spies like Oliver, or professional agitators unconnected with Luddism like the Watsons or the Irish delegates of whom the spies were always talking. The Government took great pains to prove

[1] Fletcher to H.O., Nov. 21, 1811, in H.O. 42. 117.

[2] Bulkley to H.O., Dec. 26, 1811, in H.O. 42. 118.

[3] Lloyd to Bulkley, Feb. 11, 1812, in H.O. 42. 120.

[4] J. Meyer, Feb. 11, 1812, in H.O. 42. 120.

[5] Peel, op. cit., p. 56.

[6] See reports in letters from Nottingham to H.O., particularly from Mr. Coldham and Mr. Enfield, in H.O. 42. 142 et seq.

connexion between the different districts, tapping the mails, watching the post-offices, making a free use of spies and informers.[1] It could prove nothing. There is no actual evidence to show, and no reason to assume, that the Luddites in any one area were connected with those in the others, or possessed any regular system of delegates.

There is also nothing to show that they were, as the parliamentary committees charged, associated upon oath. Only in the north of England in 1812, and only upon the evidence of spies, is there any evidence of secret oaths being administered. There is no case of any person convicted of administering or receiving an illegal oath being also convicted of machine breaking, nothing whatever other than the uncorroborated testimony of spies to prove the Luddites ever took any secret or illegal oath at all. It was positively denied in Yorkshire in 1813, when men were coming in to confess their offences and take the Oath of Allegiance, that any secret oath had ever been administered in that district.[2] There is no evidence whatever of the midland Luddites having done so. Only around Stockport and Bolton were any workers willing to confess that they had taken illegal oaths. Even there the numbers involved ran into hundreds rather than into thousands, and it was specifically charged that the spies had been prime movers, and the men unwilling assentors, in the administration of oaths.[3]

The only cases proved before the courts were proved upon spies' evidence. Several of these cases are frankly suspicious. The men convicted on the evidence of Sergeant Holland Bowden, for instance, of administering an illegal oath to him upon Dean Moor near Bolton in April 1812, were obviously the frightened tools of the spy Stones and of the ten or a dozen spies, members of the local militia,

[1] See Chap. XV.

[2] See depositions and reports in letters from the West Riding to the H.O. during the first few months of 1813, H.O. 42. 131–4.

[3] See depositions of Bolton weavers before Sir Richard Clayton, enclosed in letter to H.O., Oct. 18, 1812, in H.O. 42. 128.

whom he had had with him on that occasion, stirring up and driving forward the unwilling 'Luddites'.[1] The men convicted at York for receiving illegal oaths at Halifax[2] and Barnsley[3] in the summer of 1812 swore that they had not done so. The cases against them rested on the evidence of the spies MacDonald and Gosling and Taylor and Whitehead respectively, men sent up to Yorkshire with instructions to find such evidence, and, according to their own accounts, successful in doing so within a few hours of their arrival. To make their testimony still more doubtful, McDonald, the major witness, was himself at the time of the trials under indictment for criminal assault.[4] Even the Crown Attorney had expected his evidence to be discredited under cross-examination.[5]

To make these tales still more unworthy of belief is the case of the thirty-eight Lancashire men accused of administering an illegal oath at Manchester in June 1812 but acquitted at the assizes at Lancaster later that year.[6] These men were accused on the testimony of a spy, Samuel Fleming, who attended their meeting at the Prince Regent's Arms, Ancoats Lane, Manchester. He had been sent to get evidence of illegal oaths. He was followed almost immediately by his employer Nadin, Deputy-Constable of Manchester, and a number of constables, who arrested every one present (as they thought). They confidently expected convictions, Fleming being willing to swear that, despite the ostensible purposes of the meeting, to petition for peace and parliamentary reform, purposes substantiated by the papers taken up by the police, he had been administered an illegal oath by Knight, the Chairman of the meeting. Unfortunately for the prosecution, however,

[1] See depositions of Bolton weavers before Sir Richard Clayton, enclosed in letter to H.O., Oct. 18, 1812, in H.O. 42. 128.

[2] i.e. Baines and others, see Hansard's report of the York trials.

[3] Ibid., Wortley to H.O., Sept. 6, 1812, in H.O. 42. 127.

[4] Hobhouse to H.O., Jan. 9, 1813, in H.O. 42. 132.

[5] Ibid.

[6] See H.O. series 42, bundles 123, 124, and 125, and local Manchester and Leeds press.

one member of the company had hidden on the stairs and escaped. He corroborated the tale of the prisoners that the meeting had been a legal, peaceful one, and that no oath had been administered. His evidence was believed rather than that of the spy. One is inclined to think if similar testimony had been available in other cases no person would have been convicted on the charge of administering or receiving an illegal oath.

It is evident that, even if secret, illegal oaths were sometimes administered, as they may have been around Bolton and Stockport, they were not a feature of Luddism properly so called. Like the secret committees in the same area, and like robber gangs on the one hand, and legal trade associations on the other, in every disturbed area, they were, at the most, features of the situation contemporaneous with Luddism and often, though wrongly, confused with it. Some of the Luddites, as for instance those accused of the murder of Horsfall and the attack on Rawfolds Mill, may have taken, and have forced their fellows to take, an oath of secrecy on that particular matter.[1] Some of the Luddite gangs, like the robber gangs, may have taken an oath of loyalty to one another. The alarming tales of extensive, mysterious oath-bound conspiracies are, however, a spies' invention.

Similarly exaggerated were the stories of bands of Luddites armed, disguised, and drilling by night. No actual, as apart from rumoured and hearsay, evidence upon this point was ever uncovered. No witness was ever found ready to swear to having attended, or even to having received a first-hand account of, such a nightly drill. No dumps of arms were found, nor could the authorities upon their search of individual houses for arms discover any large number of them.[2] It was even believed towards the

[1] See account in Peel, op. cit.

[2] e.g. the failure of searching parties to find any of the dumps of arms about which the informer Barrowclough was talking in June 1812; letters from Hay, Lloyd, and Maitland to H.O., July 1812, in H.O. 42. 125.

end of 1812 that many people had never really lost their arms at all, having pretended the Luddites had stolen them as an excuse for not surrendering them to the military, and having accounted for their later possession of them by saying the Luddites had mysteriously and suddenly brought them back.[1] There were certainly large Luddite mobs, some of who were disguised and armed, turning out in 1811 and 1812, in the midlands and in the north of England, to break machinery, to collect arms, or lead, or to steal goods. Some of these were Luddite gangs, others were only pretending to be. The members of these gangs, usually a much smaller number than was rumoured by the terrified householders, were sometimes accustomed during the height of the disturbances to be out at night, alarming the villagers with the noise of their marching feet, and by letting off rockets or stray shots, even when they had no specific attack in view, general terror being a powerful weapon for their purpose. But nothing more than this can be proved.

One is tempted, moreover, to doubt many of the stories current at the time because the few that one can check up on were so grossly exaggerated. The nocturnal meetings near Bolton,[2] for example, upon which the authorities largely relied for their conclusion that great bands of men disguised and armed were drilling on the northern moors, were small, feeble things, attended by less than fifty people, many of them spies, and all of them frightened and unwilling except upon pressure to resort to more than violent speeches. The largest actual assemblages of which definite reports survive, the attack on Rawfolds Mill[3] in Yorkshire in April 1812, and some of the Nottingham riots[4] in

[1] Letters from Hay, Lloyd, and Maitland to H.O., July 1812, in H.O. 42. 215.

[2] Accounts in letters of Fletcher to H.O. for April 1812 in reports of Stones, in ibid., and in depositions of Bolton weavers in H.O. 42. 128.

[3] Most vivid account in Peel, op. cit., pp. 50 et seq.

[4] Especially in March and Nov. 1811, e.g. thea ttack on Betts's frames at Bulwell; depositions of accomplices in H.O. 42. 118.

November 1811, were attended by from 70 to 150 men, many of whom, especially in Yorkshire, were there unwillingly, under compulsion by their more adventurous fellows,[1] and only a portion of whom were armed. Their discipline was very limited and their purpose solely the destruction of machinery. It is extremely unlikely that nocturnal meetings of which no precise accounts survive were very different from the few upon which definite evidence is available. Luddite mobs, except in so far as they were embarked upon a specific piece of framebreaking, were seldom more than fifty strong, if so numerous, and had little definite purpose, being pieces of bravado, designed to keep up the spirits of the disaffected and the alarm of the authorities.

There was no army, no national organization of the Luddites, no extensive secret conspiracy.[2] There were only little persistent, and sometimes professional, gangs, larger *ad hoc*, more or less spontaneous mobs on particular occasions, and a general feeling of irritation likely to issue in acts of violence against unpopular employers and merchants.

[1] Note account of Bolton meetings of April 7, 19, and 24 (in Fletcher to H.O.) and of Rawfolds attack, April 11, 1812 (in Peel), at all of which precautions had to be taken to prevent great numbers of half-hearted men from deserting.

[2] Cf. Maitland's conclusion (Nov. 4, 1812, in H.O. 42. 129. 'There was no real bottom in this Luddite system').

X

THE CAUSES OF POPULAR DISORDER

THE major cause of popular disorder in Regency England was undoubtedly distress. There were many other causes of discontent, political as well as industrial. Mobs provoked to riot for any reason could generally hope to find support from people with other reasons hoping to obtain different advantages, or moved to protest against a different grievance.[1] There was, as we have seen,[2] plenty of cause for bitter disputes between different sections of the people, and between the people and the government. On the whole, however, these causes of dispute, these bitter social and economic discontents, did not issue in disorder except upon occasions of unusual distress.

Contemporary authorities were quick to anticipate trouble when there was extreme distress. We find, for instance, the Bolton and Stockport authorities wondering, in the winter of 1811–12, how the labouring classes could get through the year, popular distress being what it was.[3] Lord Liverpool in the debate in the House of Lords upon the midland framebreaking said in February 1812 that the decline in trade and consequent want of employment had issued in bitter disputes between masters and workmen and in disorder, which was quite natural and in the normal course of things.[4] There was, as General Maitland remarked with regard to the history of Manchester, 'no instance of a considerable stagnation of trade, accompanied by a high price of provisions, where something of the same kind (i.e. popular rioting) has not ensued.'[5]

[1] Note the support of colliers and other outsiders in the attack upon Mr. Burton's steam looms at Middleton, April 1812 (Chippendale to Fletcher, April 23, in H.O. 40. 1).

[2] Chaps. I, II, III, IV, VIII.

[3] e.g. Pilkington to H.O., Nov. 12, 1811, in H.O. 42. 117.

[4] *Parl. Debates*, xxi. 971.

[5] Maitland to H.O., June 22, 1812, in H.O. 40. 1.

It was natural that there should be disturbances in 1801–2, 1811–12, and 1816–17, since these were years of unusual distress, of high prices, of stagnation of trade, of unemployment and low earnings. It was almost normal in England during the entire reign of George III, while the social and industrial situation of the English people was altering so rapidly and profoundly but before the political machine was brought up to date, for periods of poor trade, accompanied by want of employment and famine prices, to be characterized by popular disorders of some kind. There were many instances of this, although other causes often entered into the disturbances besides distress. There was framebreaking in Nottingham in 1777–8, a period of very poor trade. A decade later there were the Gordon Riots, in which popular distress, though a minor, was a contributing factor. In 1801–2 there were riots in Gloucester and Somerset on the introduction of gig mills and shearing frames, which seemed especially untimely because of the prevailing high prices and want of employment. In 1811, '12, '14, '16, and '17, there were Luddite outbreaks and, in the latter years, agricultural disturbances. After 1817 there were further disorders, Peterloo, the tumults which provoked Castlereagh and Sidmouth to resort to their famous repressive 'Six Acts', the public demonstrations in favour of Queen Caroline, the Cato Street Conspiracy, the riots which accompanied, and contributed towards, the passing of the Reform Bill, and further agricultural disturbances. In all of these instances of popular disorder, some serious, some of purely local, temporary importance, although there were other and often more important causes, popular distress was always a contributing cause.

There was no comfort in the Poor Law or in public charity to dissuade the working classes in periods of distress from resorting to disturbance. Their normal situation allowed them no margin to create reserves to carry them through a depression. Their situation was permanently so nearly desperate that it needed little to provoke them into riots, which though useless as a means of securing redress of grievances, were at least a method of letting off steam. There was no adequate method of obtaining in a peaceful manner, by trades union negotiations or petitions to Parliament, or even by strikes, the protection and improvement of their standard of living that many groups of workers so badly needed. There was no effective police or system of order to prevent an angry meeting from degenerating into a dangerous riot, or a temporary riot from becoming a long-drawn-out disturbance.

This connexion between distress and disorder was particularly recognized in connexion with Luddism. Maitland traced an historical connexion between the two, so far as the cotton country was concerned.[1] The Trade Associations, which were permanently working for the protection and improvement of workers' wages and conditions of work, were very apt to lose control of their membership and to see negotiation discredited in favour of direct action, upon occasions of unusual distress, such as undoubtedly existed in the years 1811–12. The high price of provisions,[2] the reduced level of earnings,[3] the want of employment,[4] all of which were unusually severe, were a sufficient cause in his opinion for the disturbances in the area under his command. Brougham tried similarly to trace a geographical connexion between distress and disturbance.[5] He had served on the committee of the charitable society which was raising a subscription in 1812 for popular relief. 'In examining these records he found it completely confirmed that the distress was great, general, and unexampled.

[1] Maitland to H.O., June 22, 1812, in H.O. 40. 1.

[2] Ibid., May 4, 1812, in H.O. 40. 1. [3] Ibid.

[4] Cf. Mr. Hayne's statement with regard to disorders in the lace trade: 'the disturbances at Nottingham have arisen more from want of work than the prices given for their labour, and generally speaking they would have been content with the prices if they could have had full employment'. Hayne to H.O., Feb. 12, 1812, in H.O. 42. 131.

[5] *Parl. Debates*, xxiii. 1014 et seq.

He had looked over the correspondence for twenty-two districts and found that the disturbances were so much connected with distress that they might be directly traced to it; and whenever a district was found in which the distress was great, in that district also would be observed a proportionate disturbance.' When adequate measures for the relief of distress were taken, as they were, for instance, at Walton in Lancashire, despite the depression, there were no disturbances. When no adequate measures for relief were taken, as at Huddersfield and Bolton, places in which the original distress was no worse, considerable public disorder was experienced. He agreed completely with Maitland that 'exactly in proportion with the necessities of the People the Spirit of Disaffection has shown itself more or less'.[1]

This conclusion seems to be proved by the fact, which the *Annual Register* noticed after the disturbances were over, that order was restored as conditions improved. As they put it:[2]

'Gradually, however, order was restored; and the revival of trade, and consequent increase of wages, by manifestly contributing to this effect, unequivocably proved that one cause at least of the disturbances was the distressed state of the labouring classes, arising from the decay of trade, the lowness of their wages and the extreme dearness of the necessaries of life.'

It is also necessary to make the same assumption in order to explain why it was, when frauds had existed, and the new machinery been employed, for so many years in each of the disturbed industries, that there should have been no disorder until 1811. The only thing which was new in that year was the distress, and the breach of intercourse with America which was the prime, immediate cause of distress. Steam looms, shearing frames, wide stocking frames, had all been employed before. There had been disputes before between the cotton weavers, the croppers,

[1] Maitland to H.O., June 30, 1812, in H.O. 42. 124.
[2] *Annual Register*, 1812, p. 306.

and the framework knitters and their employers upon this point, and on the matter of wages and other conditions of work. The thing which turned these classes of workers from negotiations to riot, and which made them smash the machines upon which they had been working, was partly the break-down of negotiations, but mainly the collapse of the market. The immediate cause of Luddism was not the invention of new machinery but the stoppage of trade with America.[1]

Depression in trade due to the American Non-Intercourse Act was not, however, the only cause of distress, and therefore of disturbance. The bad harvests, and the consequent high price of provisions, were, as we have seen,[2] immediately and generally recognized to be major causes of disorder. Nothing was more likely than a sudden rise in the price of provisions to provoke disorder in Regency England. This was the cause of the most widespread of the disorders in 1812, the riots in the month of April in provision markets from one end of the kingdom to the other. It was an important cause of all the disturbances of the period.

A third cause of distress, and therefore of disturbance, was the business depression, the collapse of the market in 1810 following the speculative boom of the preceding years, and consequent especially upon the failure of the South American trade to realize the expected profits.[3] The restriction of credit, the wave of bankruptcies, the sudden glutting of the market, which were features of the year 1810, produced their inevitable consequences, unemployment, diminished earnings, bitter trade disputes. These in their turn degenerated into riot.

[1] Note the decline in the value of exports to America from more than eleven million pounds in 1810 to less than two million in 1811, *Accounts and Papers*, 1812, x. 25.

[2] Note evidence on this point by Maitland (to H.O., May 4, 1812, in H.O. 40. 1), Newcastle (to H.O., Nov. 16, 1811, in H.O. 42. 119), Coldham (frequent letters in H.O. 42. 117 et seq.), and other contemporary authorities.

[3] Note speech by Ryder, *Parl. Debates*, xxi. 11. 811.

There were also other causes of distress, and of Luddism, the difficulties of trade with the Continent, the changes of fashion due to war and other factors,[1] the terrible pressure of war-time taxation, all of which were, especially at a time of trade stagnation and poor harvests, likely to accentuate the unemployment and low wages from which the working classes were suffering.

Finally in this connexion there was the effect of the Industrial Revolution, and especially of the introduction of labour-saving machinery, which was undoubtedly pressing hardly upon particular classes of workers, even if it was benefiting the country as a whole. The croppers, the hand-loom weavers, the framework knitters, and domestic lace workers, were all losing their relative status, and were to continue to do so, partly, at any rate, because of the industrial changes which were taking place, because of the mechanization and urbanization of industry. They were not merely being thrown out of work, or having to accept lesser wages, because they could produce less than men working on the new improved machines, they were tied to domestic hand industries which could have no prosperous place in the industrial system which was slowly being established. It took a long time for changes to proceed far enough for these old hand industries to die. Until the late thirties the hand-loom weaver, until the sixties the domestic framework knitter, continued to exist in undiminished numbers. Machine and factory production did not replace, they only supplemented the old-established methods and workers. They did, however, perhaps inevitably, tend to degrade the relative, if not the absolute, status of these workers, whose pitiable later condition is reflected in many parliamentary reports.[2] Though they did not know it, except perhaps in the West Riding

[1] For instance the going out of pantaloons (see evidence before the committee on Framework Knitters' Petitions).

[2] See parliamentary inquiries into Framework Knitting Industry, 1812, 1819, and 1845; and into condition of Hand-Loom Weavers.

cropping shops, the Luddites were fighting against a distress which was due not merely, or mainly, to war or trade depression or bad harvests, which were temporary, but to the slow, permanent decline of their callings, left stranded by the advance of industry.

It is also necessary to recognize, besides distress, due to so many different factors, trade disputes as a major cause of Luddism. Distress in 1811–12, and in 1816–17, was universal. Luddism was localized. There must have been some reason why riots should have taken place in three main areas only while every area was distressed. The cotton area around Glasgow shared in the same depression of trade as that around Manchester. Petitions poured into Westminster in 1811 from both areas alike.[1] Petitions in 1812 came to Parliament even more urgently from Birmingham than from Nottingham.[2] Unemployment and pauperism in Liverpool equalled that in Manchester and Leeds.[3] And yet Nottingham, Manchester, and Huddersfield, and their environs, alone were the scenes of extended disorder.

Even within particular districts, though distress was general, disturbances were localized. In the woollen industry, although depression of trade and high prices were to be found everywhere, only in the Spen valley between Huddersfield and Leeds were there disturbances. In the cotton area, though distress was universal, machines were broken only at Westhoughton, Middleton, and Stockport. In the three hosiery counties, though conditions were difficult throughout the industry, and although cut-up goods were manufactured in Leicester even more generally than in Nottingham, the Nottingham area was alone the scene of extended framebreaking.

[1] *Parl. Debates*, xix. 1017 and xx. 906 et seq.

[2] *Parl. Debates*, xx, and evidence before Committee on Petitions for the Repeal of the Orders in Council.

[3] *Leeds Mercury*, Feb. 22, 1812, says that one-sixth of the inhabitants of Liverpool and one-fifth of those in all the large towns of Lancashire were in the condition of requiring charitable relief.

Similarly in 1816–17, although distress and discontent was general, disturbances were restricted. In the summer of 1817, although the whole country was afraid of trouble, only around Manchester, Derby, and Huddersfield was trouble realized. Distress and discontent were never the only, though they were a necessary, factor in popular disturbances in Regency England. A further factor was necessary at all times, and it was provided in local trade disputes and, towards the end of the period, in the activity of the agent provocateur.

The framework knitters had, as we have seen,[1] been long fighting to prevent the manufacture of cut-ups, of single press, single thread, and two-course hole. They had been trying to prevent frauds in the manufacture, which they believed were bringing the trade into disrepute and were the cause of their distress. They had been trying to prohibit 'colting', payment in 'truck',[1] arbitrary deductions and assessments, and other long-standing abuses. They had tried unsuccessfully to achieve these objects by negotiation,[2] by appeals to the Framework Knitters' Company[3] and to Parliament,[4] by every sort of peaceful means. They had been almost incited by some of the hosiers, who really wished as much as the men to end these abuses, to coerce the recalcitrant hosiers and bring the whole trade into line.[5] Framebreaking with them was caused not only by distress, but by frauds in the industry and by the breakdown of attempts to correct them by peaceful means.

Similarly in the West Riding the croppers had long tried, and for some time successfully, to prevent the introduction of shearing frames and gig mills. They had the sympathy

[1] Chaps. II, IV, VII.

[2] See evidence of Thomas Hayne to H.O., Feb. 12, 1812, in H.O. 42. 131 for proof of the great importance of this matter.

[3] Cf. ultimatum of Brocksopp and Parker, Feb. 1811, that they would reduce prices unless workers could get rest of trade to give up cut-up spurious work and pay full rates (Felkin, op. cit.).

[4] e.g. in 1804–5 (Felkin).

[5] Before appealing to the Framework Knitters' Company in 1804 and in 1812.

of many of the masters in this attempt.[1] They were driven to machine breaking as much by the failure of their peaceful campaign against machinery as by the trade depression.[2]

So also the cotton weavers, and the other workers who supported them, who attacked steam-loom factories in Lancashire and Cheshire, did so because their attempts to secure redress of grievances by trade-union action, and by petition to the magistrates and to Parliament,[3] had all failed, as well as because the trade depression had caused sudden exaggerated unemployment and distress. In every disturbed area the break-down of peaceful means of preventing abuses and redressing grievances was a prime cause of Luddism. It was the existence of such local situations, in which long-standing trade disputes between the masters and workmen had reached a state of deadlock, which explains why disturbances should have occurred only in a few areas while distress was so general. Trade disputes explain why Luddism should have been localized in respect of place just as distress explains why it should have been restricted in point of time.

An added cause of disturbance was undoubtedly the situation of the country, making disorder easy. The employers were vulnerable, since their machines were, in the midlands and the West Riding, situated in small country workshops, too many and too remote to be adequately guarded. Especially in the midlands, where the frames were actually in the possession and under the care of the stockingers, the property of the employers was dangerously exposed to the workers' attack. Luddism

[1] Note instances in 1809 and 1811, when an agreement with the better hosiers was in sight on condition that the men brought the whole trade into line and put an end to abuses (see accounts in Felkin and in parliamentary inquiry into Framework Knitters' Petitions).

[2] Grey to H.O., April 16, 1812, in H.O. 42. 122.

[3] See pamphlet *The Beggar's Complaint against Rack Rent Landlords . . . also some Observations on the Conduct of the Luddites* . . ., Sheffield, 1812, pp. 106 and 107.

was too easy and inviting a method of coercing unpopular employers when their machinery stood open to attack, in some country shop on the Yorkshire moors, or in the very houses of the discontented Nottinghamshire stockingers.

To make matters worse the population was so unanimous in sympathizing with the Luddites.[1] No one would give evidence against them. No bystanders would stir a hand to stop the attacking parties or to warn the authorities. Many a householder in charge of the hated machinery was himself a sympathizer, if not an aider and abettor, of the attacking parties. Even when, as in Yorkshire, the householder, being the owner, might wish to protect the machinery in his care, he was usually too terrified to do so, or to give an alarm, and was, besides, more than half in agreement with the Luddites, that the new machinery, which the competition of more enterprising manufacturers forced him to employ, was to the disadvantage of the trade.

The forces of order were also, as we shall see,[2] so very inadequate, that there was little to prevent reckless young workers from carrying out their wild plans. Framebreaking might never have become a widespread campaign if it had not been so easy, if the authorities had been better organized to prevent it. The non-existence of a police force was as important a cause of disorder in Regency England as the efficiency of the police is of order in modern England.

A further cause of disorder was the activity of some at any rate of the many spies employed by the government and by local authorities. In certain instances, at Bolton in 1812, and with regard to the 'Pentridge Revolution', the 'Huddersfield Rising', and the 'March of the Blanketeers' in 1817, the activity of the secret informer was an important contributory cause of the disturbances which took place. The spies, as we shall see,[3] so far from preventing,

[1] Coldham to H.O., Jan. 14, 1812, in H.O. 42. 119, and Grey to H.O., April 16, 1812, in H.O. 42. 122.

[2] Chaps. XII, XIII, XIV, XV.

[3] Chap. XV.

actually aided and abetted the disorders, which might never have taken place but for their misdirected activity.

Popular disturbances in Regency England, of which Luddism was the most serious, were the result of a complicated chain of causes, the severity of popular distress, the bitterness of trade disputes, and the lack of effective means peaceably to settle them, the pressure of new changes upon particular classes of the population, the vulnerability of employers to direct action on the part of their employees, the inadequacy of the internal defence and police arrangements, and the tendency of spies to become agents provocateurs. They usually occurred only, as with Luddism, when many of these causes were present at the same time.

XI
THE EFFECTS OF LUDDISM

THE immediate and most obvious consequence of the Luddite disturbances was the destruction of an immense quantity of property. Rather more than 1,000 stocking frames had been destroyed in the three midland counties by February 1812.[1] Upwards of 100 were destroyed in that area later that year and in the first few days of 1813.[2] It is impossible to estimate at all exactly how many frames were broken in the two later midland Luddite outbreaks in 1814 and 1816. It is probable, however, that at least 100 were broken in each period.[3] This would make a total loss during the whole period of Luddism of between 1,300 and 1,400 stocking frames. The value of this property when new would have been between £30,000 and £40,000.[4] Even at the then depreciated value of the stocking frame the monetary loss was more than £13,000.[5]

There were also broken at this time a certain, much smaller number of lace frames, and, in 1816, some new improved lace machines. These latter machines were very costly, so much so that the damage done in one attack alone, that on Heathcote and Boden's Loughborough factory, was estimated at more than £8,000.[6] The value of all other lace frames and machines damaged or broken by the Luddites may well have been at least as much. In

[1] Ryder to H.O., Feb. 14, 1812 (*Parl. Debates*, xxi. 11. 811) and Becher to H.O., Feb. 11, 1812, in H.O. 42. 120.

[2] Estimated from accounts of outrages listed in H.O. correspondence and press.

[3] Ibid.

[4] A new, simple stocking frame sometimes cost as much as £30 (see evidence before Parliamentary Committee on Framework Knitters' Petition).

[5] Coldham (to Newcastle, Nov. 28, 1811, in H.O. 42. 119) and Becher (to H.O., Feb. 11, 1812, in H.O. 42. 120) each estimated the depreciated value of the broken stocking frames as being £10 apiece on an average.

[6] Felkin estimates the loss on this occasion as being from £8,000 to £10,000.

this case the loss in the lace trade must have been even larger than in the hosiery, amounting perhaps to as much as £16,000. The Luddites may well have cost the three midland counties, directly and indirectly, apart from the cost of defence arrangements and of prosecutions and rewards, upwards of £30,000.

No estimates survive of the extent or cost of the damage done in the other Luddite attacks, in Lancashire, Cheshire, and Yorkshire, and in other contemporary disorders. It must, however, have been considerable. A great number of shearing frames were destroyed in the West Riding. Two complete factories were destroyed and several others seriously damaged in Lancashire and Cheshire. It cannot be an exaggerated estimate to place the total monetary loss on account of machinery destroyed by the Luddites at more than £50,000,[1] even at current depreciated values. When one adds the cost of the damage done in attacks upon provision and other shops, the Sheffield armoury, the Manchester Exchange Hall, and other scenes of disorder, and the loss of trade to the manufacturers during the course of the disturbances, and the expenses in which they were involved because of them, the total monetary cost of Luddism must have been very high.

The burden of this loss fell upon the manufacturers affected, although it was argued that the county in which the disturbances took place was responsible.[2] In one case, that of Heathcote and Boden, a verdict of damages against the county in favour of the injured manufacturer was returned. But the sum involved was never paid, because Heathcote moved his factory to Tiverton and the county pleaded successfully that it was only liable to replace broken machinery within its own area.[3] In another case, that of William Cartwright of Rawfolds, the Government

[1] A conservative estimate for the whole country, allowing just under £30,000 for the midlands.

[2] Request of Nottingham hosiers for the opinion of the Attorney and Solicitor-General, Nov. 30, 1814, in H.O. 42. 141.

[3] Felkin, op. cit.

did finally make a compassionate grant, as a matter of grace and not of right, in respect of the damage which he had suffered, which seems to have rendered him almost bankrupt.[1] In other cases, like that of Messrs. Oates, Wood, and Smithson of Leeds, the manufacturers were able to collect from their insurance companies.[2] In the majority of cases, however, the individual manufacturer had to stand the burden of his own loss.

It was a very heavy one. The destruction of frames in the midlands, upon which alone accurate figures are obtainable, amounted to more than four per cent. of all those then existing in the United Kingdom, more than five per cent. of those in the three midland counties, more than nine per cent. of those in the two counties, Nottingham and Derby, in which framebreaking was general, nearly twelve per cent. of those in the country districts in which most of the framebreaking took place.[3] Even though it was generally admitted that the industry had been so over-expanded that even after all this destruction there were still more than enough frames surviving to meet all reasonable requirements of the trade,[4] so that machine breaking could not be said to have had, from a general and ultimate point of view, a fatal effect, it was still a serious matter to the individual hosiers affected. Machine breaking was equally, if not more serious, to the owners of steam looms, shearing machines, gig mills, and improved lace machines, which also suffered from Luddite attacks, and which were new and costly machines, in which their owners had invested large amounts of (often borrowed)[5] capital. Machine breaking was a costly matter to the

[1] Cartwright to H.O., in H.O. 42. 130 and 147.

[2] *Leeds Intelligencer*, advertisements in Jan. and Feb. issues.

[3] Estimate of number of frames in the area and in the country taken from Blackner, *History of Nottingham* (quoted in Felkin, op. cit., p. 437).

[4] Felkin, op. cit. (notice also continual talk by contemporaries of the trade being overstocked with frames and hands).

[5] A vivid and fair, though fictitious, picture of the actual effect of Luddite attacks upon manufacturers affected is to be found in Phyllis Bentley's *Inheritance*, London, Macmillan, 1932.

manufacturers affected and therefore a powerful coercive weapon in the hands of their employees.

It was no wonder that an immediate result of machine breaking should have been, in the midlands and in the West Riding, that most of the smaller manufacturers should have ceased to use the hated methods and the obnoxious machinery.[1] Only in Lancashire and Cheshire, where the factories using steam looms were few and large, and where the owners affected were wealthy, powerful, and little open to such arguments, was Luddism an ineffective method of securing at any rate temporary redress of grievances. Elsewhere, where the owners and employers were often small men, very liable to terror, and where the machinery was in small and often lonely houses, which could not possibly be guarded, Luddism was quickly effective. The Yorkshire woollen masters laid up their new shearing frames. The Nottingham hosiers gave up making cut-ups and took their frames under guard into Nottingham for safe keeping.

In the midlands, where the object of the Luddites was not to prevent the use of machinery but to secure better conditions of work, negotiations rapidly followed. Within a few days of framebreaking commencing on a great scale in November 1811 individual hosiers had surrendered to the men's terms and general negotiations were set on foot.[2] Many hosiers announced during the following weeks that they would pay the desired advance in price and would refrain from the hated methods of manufacture.[3] The Luddites could very soon congratulate themselves with having raised the average rate of wages by 2*s*. per dozen.[4]

This success was, however, temporary. Very soon wages relapsed again. Comparatively soon the old fradulent methods of manufacture were revived. The negotiations

[1] See report of Huddersfield Committee to H.O., April 1812, in H.O. 40. 1.

[2] For account of negotiations see local press for Nov. and Dec. 1811 and Jan. and Feb. 1812.

[3] Ibid.

[4] Felkin, op. cit., p. 439.

between masters and men, which had looked like being a success, broke down again upon the old rock, the irreconcilable attitude of the minority of the hosiers.[1] Within a few months in the midlands, within a year in Yorkshire, conditions had relapsed into their previous state. The situation of the workers was worse and not better in that Luddism had been tried and failed so that the men had no longer any weapon in reserve. The moment the employers and owners of machinery regained confidence, which they did rapidly once the Luddites had been suppressed, they recommenced their old practices, with even greater confidence and less willingness to give way to their men than before the Luddite outbreaks, the fear of violence no longer being a bogy to men who had experienced it in actuality. The Parliamentary Committees of 1812 and 1819 with regard to the midlands show that conditions there after Luddism were at least as bad as they had been before. The further inquiry in 1845 shows that these deplorable conditions endured and became normal. Similar evidence is available in the north. The croppers and the hand-loom weavers were no more successful than the framework knitters in securing from Luddism any permanent improvement in their conditions.

The experience of other rioters was similar. The mobs who raided provision shops secured only a momentary advantage, prices reverting to their former level the moment the military had restored order. Here and there a mayor or a magistrate would try to improve conditions, arranging for provisions to be obtained from ships in port, as at Falmouth,[2] or trying to bring workers and masters together,[3] or to prevent regrating and speculation.[4] But such attempts were infrequent. They were seldom even temporarily effective. They never endured. Agricultural

[1] *London Times*, Dec. 27, 1811. [2] Reports in H.O. 42. 122.

[3] As at Nottingham (see Conant and Baker's report in H.O. 42. 119) and Stockport (see pamphlet, *A Beggar's Complaint* . . .).

[4] As at Carlisle and Plymouth (letters in H.O. 42. 122.).

labourers whom distress provoked to rick burnings and other acts of riot, and the hapless participants in such ventures as the 'March of the Blanketeers' were even less fortunate. They did not succeed in achieving even a momentary or local success. A brief hour or two of riot won for them only sentences of death and transportation.

The machine breaking did not have, except in one case, the effect that the masters and the government, and students of affairs, insisted that it would,[1] that of driving the trade to other more peaceful areas. Machine breaking had had this effect before. Machine breaking in Leicester in the 1770's had driven the woollen and worsted industries away from the midlands, so that midland hosiers in 1812 had to buy their raw material from far afield.[2] Machine breaking at Loughborough in 1816 induced Mr. Heathcote to transfer his lace factory to Tiverton in Devon.[3] But upon the whole Luddism was too quickly suppressed for a tendency for the migration of industry to set in. Long before employers could have had time to transfer their factories, or before other areas could have taken advantage of the situation created by Luddism to capture markets hitherto held by manufacturers from the Luddite districts, the machine breaking had been suppressed. It was a temporary phenomenon.

The workers, upon the relapse of Luddism, reverted to other methods of securing a redress of grievances, to trades union action, to petitions to Parliament, to attempts to secure peace and parliamentary reform. They entered into such activities with greater enthusiasm because direct action had been proved in the end, and after a short period of easy success, so dangerous and so ineffective. It would be possible to show, though it is outside the scope of this work, that Luddism was merely an episode in the history upon the one hand of trades unionism, and on the other of working-class political activity, both of which had been

[1] See pamphlets exhorting workers not to break machinery (copies in H.O. 42). [2] Felkin, op. cit. [3] Ibid.

temporarily discredited in the Luddite areas in favour of machine breaking and riot, both of which came into their own again, and absorbed the energies of former Luddites, when Luddism had been suppressed. The distressing situation of the labouring classes, of which Luddism was an effect, and the impossibility of improving it by direct action, which the suppression of Luddism impressed upon the people generally, combined to create a great incentive to all discontented people to build political and industrial instruments to serve the purposes that Luddism had failed to serve, the protection and improvement of the wage earners' conditions of work and standard of living. The Petitions to Parliament, the Nottingham Union, the strikes, and the other political and industrial activities which occupied the attention of midland workers after 1812, though temporarily, upon occasions, accompanied by machine breaking, very soon entirely replaced it. Similar activities absorbed the interest of workers in other areas, in all of which the failure of riot and disturbance had the effect of increasing the support given to other means of securing a redress of grievances.

The disturbances had also had the effect of attracting the attention of the public and of Parliament to the situation out of which they had grown. On the one hand, as we shall discuss in later chapters, the authorities and the public had been alarmed at the difficulty of suppressing the outbreaks. They had realized more clearly than before the urgent necessity of having a better system of police. They began to realize also, for a similar reason, the necessity of improving the system of internal government, of reforming the Home Office, the magistracy, the municipalities, things which were obviously necessary if similar and even more dangerous outbreaks were not to occur again. Disturbances under the Regency had the effect of accelerating the tendencies towards political reform that issued during the next decades in such innovations as the new police, the Reform Bill, and the Municipal Corporations Act.

On the other hand Parliament and the public had their attention called by the Luddites, and during these frequent disturbances between 1811 and 1817, to the industrial situation. Free Trade legislation, Factory Acts, the legalization of Trades Unions, the very many attempts that Parliament was to make during the nineteenth century to correct the more obvious injustices of the new social order, the whole decline and fall of *laisser-faire* philosophy, though following long after the last Luddite had been swung off the gallows, owed something to the Luddites' hopeless battle against fate. Parliament in 1812 repealed the Orders in Council because of their effect upon the industrial districts.[1] A committee of Parliament was ready to pass a Bill regulating those frauds in the lace trade which had provoked the Luddites.[2] The public, including many members of Parliament and leaders of opinion, subscribed during the course of 1812 as readily and freely to subscriptions for public relief as they earlier had to those for the suppression of disturbances.[3] Parliament was not yet an effective instrument for the relief of such distresses as those which provoked the Luddite movement. Its members were, as we shall see, as yet too little conscious of internal conditions, and of the necessity for public interference in industrial matters, and was besides too inhibited by a doctrinaire policy of *laisser-faire*, effectively to redress the grievances of the disorderly. But the disturbances of the time, and the sense that they gave to Parliament and the public of the necessity of doing more than just wait for

[1] But not because of the disturbances. Brougham, as counsel for the petitioners, was very careful to keep all question of disturbances out of his case, he and other witnesses stressing the orderliness rather than the rioting of the distressed populace.

[2] The hosiery clauses were struck out of the Bill because the industry was an old one which there was a strong *laisser-faire* prejudice against restricting or controlling.

[3] See advertisements in the press in May and June 1812 with regard to subscriptions for relief. A subscription for suppression of disturbances had been taken up in Nottinghamshire in January (see Nottingham press).

and suppress disorders, were a powerful factor in educating opinion. One can see the advance in this respect even as between 1811 and 1817; in the latter year there was a greater knowledge of and interest in internal and industrial conditions than in the former. But for the Luddites and the Blanketeers Manchester and Birmingham might have been unrepresented in Parliament, as well as without local systems of police, wage-earners might have been without the right to form trades unions, factory acts might have been delayed much later than they were. For it was the hapless rioters more than the publicists who made the Home Office and internal matters generally of major and not of very minor importance.

The Luddites failed hopelessly in their immediate objects. They succeeded, however, just a little in what was, though they did not know it, their ultimate function, to prove the necessity of taking consciously in hand, and not leaving to follow their own distressing, undirected course, the readjustments that were an inevitable part of the political and industrial revolutions of the nineteenth century.

XII

THE MACHINERY OF ORDER

PARLIAMENT,[1] preoccupied with a European war, was in the first two decades of the nineteenth century little apt to act as a regular check upon the Executive. In the days of *laisser-faire*, before the nice distinction between politics and economics had been broken down, its deliberations were seldom disturbed by the jolting and straining of the industrial machine. In the period of parliamentary history before the question had developed its full importance it was not easy to bring the situation of the moment to the attention of the House. And when interference with the natural laws which were thought to govern industry was strongly deprecated, to trouble the House with a local or temporary dispute or disorder was neither necessary nor useful.

Therefore, although Parliament as the supreme organ of government was certain to be troubled sooner or later with business arising out of a protracted or serious internal disorder, it would not be concerned with the initial stages of the disturbance or with the routine business of its suppression. Only when emergency powers were needed or when it was desired to strengthen the penalties of the law were industrial disputes or popular disturbances brought to the attention of the two Houses of Parliament. Money could be spent by the Government or granted to the local authorities; troops could be dispatched to the scene of disorder; efforts could be made to mediate the disputes; offenders could be brought to justice in the regular

[1] See reports and minutes of evidence of committees (of Secrecy, 1812 and 1817; on petitions for the repeal of the Orders in Council, 1812; and from Framework Knitters, 1812 and 1819) and debates thereon and upon relevant bills (Framebreaking; Nottingham Peace; Unlawful Oaths; Lace Regulation; Preservation of the Public Peace (or Public Safety); Indemnity, 1812; Suspension of Habeas Corpus, 1817; and Nottingham Peace (renewal) 1813) in *Parliamentary Debates* for 1812, 1813, and 1817.

way or by means of a Special Commission; without resource to Parliament. Although all these policies might have been resorted to, and though the press might have made universal a knowledge of the gravity of the situation and of the activity of Government, not till parliamentary action was needed would the Ministers think it necessary to tell Parliament what had occurred. Even then their action would be limited to justifying the measures they had to propose and they would not think of embarking, or of allowing the House to embark, upon an extended inquiry into the situation as a whole.

Thus in 1811–12, although there had been reports of impending trouble for more than a year, and though dangerous disturbances had actually been raging without intermission for more than three months, it was not until February 1812, a short ten days before the Government was planning to present its emergency Bills in connexion with the disorders, that Luddism aroused any comment in Parliament. Then, and again later, during the passage of the five Bills which were presented in connexion with Luddism, there were brief parliamentary discussions with regard to these unprecedented civil disorders. With the passage of the last of these five Bills in July parliamentary attention to Luddism ceased. In the autumn of 1813 one of these Bills, The Nottingham Peace Bill, was renewed until March, 1815. Thereafter, despite the occurrence of disorders in the country, there was no further parliamentary notice of them until the beginning of 1817.

In that year, when the post-war depression with its long, sad train of consequences was forcing itself upon the attention of the nation, Parliament again gave its full attention to disorders in the manufacturing districts. In February and in June Secret Committees of both Houses were appointed to study reports from the disturbed localities. The evidence was considered sufficient to justify alarming reports and to induce Parliament to grant the Government the powers for which it asked, including suspension of the

Habeas Corpus Act. There were several full and interesting debates, in one of which the spy system was very trenchantly exposed and attacked. There were signs of a greater interest in, and knowledge of, internal and industrial conditions, amongst the members, as compared with the situation five years before. Parliament, like the nation, was now no longer preoccupied with problems of war and foreign affairs. The forces in the House of Commons, like those in the country, were beginning once again to shape themselves for the party conflicts of peace. There were already signs of an effective radical opposition, a factor which had hardly existed, so far as disturbances and internal policy were concerned, in 1812.

But even in 1817 it is astonishing to note how little real knowledge of or interest in these internal matters existed. Concern for such matters was growing, but it was still small. A very meagre House was all that usually came in to listen to speeches on disturbances and trade disputes. It was even now, when there were no great battles abroad to dwarf the importance of riots at home, not until the last moment, when emergency powers were needed, that Parliament was consulted. Even now an attempt was successfully made to keep such discussion as there was strictly to the business on hand, to the proposed legislation, and to the acts of the Government, and not to allow it to stray over the whole background of the problem. Parliament was still content to act as a cipher of the administration, leaving it free to act as it pleased within the law, giving it promptly any further powers it requested.

This neglect of internal matters, this willingness to leave policy with regard to them to the Government, was even more strikingly exemplified in 1812. The Opposition in the House of Lords and the House of Commons, the Whigs mostly opposing the Government's measures in the Upper, and the Radicals only in the Lower House, mustered usually only about 17 votes on each division called against the administration's measures. The Government's majorities too were small, varying from a mere 15, on a total vote of 59, on the Framebreaking Bill in the House of Lords in February, to slightly more than 100, out of a total vote of less than 150, on the Public Safety Bill in the House of Commons in July. The average attendance when Luddism and other disturbances were being discussed was very, very small. The Government's supporters, who were united in favour of the Bills presented, were not interested enough in them to turn out in any numbers to carry them through. The Opposition, which was divided, some members inclining to oppose the Government's measures on principle, others supporting them because the entire governing class was really at one in its attitude to disturbances and its feeling that they must be put down, was equally slack in its attendance.

Parliament was actually forced to give a good deal of attention to this matter of disturbances. It passed the five Bills requested of it, the Framebreaking Bill, the Nottingham Peace Bill, both in February, the Unlawful Oaths Bill in May, the Preservation of the Public Peace (or Public Safety) Bill and the Act of Indemnity in July 1812. It appointed Committees of Secrecy in June 1812, basing its subsequent legislation upon their reports, which were based in turn upon reports to the Government from local magistrates and other informants. It also conducted lengthy inquiries into larger aspects of this problem, the inquiry of the Committee of the Whole into Petitions against the Orders in Council in April and May, the inquiry of the special Committee on Framework Knitters' Petitions in June and July 1812. In consequence of these inquiries the Orders in Council were actually repealed, with immediate, beneficial effects upon the trade situation and upon the disturbances, while the House of Commons passed a Bill regulating those abuses in the lace trade against which the Luddites had been protesting, only to see the measure badly defeated in the House of Lords.

These latter inquiries and measures were, however, not taken in relation to one another or to the Committees of Secrecy or the Luddite legislation. It does not seem to have been realized that the disturbances, since they had clearly grown out of the distress, might be relieved by such measures as repeal of the Orders in Council and regulation of the hosiery and lace trades, which might be a solvent to distress. Each committee, each separate bill, seems to have been considered by itself, without relation to other matters before Parliament. So far as Luddism was concerned all that the Government recommended, and all that Parliament, with the exception of a very small minority, wished to do, was to suppress it, by enlarging the penalties of the law and improving the organization of the police. They did not believe that relief of distress or redress of grievances was practicable, or was, in any case, any substitute for punishment of the guilty. It was a coincidence, and so far as the hosiery and lace trades were concerned a consequence of the suppression of Luddism, that Parliament should have happened during this year to have dealt in some measure with the broad situation out of which disturbances had arisen. That it might have some relation to disturbances was never even suspected by those members of Parliament who studied the evidence which lead to repeal of the Orders in Council and to a vote upon the Lace Regulation Bill.

Similarly in later years Parliament kept disturbances and distress quite distinct in determining its policies. It recognized that distress was a powerful cause of disturbance, but it did not believe that anything could be done about disturbances other than to try to put them down by whatever repressive measures were required. When it dealt with distress, as it sometimes did, it never was rude enough to mention the word disturbance. The debates in 1817 on popular distress and popular disturbances were quite distinct, no attempt being made to connect the two, to delay action on suppression of the disturbances because of distress, or to hasten action on distress because of disturbances. Parliament was accustomed, apparently, not merely to act but to think in water-tight compartments. It dealt with different aspects of disturbances separately, and upon the whole it limited its action to doing what the Government requested of it.

It was very poorly informed upon such matters. It is striking the differences of opinion which existed at the time amongst members with regard to events taking place within 200 miles of Westminster. Although many members of Parliament were themselves magnates and magistrates from the disturbed districts, first-hand witnesses with regard to the situation out of which the riots had grown, they allowed themselves to be strangely deluded. A very few of them were found sceptical enough not to believe the obviously exaggerated reports of the Committees of Secrecy, which, as Mr. Whitbread remarked, were totally unjustified even by the evidence which the Committees themselves had seen, evidence which was in itself, very often, highly untrustworthy. Parliament was slow to act. It was behindhand in its information, dealing, for instance, with midland Luddism only in February 1812, when it had already substantially ceased, and with northern Luddism in June and July, when it was well on the way to being suppressed. It was ill-informed enough to think that the riots were increasing when in fact they were almost finished, credulous enough to think that there were large and alarming designs behind the riots when the Government's own agents were ready to state definitely that there were not. With a few notable exceptions the members of both Houses of Parliament were with regard to Luddism and other internal disorders as dependent upon the information presented to them by Ministers as they were with regard to matters of distant and foreign importance. Parliamentary debates and the reports of Parliamentary committees are seldom a good source of information, almost never a primary one. They merely echo the conclusions of Ministers, themselves founded upon reports from local magistrates.

It was not surprising therefore that Parliament's role in these affairs should have been a minor one. It was not surprising that the Acts of Parliament should usually have come too late to be of any real use. The Framebreaking Bill, which was opposed by Nottingham local and informed opinion, was never put into effect, framebreaking having substantially ceased before it was enacted. The Nottingham Peace Bill, strongly backed by informed local opinion and founded upon their suggestions, was only made use of to the extent of taking names of persons who might be called upon for service in the Watch and Ward in case of necessity. No actual necessity to use the forces thus available ever at that time arose. The Unlawful Oaths Bill was just as vain, all the persons arrested and charged being liable to conviction under the existing law prior to the enactment of this bill, and the administration of oaths being in fact, though Parliament did not know it, no real part of the Luddite campaign. The Public Safety Bill and the Act of Indemnity were applied, but only after the disturbances had been brought substantially to an end without their help. The repeal of the Orders in Council, which did have a temporary good effect, came too late to prevent the American Declaration of War, which once more closed the all-important American market. The acts of government in 1817 came similarly after rather than before the height of the crisis and cannot be said markedly to have affected the situation or contributed to the restoration of order. Parliament was at this time, in relation to internal disorders, a mere instrument of government, and an unwieldy, ineffective instrument at that.

The real national authority lay with the Cabinet. It was only on the Cabinet's advice, when the Cabinet wished it, that Parliament dealt with disturbances. There is in this matter no evidence of Parliament as a body controlling, or indeed influencing, the Cabinet, although individual members of Parliament, men like Eyre of Nottinghamshire and Wilberforce of Yorkshire, who interviewed the Home Secretary and brought pressure to bear on him to accede to local requests, did have some influence over the administration's policy.

But even the Cabinet was content upon the whole to neglect such matters as internal disorder. It was not until the end of January 1812, less than a fortnight before parliamentary action was requested, and long after grave disturbances had commenced, that the Cabinet as a body, so far as we know, first discussed Luddism.[1] Then it did receive a full digest of the correspondence from the localities and of the other material in the hands of the Home Secretary. It approved of the Bills the Secretary had drafted. It recommended the issuance of pamphlets proving to the rioters how shortsighted their policy was and how certain to defeat its own ends and drive their trade away to other safer regions. But it does not seem even then to have regarded the matter as of the first importance or to have contributed anything material to the policy that was being pursued or that had been decided upon. And prior to that, although very great exertions had been made by the authorities national and local, including the use of an hitherto unprecedented number of troops, it does not seem even to have asked for information. The Prime Minister had been interested in the matter and had had some correspondence with the Home Department with regard to it.[2] There is no evidence, however, of his other colleagues having done so. They had been content to leave the matter to the responsible minister, the Home Secretary. Now, when their approval had to be secured, since Parliament was to be approached, they were content to accept his report and his measures.

[1] Reports of meetings in letters to Conant and Baker from H.O., Jan. 29, 1812 et seq. in H.O. 79. 1.

[2] e.g. Perceval to Ryder, April 10, 1812, in H.O. 42. 122, with implied reference to previous correspondence.

The same thing happened the next time that popular disturbances became important enough to require parliamentary attention. From 1812 to 1817 the Cabinet seems to have neglected such matters, which required only local measures of action. In 1817, when national and emergency measures were thought necessary, the Cabinet was again consulted, on the 19th and 24th of January, a few weeks only before the matter was brought up in Parliament and Secret Committees appointed.[1] The Cabinet then, as in 1812, seems merely to have received a report from the Home Secretary, and abstracts of his correspondence with the disturbed districts, the same material that went before the parliamentary committees. It accepted his conclusions and endorsed his measures.

The real authority therefore lay with the Home Department. Of all the offices of state this was the one least likely to attract the attention of the Cabinet or to hold that of Parliament. So much was this the case and so little had the Home Department been regarded as important that in July 1812 *The Times* attributed to its incompetence a large measure of responsibility for delay in putting down Luddism. It printed a strong attack upon the personnel of the office.[2]

'There is too, we believe, less of talent and energy in that office by which our Home concerns are chiefly directed than in all the rest put together. We say nothing of the head of it, his is a recent appointment, but his subordinate officers are men who, through a long series of years, whatever might be their competence to more arduous stations, have been at least thought sufficiently qualified for a department wherein no difficulty has ever till now occurred, so that it is evident to common reason that the Home Office must have become the sink of all the imbecility attached to every Ministry for the last thirty years, and should, therefore, at this period, when occurrences requiring more capable minds have taken place, be instantly and radically reformed.'

[1] Schedules of letters submitted to Cabinet in H.O. 42. 158.

[2] *London Times*, July 1, 1812.

On the 4th, replying to comments that had been aroused by this attack, *The Times* leader-writer re-emphasized his point. He admitted that it was true that the charge probably affected the heads as well as the subordinates. Indeed it would have been surprising if a critic, who thought that the Home Office attracted the least able and energetic, had failed to note the significance of the fact that this was the office to which 'Doctor Addington' had been appointed. But he was not content to blame on Lord Sidmouth, then Secretary, all the shortcomings of his Department. He continued:

'We complained then, as we do now, that a Department, notoriously composed of persons only deemed adequate to the common business of the most unimportant of the three offices of State, should receive no accession of strength (we do not mean numbers) at a time when that office has the most delicate and difficult affairs assigned to its management.'

Even the Home Office apologists admitted that the growth of business had made some enlargement of the Department really necessary. *The Times* went farther and felt that a more competent Department was needed. Either the talent was insufficient now or it had been superfluous before.

It was then to this 'most unimportant of the three offices of State' that the major responsibility for the maintenance of internal order was entrusted. At its head during the Luddite disturbances were two Secretaries of State In the Perceval Government the Secretary was Richard Ryder. A clear-headed and fair-minded politician of the second rank, Ryder held office until the formation of the new Liverpool Government in June 1812. He was then succeeded by Henry Addington, Viscount Sidmouth. Sidmouth had been respected as an amiable though not very resourceful politician, an admirable Speaker but a poor Premier, well fitted for his present normally unimportant office. He was to gain during his ten years at the Home Department a very different reputation. As the minister responsible for the last and longest suspension of the Habeas Corpus Act; as the author of the 'Six Acts'; as the mouthpiece of the Government in expressing approval of the 'Massacre of Peterloo'; as Home Secretary at a period when Home Affairs were of the first importance and when the apprehensions of disorder were very grave; Sidmouth became widely regarded as a ruthless enemy of popular liberty. Few British governments have been so unpopular in the country as that of Lord Liverpool. Few ministers have been more generally hated than the two who were held responsible for the Liverpool Government's repressive policy, Sidmouth and Castlereagh.

Under the Secretary of State and conducting most of the correspondence with the localities was the permanent Under-Secretary, John Beckett (later Sir John Beckett of the Colonial Office). Alongside him, and acting apparently in a more personal relation with the Home Secretary, was during the later years of Luddism the other Under-Secretary, Mr. Hiley Addington. The Department at this time was still a small one and its heads kept a close touch with all its work, personally interviewing magistrates, members of Parliament, and even spies and prisoners, with information from the localities, and being not merely nominally but actually responsible for even minor departmental acts.

Acting in conjunction with this office was the Treasury Solicitor's office. Mr. Lichfield and Mr. Hobhouse at Lincoln's Inn were in frequent communication with the permanent Under-Secretary of State. Through this department were arranged official prosecutions, Mr. Hobhouse himself conducting some, as at York in January 1813, spending some months in the north to prepare the cases, and he and his colleagues in the Lincoln's Inn office supervising and assuming financial responsibility for all. Through the medium of the Treasury Solicitor cases were sent by the Home Office to the Law Officers of the Crown for their opinion. In conjunction with the various law officers and with the Lord Chancellor and the Lord Chief Justice the Home Office was also in touch with the Judges, who had to send reports and recommendations for mercy into the Department after each Assize, and with whom the Home Secretary was often in correspondence or consultation.

The Department thus situated controlled from its office in Whitehall the whole interior government of the country. Through it passed all petitions to the Crown. The Home Secretary managed much of the business of the Privy Council and arranged audiences with the Prince Regent. On his recommendation were appointed or removed the Lords Lieutenant. On their recommendation the Home Secretary appointed the Deputy Lieutenants. Though the magistrates were appointed by the Lord Chancellor on the recommendation of the Lord Lieutenant of the county, the Home Secretary had an important, though unofficial, responsibility in connexion with the policy these other officials followed in making recommendations and appointments. The Justices of the Peace were, besides, in regular communication with the Home Office, to which they were responsible in their administrative capacity. Even closer was the relationship between the Home Department and the Stipendiary Magistrates, Police Officers, and Bow Street Runners in the metropolis.

The Home Department had thus very extensive powers. In these London Police Offices it controlled the only professional police force in the country, members of which it could and did dispatch at pleasure to any part of the kingdom. Through its control of the Secret Service Fund the Department had money available for almost any purpose connected with the public security. From this fund and from the ordinary funds of government the Home Secretary made grants for public rewards for information, for the payment of spies and informers, for the expenses of prosecutions, for the cost of procuring, guarding, and rewarding witnesses, and for other purposes connected with the detection of offenders and the suppressions of disturbances. The approbation of the Crown through the medium of the Home Department was needed for the calling out of the militia and yeomanry. On the orders of the Home Secretary alone would the Secretary at War make provision for the issue of pay and allowances to the local forces thus mobilized. It was through the medium of the Home Department that approach was made to the Commander-in-Chief or to the local area commanders for regular forces for internal duty, and action by the Horse Guards was usually a matter of course after decision by the Home Office. It was the Home Department which was the medium of communication between the local authorities and the various organs of Government and between the local authorities and Parliament.

Immediately below the Home Department stood the Lords Lieutenant. Normally absent from their Lieutenancies and unconcerned with routine business they were yet far from being ciphers. On occasions of emergency they would go down to their counties and take charge of local defence arrangements. They presided over meetings of the Lieutenancy or of the county magistrates. They passed on to the Home Secretary local requests for reinforcements or for enlarged powers. They represented the Crown in the country and the country in London, taking down to their Lieutenancies the exhortations of the Government, bringing to the Government the requests of their subordinates, the local Justices and Deputy Lieutenants. They were not merely legally and in point of precedence but by tradition and in fact the leading men in their respective counties, and they were expected to set an example to their Lieutenancies. It was to them that the Home Secretary applied in the first place when he wished to communicate generally with the magistrates throughout the country. The first sign of widespread disaffection and of government alarm was apt to be a circular letter from the Home Office to the Lords Lieutenant.[1]

Of the Lords Lieutenant in the disturbed districts the Duke of Newcastle, Lord Lieutenant and Custos Rotulorum of Nottinghamshire, was the most active. He was during the first Luddite disorders in 1811–12 almost permanently in residence at Clumber. He took an active part in measures for the suppression of disturbances. He was one of the most regular and informative of the correspondents of the Home Secretary.[2] He arranged, firstly at his own expense and later at that of the Government, for the employment of informers.[3] He called out the militia. He took the lead in subscriptions for the prosecution of framebreakers and for the relief of distress. He took the chair at that meeting of county magistrates which recommended in January 1812 the reorganization of the Watch and Ward, recommendations upon which the Government's later Bill was based.[4] He presided at later meetings of the Lieutenancy. He paid a special visit to the county in May. He was active again in the winter of 1812–13 and in 1814. No disturbance ever happened in the county without his taking an interest in it and reporting on it to the Home Secretary.

While the other Lords Lieutenant were hardly so active as this, all those whose areas were disturbed seem at any rate to have made special visits to their Lieutenancies. The Duke of Rutland, as Lord Lieutenant of Leicestershire, was often resident in the county and sent up a number of reports and suggestions.[5] The Earl of Derby and the Earl of Stamford went down to Lancaster and to Cheshire

[1] e.g. in 1817 the first sign of recognition on the part of the Government that the situation was serious is to be found in a circular to the Lords Lieutenant (copy in H.O. 42. 158).

[2] Frequent letters, mostly in series H.O. 42. 117–59.

[3] Exchange of letters between Newcastle and Ryder, Dec. 16 and 18, 1812, in H.O. 42. 118.

[4] Report and resolutions in H.O. 42. 119.

[5] Particularly depositions with regard to forced collections of funds in Leicestershire in Dec. 1811, in Rutland to H.O., Jan. 5, 1812, in H.O. 42. 119.

respectively to hold meetings of their Lieutenancies in May 1812. Earl Fitzwilliam not merely did the same, he also returned to the West Riding later that year. Both at this time and again in 1816–17 he kept in close touch with events in his Lieutenancy. He wrote up occasionally to the Home Office. He presided at meetings of the Lieutenancy. He was sufficiently interested in its affairs to make suggestions from time to time as to policies to be pursued. He joined with the military authorities in impressing upon the magistrates and on the local population the most strenuous measures for their own defence.[1]

Alongside the Lord Lieutenant stood the High Sheriff. Possessed of similar powers for calling out the yeomanry and militia and holding a position of only less dignity and even greater antiquity, the Sheriff might have become a rival of the Lord Lieutenant. Being more often than not a local landowner of the second rank, seldom absent, like the greater landowners, abroad or in London or at some other seat, he had fewer outside interests to preoccupy his time. More on a level with the magistrates with whom he would have to co-operate he might have played a large part in the suppression of disturbances. That in general he did not and that the Sheriff was in most counties distinctly less active than the Lord Lieutenant was due to the normal inactivity of the office and to the way its prestige had declined. It had become difficult to get important people to serve. The office was an annual and a thankless one.[2] It was seldom held by a vigorous influential individual.

There was in fact only one Sheriff who played any considerable part in the suppression of Luddism, Mr. Wright, the High Sheriff of Nottinghamshire in 1811.[3] He called

[1] See letters from or to Maitland, Wood, and Fitzwilliam for May and June 1812, in H.O. 40. 1 and 42. 123 and 124.

[2] The best account of English Local Government, and one from which some of the facts in this chapter are taken, is *The History of English Local Government*, by S. and B. Webb.

[3] Letters in H.O. 42. 118 and 119.

out the local militia early in November of that year. He took the field at their head. He was at great pains to gather all the threads of authority into his own hands, so much so that the Duke of Newcastle complained that he was being kept in ignorance of what was going on, was being shouldered out of his proper precedence and authority.[1] This was, however, the only instance of such conflicts between Sheriff and Lieutenant, or, indeed, of such activity on the part of any Sheriff.

Beneath these county officials stood the general organization of the Lieutenancies and of the Justices of the Peace. The Vice-Lieutenant and Deputy Lieutenants individually and collectively had a responsibility not merely for the defence of the county in the event of invasion, but also for the maintenance of internal order. Usually gentlemen of greater prestige than the Justices of the Peace the Deputy Lieutenants had a less arduous office, being free from the great mass of petty judicial and administrative business piled upon the Justices. It was only when there was an emergency that the Lieutenancy was called together. Then it would meet and consider the situation of the locality. It would arrange for the calling out of the county forces according to plan. It would determine whether the situation was such as to necessitate the institution generally or in particular districts of the Watch and Ward. Through the medium of the Vice-Lieutenant, of the Clerk of the Peace, or of a committee representative of the Lieutenancy, it would supervise the carrying into effect of its decisions, and would develop a comprehensive policy of local defence. Meetings of the Lieutenancy were called for these purposes and especially to initiate the organization of the Watch and Ward, in Nottinghamshire, Cheshire, the County Palatine, and the West Riding, in the spring and summer of 1812. Especially in the north, where the number of magistrates able and willing to act was very small, a great burden fell during May and June 1812 upon the Lieu-

[1] H.O. to Wright, Dec. 2, 1811, in H.O. 43. 19.

tenancy, who had to exert all their influence in order to stir the local population to take adequate measures for its own defence.[1]

Parallel with the Lieutenancy stood the organization of the Justices in Sessions. A general meeting of the magistrates of the county might be a more convenient method of instituting the necessary measures of defence. The Justices would be meeting in any case every quarter, and often, by a system of adjourned meetings, more frequently, at one or other of the less inconvenient county centres. They could, and did, easily in case of necessity call special meetings, or make use of regular ones, to plan necessary defence measures. It was such a meeting of Nottinghamshire Justices presided over by the Lord Lieutenant which recommended the reorganization of the Watch and Ward in January 1812.[2] The Justices in Sessions possessed co-ordinate powers with the Sheriff and Lord Lieutenant for the calling out of the militia. Not merely could a group of justices call out on their own authority detachments of the yeomanry and militia in case of emergency,[3] but in practice the Sheriff and Lord Lieutenant would act in this matter on the advice of the magistrates.

The Justices were, as we shall see, very quick to exercise these collective powers, calling out the militia, for instance, more speedily and in greater numbers than the Home Secretary, the Lord Lieutenant, or the local regular officers often thought was necessary.[4] They were not so quick, however, to institute those local defence associations upon which experts believed the restoration of order really depended. It was difficult to do so, the population being

[1] See p. 232, n. 1.

[2] Account in H.O. 42. 119.

[3] In the absence of the Lord-Lieutenant and Vice-Lieutenants of Lancashire, Hay, Wright, and Barton, two other J.P.s, and one D.L. called our nearly 1,000 men of the local militia in Lancashire on April 28, 1812 (H.O. 42. 122).

[4] Note comments of Ryder, Maitland, and Sidmouth during the 1811–12 disturbances.

so united in fear of or sympathy with the Luddites. Whole villages petitioned against such measures being taken, or a Watch and Ward instituted, in them.[1] Especially in the north, in the West Riding in 1812, very few places took adequate defence measures despite the decisions of the Lieutenancy and despite the efforts of the military.[2]

There was also the difficulty that the execution of the decisions of Sessions or Lieutenancy depended usually upon the energy, courage, and ability of individual justices. Some one had to take in hand the actual organization of a defence association, the actual command of a system of patrol or Watch and Ward. Many magistrates were unwilling to attain a dangerous notoriety by doing so, or by taking a prominent part in executing collective policies. If they did not do so the whole machinery of order collapsed.

The burden of local government fell, indeed, in an unusual degree upon the individual Justice of the Peace in the early nineteenth century. By tradition the many matters which could be settled by a single justice acting alone, or by two or three together, were left in each district to the justice or justices resident there. Action might legally be taken, but in practice it seldom if ever would be, by some other member of the Commission. If the local justice were inactive, or if there were no justice within easy reach, all but the most urgent magisterial duties were apt to be neglected. The conscientious justice had a busy time. It was his responsibility to read the Riot Act to disorderly meetings; to order angry mobs to disperse within the hour; to enroll special constables; to call on the local regular forces, if any; to issue warrants for the arrest of offenders; and to take all necessary steps for the maintenance of order, the suppression of disturbances,

[1] Memorial of Huddersfield Committee to H.O., April 1812, in H.O. 40. 1.

[2] *Leeds Intelligencer*, Sept. 21, gives an account of arrangements then, when confidence had returned and inhabitants were willing again to act, as they had not been in June 1812.

and the detection of offenders. If he did not act no one would act in his district. The military, the militia, the constables would none of them act except at his request.[1] He and his fellows on the bench had the responsibility of deciding whether the local militia and yeomanry should be called out; whether the Sheriff or Lord Lieutenant should be asked to call out the entire county force; whether further special constables should be enrolled; whether a regular nightly watch was needed; whether the point had been reached when further regular troops were needed for the safety of the district. The real responsibility for the suppression of disturbances rested upon, and could not be avoided by, the individual Justice of the Peace.

This was true even in the few corporate towns. While the corporation might take its own measures for defence it was the responsibility of the county magistrates to determine whether or no the county militia and yeomanry should or should not be kept within the town.[2] When, as was usually the case, disorders extended past the borough boundaries, or originated outside the town, there was nothing that the borough corporation, with its limited jurisdiction, could usefully do. The major responsibility rested upon the county justices, who had jurisdiction throughout the county, including for many purposes its corporate towns.

There were also, in point of fact, very few corporate towns amongst the growing manufacturing centres which were the chief seat of the Luddite and other Regency disturbances. Just as the Political Reform movement owed so much of its impetus to the fact that the great centres of population in the early nineteenth century had no representation in Parliament, so the anxieties of the authorities at that time were largely increased

[1] There was some friction between General Hawker and Mr. Becher with regard to the stationing of troops in Southwell, Notts., as a result of which the order was again issued to all regular officers that they should only act at the request and on the warrant of a magistrate (Letters in H.O. 42. 121).

[2] Coldham to H.O.

by the fact that so many of these same centres were without any effective local government. Manchester was still a manor, governed by a borough-reeve and constables, appointed by the lord of the manor, and by the county justices. Birmingham, Bolton, Stockport, Huddersfield, Halifax, and other important centres of industry (and of disorder) were only geographical expressions and had no corporate existence. Not merely were many of the large villages and small towns in which industry was still situated without any organized local government but some even of the larger manufacturing towns, particularly in the north, where population had so recently begun to grow, had still only medieval manorial systems of government. Even where there was a Mayor and Corporation, as there was at Nottingham, Leicester, Derby, Liverpool, and Leeds, to mention some of the more important towns within the disturbed districts, it was, as the inquiry which preceded the Municipal Councils Act of 1834 strikingly exemplified, very often an antiquated, corrupt, and inefficient oligarchy.

Where there was a Mayor and Corporation the responsibility for the maintenance of order, with the limitations we have mentioned above, rested naturally with them. Sometimes, as at Leicester, they did little or nothing to live up to their responsibilities. Elsewhere, as at Nottingham, they pursued an active, intelligent policy. Usually such towns, however inefficient and cowardly their officials, maintained better order than the unorganized towns and the country districts. It was easier to enrol adequate police forces, there being a large middle class of shopkeepers and small business and professional people able to act as special constables. The task of patrolling was easier and less hazardous. It was more difficult for criminals and machine breakers to escape detection. But apart from this the mere existence of an authority equipped to act was a source of strength. It was noted, for instance, at Leeds, that the number of magistrates always resident in the town and available, and the number of troops garrisoned there, had served to maintain order without it being necessary to take special or complicated measures.[1] It was obviously the case in Nottingham that the quickness with which the Corporation acted, and the fact that it possessed the powers, the funds, the machinery, the officials necessary for carrying a police policy quickly into effect had a very great effect in restoring order more quickly there than was the case in the surrounding country.[2]

The amazing contrast between the, upon the whole, orderly record of the corporate towns, Leeds, Liverpool, Nottingham, and Leicester, and the very disorderly record of the unincorporated towns, Manchester, Bolton, Huddersfield, and Stockport, was clearly partly, if not chiefly, due to the fact that the former possessed and that the latter lacked any responsible authorities able to act quickly, regularly, and effectively for the suppression of disturbances. Similarly the contrast between the speed with which order was restored in the towns as compared with the open country was not due wholly to the greater difficulty of policing the country but also partly to the presence in the towns and the absence in the country of responsible officials and adequate forces near to the scene of riot, wherever that might be.

The trouble in the unincorporated towns and in the country was twofold. On the one hand there were too few resident justices. In Nottingham or Leeds it was possible within a few minutes of an alarm being given for a justice's warrant to be obtained and for a party to be commissioned to pursue the offenders. Within an hour or so of any riot a meeting of magistrates or of the Corporation as a whole could take whatever measures might be needed to guard the town against further such disorders. In unincorporated towns and in the country villages there was very often no justice nearby and easily available. It was very often

[1] Campbell to Grey, May 9, 1812, in H.O. 42. 123.

[2] See conclusions of Conant and Baker, Feb. 1812, in H.O. 42. 119.

too late to do anything before a responsible magistrate could be reached to give orders. It was also a cumbersome process, taking usually quite a period of time, to summon together the district Sessions or county bench that was needed if a general system of defence were to be instituted.

This deficiency in the number of justices available was particularly felt in the north.[1] It was often hard, particularly at a time of emergency, to get people to accept appointment to the Commission of Peace. Numerous instances are known of persons nominated failing to take out their dedimus, and thus avoiding actual service.[2] But even apart from this there was in the north, where rapid population growth was very recent, and where the homes of the responsible landed gentry or of suitable clergy, from whom the justices were mainly recruited, were few and far between, an actual shortage of suitable magisterial timber. The result was that during the Luddite disturbances the authorities were greatly embarrassed by a shortage of local magistrates. The whole system of defence looked like breaking down for lack of energetic local magistrates to administer it.[3]

To remedy this defect various measures were proposed. Magistrates and officials from other counties, as, for instance, Hay from Manchester and Lloyd from Stockport, busied themselves in the West Riding. General Maitland took legal advice as to whether it would be proper to appoint regular officers, upon whom a large part of the actual burden of defence was falling, to the Commission of the Peace for one or more counties.[4] Advised against this he was at the same time given permission to have regular soldiers under his command sworn in as special

[1] See Maitland's correspondence in H.O. 40. 1 and H.O. 42. 122 et seq.

[2] See Webb's *English Local Government* and Chambers's *Nottinghamshire in the Eighteenth Century* for evidence as to how general, even in other places and previous years, this practice of avoiding duty was.

[3] See statements of Wood, Vice-Lieutenant of the West Riding, in H.O. 40. 1.

[4] H.O. 40. 1, June 1812, correspondence of Maitland and H.O.

constables.[1] He took steps to discover some energetic young men, if necessary from other districts and of a rank and wealth not usually adequate to the office, who might be appointed Justices if only they would promise to act.[2] Finally power was taken, under the Public Safety Bill of July 1812, to give justices from adjoining counties formal jurisdiction in the counties other than their own within the disturbed districts, and to dispense with the necessity of the presence of a justice and of the reading of the Riot Act when dispersing disorderly meetings.

On the other hand there was a further defect in the system, the slackness or cowardice of justices even in areas where the number was adequate. It was repeatedly said that magistrates were afraid to act, were unwilling to win a dangerous notoriety by any unusual effort against the disaffected. Especially in the north, where the situation of the normal justice's house was a lonely and dangerous one, despite the guards that were accorded to them in case of need, many magistrates were unwilling to do more than was absolutely necessary. They were, as Lord Fitzwilliam complained,[3] sadly relaxed in their duties unless danger was actually staring them in the face. He and other officials here and elsewhere, throughout the period, had frequent occasion to complain that there were very few justices who did their full duty. This trouble was even felt in Nottinghamshire, where the number of large estates should have given the magistrates confidence because of the propinquity of friends. The members and magistrates of the town of Nottingham were apparently justified in their charge[4] that if the county magistrates had been as active as the town ones emergency powers would not have been needed and Luddism might quickly have been suppressed.

1 H.O. 40. 1, June 1812, correspondence of Maitland and H.O.

2 Maitland to H.O., June 19, 1812, in H.O. 42. 124.

3 Acknowledged in Sidmouth's of July 16, 1812, in H.O. 43. 21.

4 Mr. Smith, M.P. for Nottingham in House of Commons debate on Framebreaking Bill, Feb. 1812, *Parl. Debates*, xxi.

The trouble was not merely that justices were afraid or lazy or inefficient, it was also that there was no clear concentration of responsibility upon them. The town corporations had responsible officials whose clear duty it was to act for the whole body. The Mayor and the Town Clerk, as at Nottingham, were quick to call the Corporation together, to devise measures to submit to it, to carry out its resolutions, to act in its name. In the county there were no such responsible officers to see that the bench did its duty and that its decisions were carried out. Each bench of justices had a Chairman of Sessions and a Clerk. Each county had its Clerk of the Peace. Unfortunately, however, these officials were sometimes very inactive. The Chairman of Sessions, who was still sometimes, as he had always originally been, a temporary officer, elected at each meeting to preside only over that session, was usually content to be merely the presiding officer of the meeting, and seldom acted as the leader and executive of the bench. The Clerk to the Justices was in the process of becoming, not a mere adviser and secretary to the justices as individuals, but a formal and executive Clerk to the Court. But he was still too often content to do as little as he must rather than as much as he might.

In three cases only during this period did Chairmen of Sessions take an active part with regard to disturbances. The Rev. W. R. Hay of Manchester, who was for nearly twenty years Chairman of the Manchester and Salford district bench, and who saved his colleagues the necessity of doing what since 1804 they, almost alone in the country, had been empowered by private Act of Parliament to do, that is to appoint a permanent paid Chairman, was very active. He was in frequent communication with the Home Secretary, with other magistrates, and with the local military officers. He was in charge of an elaborate spy system. He was not content to confine his activities to Manchester, being busy even in West Riding matters. He was one of the most regular and trusted agents of the Home

Office, continually on the look-out for trouble and quick to take measures to prevent it. His example was an infectious one and the greater activity and efficiency of the Manchester justices was largely due to his leadership. This bench even went so far in 1816–17 as to organize regular meetings when the different justices, many of whom were employing informers or who had confidents amongst the disaffected, would compare and contrast the reports each had received, so that a trustworthy account could be sent on behalf of the group to the Home Office.[1] Mr. Hay's only defect was his disposition to believe the situation worse than it was and his quickness to arrest people on suspicion when the evidence was really hardly sufficient.[2]

The two other active Chairmen of Sessions, the Rev. Mr. Prescott of Stockport and Mr. Sherbrooke of Nottinghamshire, were not as outstanding as Mr. Hay, who was in fact, if not in form, a permanent police magistrate like those in London, and like his successor as Chairman of Sessions at Manchester. They were merely *primus inter pares* on their respective benches. Other individual justices were sometimes as active. These two men did, however, feel it to be their duty not merely to keep in regular touch with the Government but also to see that forces were dispatched, and the military warned, whenever there was a riot.

The only Clerks who were active, apart from the Town Clerks of Nottingham, whom we shall mention later, were Thomas Bolland, Clerk of the Peace in the West Riding, and Mr. Lloyd, Clerk to Mr. Prescott's bench at Stockport. Mr. Bolland was content to act on the orders of his Lieutenancy, merely serving as Secretary of a sub-committee of Deputy Lieutenants and Justices whom that body

[1] Ethelston to H.O., Jan. 16, 1817, in H.O. 42. 158.

[2] e.g. he arrested and later had to discharge a number of people in connexion with the 'March of the Blanketeers' and made a number of obviously exaggerated statements with regard to the probability of a general rising.

appointed to collect reports with regard to, and to encourage, the formation of adequate defence organizations in the West Riding villages.[1] Mr. Lloyd was more ambitious. He was ready to be of service anywhere, within or without his county. He was one of the most prolific and informative of the Home Office's correspondents. He took the lead of military and civil patrolling parties in person. He was always running hither and thither, from Stockport to York, ferreting out information, interviewing suspects, employing spies, interrogating, carrying off into hiding and safe-keeping witnesses, and otherwise helping to detect and arrest offenders and suppress riots. He was so active that he thought it necessary to explain his motives and to assure the government that his zeal was in no way due to desire to be appointed attorney for the trials at York.[2] Apparently his story was true and his zeal quite altruistic, for he was as active after as before the trials in January 1813, despite his not being employed in connexion with them, so much so that he had to be specifically cautioned against further arrests, it being then the policy of the government to experiment with a policy of leniency.[3]

Elsewhere other people, justices and officers of militia or private individuals, officers of local and voluntary associations, took the lead in suppressing disturbances. In Nottingham the most prominent part was taken until his death in 1815 by the Town Clerk, George Coldham. He served as Secretary to a Secret Committee appointed by the Corporation in December 1811 and given ample funds and powers to discover information, make arrests, and forward prosecutions. This Committee did not finally finish its work and close its books until the summer of 1813.[4] He served also in 1812 and 1814 as Secretary to a private committee of hosiers and gentlemen formed to

[1] *Leeds Intelligencer*, June 29, 1812.

[2] Lloyd to H.O., Nov. 1812, in H.O. 42. 129.

[3] Hobhouse to H.O., Jan. 13, 1813, in H.O. 42. 132.

[4] See correspondence between Nottingham and H.O., April 1814, in H.O. 42. 138.

prosecute framebreakers and employers paying 'truck' and committing other illegalities, and to protect the trade both against violence from the men and interference from Parliament.[1] He was a very regular correspondent of the Home Office, very active in collecting information, supervising defence measures, and carrying out the Corporation's orders. He came up to London at least once to advise with the Government against the Framebreaking Bill.[2] He was sufficiently trusted by his colleagues to be able to say that they had empowered him to present his views and amendments to the Government as theirs.[3] He was succeeded as Clerk, and in all his activities in connexion with disturbances, by his former Deputy, Henry Enfield.[4]

In the county of Nottingham different justices at different times took the leading part, the Rev. Mr. Becher of Southwell and Mr. Sherbrooke in 1811–12, Colonel Rolleston and Mr. Mundy in 1816–17. In the north the most active officials, other than Hay, Prescott, and Lloyd, were Mr. (later Sir Joseph) Radcliffe, a magistrate of Milnesbridge House, near Huddersfield, Colonel Ralph Fletcher, a magistrate and officer of militia of Bolton-le-moors, Captain Chippendale, with similar standing at Oldham, Mr. Scott, a colleague of Mr. Radcliffe's from the Spen Valley, and, until his death in April 1812, Mr. John Horsfall, a manufacturer and chairman of a committee for the suppression of disturbances at Huddersfield in 1812, and Mr. Elliston and other members of the Manchester and Salford bench in 1816–17.

These few names continually crop up in the Home Office records. There are a few other officials who at different times, when there was a disturbance in their particular locality, were active and sent up full reports to Whitehall. These few officials only, each with a different *locus standi*,

[1] See correspondence between Nottingham and H.O., April 1814, in H.O. 42. 138, and local press for June and July 1812.

[2] Coldham to H.O., Feb. 29, 1812, in H.O. 42. 120. [3] Ibid.

[4] Correspondence in H.O. letter books for 1816 and 1817.

were, however, to be counted upon as regular informants and agents of government, sure to be active in the event of any disturbance within a wide radius of their homes and jurisdictions. The activity of these individuals seems to have been due solely to their personal energy, ability, courage, and ambition. Other officials could have attained a similar prominence if they had wished. The burden of English local government fell equally upon all the justices, and upon their clerks, chairmen, and constables. Only a few of these many individuals, however, made any special effort to carry their share of the burden. The number of officials who took more than the average care in the pursuit of their legal duties was far less than the proportion which attained notoriety by taking less care even than was decent. The efficiency of English local government, particularly as regards emergency duties such as the suppression of popular disorder, depended too much on, and varied too much with, the zeal and ability of the individual local official.

Of these officials Colonel Fletcher and Captain Chippendale are particularly interesting. In their area the militia seems to have played an unusually large part in the business of detecting and suppressing disorders. Many members of the militia seem to have acted as spies, the spy system in this district being in fact organized through the permanent militia staff. The militia also was quick to function in the event of disorder, the responsible local officer commanding being also the most active local magistrate, so that the clash between the two jurisdictions, which sometimes impeded action, was avoided.

Beneath the justices were the constables of the hundred, or the permanent deputy constables of manorial towns like Manchester. These officials had formal duties to present offenders, to distribute proclamations, to carry out the orders of the justices and the resolutions of Quarter Sessions. It was their duty to enrol and command bodies of special constables, when the justices or a town corporation had ordered such a force. They had the task of supervising the actual putting into operation where necessary of a system of Watch and Ward. Beneath them were the few regular constables of the towns and villages, local officials with the thankless task of serving, in the absence of a regular police, as guardians of local order. These constables of the village, of the hundred, and of the town, were usually inefficient. The Duke of Newcastle complained in 1811 that during the disturbance of March and November of that year there had been, except in the neighbourhood of Mansfield, hardly a constable who had done his duty.[1] The office had fallen upon evil days. There was seldom in any area a constable who could be counted upon to act before, or to do more than, he was definitely ordered by some justice. The constables were seldom men upon whom the justices could rely to any extent to show energy, courage, or ability in the discharge of orders given to them. There is little evidence of any constable, except at Nottingham and Manchester,[2] taking any effective part in the handling of public disorder at this time.

The machinery of public order mounted, therefore, from the local constables and justices, through meetings of the county Sessions and Lieutenancy, and through the Sheriff and the Lord Lieutenant, to the Home Office, the Cabinet, and Parliament. The local justice was the main support of the whole machine, upon whom its efficiency rested. The Home Secretary, with whom the local justices were in continual direct correspondence, was its directing head, responsible for improvising such emergency measures as were needed. Through him the whole military strength of the kingdom, and the power and authority of Parliament, could be brought to the assistance of the normal civil power.

[1] Jan. 21, 1812, in H.O. 42. 121.

[2] For the Nottingham system see report of Conant and Baker and Mr. Coldham's letter to Mayor of Leicester, both in H.O. 42. 119. Manchester had a few special constables under the very efficient, energetic Nadin, the professional Deputy Constable.

The primary and normal responsibility for suppressing disturbances, and for arresting, and bringing to trial and judgement, any offenders against the law, lay with the local authorities, with the constables and justices. They were supposed to act on their own initiative and to use their own local forces and funds. They had, however, very often, and almost invariably in the event of serious or protracted disturbance, to appeal to the Home Secretary for emergency powers, for government funds, and for regular troops. In order to supervise the grant of these exceptional powers and forces the Home Secretary was forced to step out of his usual role of passive recipient of local reports and to become, through his own agents, magistrates like Conant and Baker, soldiers like Maitland and Byng,[1] lawyers like Allison and Hobhouse, or spies like Oliver, directly responsible for dealing with disorders. He did so unwillingly, resisting to the last the pressure to take over local responsibility. The danger of the complete breakdown of the machinery of order was, however, so urgent during the crises of some of these years, that this exceptional and undesirable step could not be avoided.

The course of events in each area, and on the occasion of each serious protracted disturbance, was the same. During the first period of trouble the local magistrates were on their own responsibility using local forces, constables, yeomanry and militia, and such regular troops as were locally available, and being exhorted by the Government, to which they invariably applied for Bow Street officers, as well as for further regular troops and for approval of local action in calling out the militia, to make do with local measures. During the second period, while the Government was willing to send down skilled professional magistrates like Conant and soldiers like Dyott, to advise and help the local authorities, and to provide very liberal reinforcements, it was still trying to restrict its role,

[1] Maitland thought it necessary to explain (May 1812 in H.O. 40. 1) that he had no intention of invading the province of the civil power.

refusing Bow Street officers or a Special Commission, throwing the responsibility of arresting and prosecuting offenders on to the locality. In the third period, as, for instance, in Nottinghamshire after about January 20, 1812, when the local system seemed obviously to be breaking down, the Government had to step fully into the breach, sending down police magistrates and officers, agreeing to pay all expenses and to assume full responsibility for prosecutions, enlarging the law, and filling the area with regular troops. Thereafter even local and civil measures were taken largely at the suggestion and under the supervision of the Government's own agents.

Responsibilities which had been at first wholly local and civil became very soon, in each area and period of disturbance, increasingly national and military. Conditions varied of course from place to place and from time to time. The local and civil power was never so completely overshadowed in the midlands as in the north in the summer of 1812, when General Maitland became almost a dictator. It was never again so hopelessly inadequate as it had been in the winter of 1811–12. Even during that period some villages, like Southwell in Nottinghamshire, felt they could maintain perfect order without any outside help. But upon the whole the tendency to rely upon national and military support was overwhelming, and increased the longer the disturbances lasted, places like Nottingham, for instance, whose patrols had been originally wholly civil, being content in the end to see the watch become wholly military.

The forces at the disposal of the local officials were, as we shall see, wholly inadequate. It was inevitable that there should be an appeal to the military and to the government every time there was a disturbance. The funds at their disposal were equally limited, their expenses falling on the already heavy county rate, so that there was great pressure upon the localities to seek financial assistance from Government. The local officials being also very often too few in number, too overburdened with other work, too neglectful of their duty, too lacking in the qualities needed for the suppression of serious disturbances, the Government was forced, whether or not it wished it, or whether the localities requested it, to intervene directly in every serious emergency. The whole machinery of order was so antiquated, and worked so clumsily, that even a restricted local disorder became a matter of emergency and necessitated emergency measures.

The heirarchy of order was clear. The system was excellent on paper, provided that the justices could be relied upon to do their duty. But it did not work in practice, and an emergency system had to be improvised *ad hoc* in each crisis by co-operation between the Government and the few officials upon whose energy and ability it could count. That emergency system involved almost invariably, as it did in the West Riding of Yorkshire in 1812–13, the effective intervention of the Government, which had to suppress riots with its own soldiers, ferret out information with its own spies, conduct prosecutions through its own attorneys. Such a method of maintaining internal order was costly and inconvenient, how much so the protracted Luddite disturbances strikingly exemplified.

XIII

THE FORCES OF ORDER

THE authorities charged with the duty of maintaining order in Regency England had four instruments to their hands, police, voluntary defence associations, yeomanry or militia, and military. The police were almost non-existent, the regular, professional police force of modern times originating in the next decade. Voluntary defence associations, or the old system of Watching and Warding, which was a compulsory substitute for such associations, were difficult to improvise and were at best clumsy expedients. The yeomanry and militia, the old substitute for the modern Territorial Army, were trained and intended rather for military than for civil duty, as a second line of defence for the kingdom in the event of invasion. It was inconvenient to make use of such forces in purely civil local disorders, except for a short space of time. The only efficient force, ready to act promptly and able to be used permanently, was the regular army, of which a considerable portion was held permanently at home even in time of war.

It was unfortunate that this should be so. It was widely recognized that an adequate system of police was alone really calculated to prevent disturbances. As the Duke of Newcastle remarked at the height of the Nottingham disorders in 1812, 'the military do not avail unless the police is good'.[1] Again and again, at Manchester, Leicester, and Nottingham, in 1812, in 1814, in 1816, in 1817, the responsible authorities, civilians like Hay and soldiers like Maitland, stressed the importance, if the disturbances were to be effectively put down, of an enlarged force of regular police.[2]

Except in the metropolis, however, no such force existed. Even there there were only a limited number of Bow

[1] Newcastle to H.O., Dec. 12, 1811, in H.O. 42. 119.

[2] e.g. Oct. 16, 1816; Allsopp to H.O., in H.O. 42. 153 says 'a permanent police establishment with regular police is the only solution'.

Street Runners available, attached to the offices of the metropolitan police magistrates. Nothing, not even the Luddite risings themselves, caused greater public alarm at this period than a few murders in the east end of London, at Wapping, in the winter of 1811–12.[1] The correspondence of the Home Office for weeks was swollen with letters complaining of the great danger to the public of a defenceless capital and advocating the establishment of some system of police.[2] The few employees of the police offices, even when they were in town, and not scattered, as was often the case, on emergency duty somewhere in the provinces,[3] were not sufficient to give any feeling of security to the public or to the authorities.

The situation in the country generally was even more chaotic. There was hardly a town which had more than a few regular constables. Leicester, for instance, in January 1812, some months after serious disturbances had commenced in that neighbourhood, had only six.[4] Manchester, where the constables were gentlemen and officials of the manor rather than policemen, had a permanent deputy constable, Nadin, who was a police officer, and who commanded a very small and totally inadequate force of paid subordinates. Oldham at the same time had two regular constables, 'Methodistical, Jacobinical' gentlemen, according to the report,[5] who fell down hopelessly upon any occasion of danger. Nottingham was somewhat better off, having an efficient, energetic municipal administration and being accustomed quickly to expand its small force of regular, paid constables upon occasions of emergency. But not even there was there a force in 1811 which was sufficient to disperse an angry mob. Even in this, in some ways the most efficiently governed of the

[1] See *Annual Register*, 1812, p. 303.

[2] Numerous letters, especially in H.O. 42. 119.

[3] Bow Street officers were on duty in Nottinghamshire in March 1811 and Feb. 1812.

[4] Mayor of Leicester to Coldham, Jan. 23, 1812, in H.O. 42. 119.

[5] Chippendale to Fletcher, April 25, 1812, in H.O. 40. 1.

disturbed towns, it was necessary on the very first occasion of riot, in March 1811, as always thereafter, to call on the regular military garrison to assist in restoring order and clearing the streets. Most towns in Regency England were little better situated as regards police than they had been two hundred years before, when the notorious Dogberry and Verges were accepted as a fair caricature of the police force of the day.

Lacking a force of regular paid constables the towns and villages of Regency England had to depend upon special constables, either paid or unpaid. It was one of the first steps of the authorities whenever danger was threatened to enrol a force of unpaid special constables. These men, recruited where possible, as at Nottingham,[1] from amongst 'the most respectable members of the community', were sworn in as constables and peace officers and given authority to disperse mobs and apprehend offenders upon a magistrate's warrant. They were usually organized in a nightly watch, patrolling the town from dusk to dawn, and serving by turns at this thankless but necessary task. They were occasionally supplemented by special ordinary constables, paid, as at Nottingham, some 4*s*. a shift, whether by night or day. Funds for these purposes might be obtained by quarterly order of the Treasurer upon the county rate.

Great numbers of such constables, mostly unpaid, were enrolled during these Regency disturbances. Nottingham swore in as many as 400 during the first week of the disturbances in November 1811.[2] This force was increased to more than 600 during the ensuing weeks.[3] As many as 1,500, some two per cent. of the inhabitants, and ten per cent. of the adult males in the Salford hundred of Lancashire, were enrolled in the latter part of April 1812.[4] More than 400, an almost equally high proportion, were

[1] System described in letter from Coldham to Mayor of Leicester, Jan. 27, 1812, in H.O. 42. 119.

[2] For Nottingham arrangements see ibid., and report of Conant and Baker to H.O. in H.O. 42. 119.

[3] Ibid.

[4] Fletcher to H.O., May 1, 1812, in H.O. 40. 1.

sworn in at the same time at Bolton-le-moors.[1] Other, usually lesser, numbers were enrolled in other towns and in the country, and during the later disturbances.

It was recognized that it was not so easy to employ this system in the open country as in the towns.[2] In the country there was no responsible middle class, the inhabitants, from whom special constables would have to be drawn, were mostly working men interested in the objects of the rioters. While some specials were enrolled, especially in rural parts of Nottinghamshire, little dependence was placed upon them, except within the urban districts. Little dependence also was placed upon them, whether in town or country, in the West Riding in 1812, there being so strong a public sympathy for the Luddites and such fear of taking a stand against them.

When volunteers failed resort could be had to a compulsory levy, to the Watch and Ward. It was then, as in theory it is still, the duty of every citizen of full age to come to the assistance of the authorities in the event of public danger from a domestic or foreign enemy. There was a general responsibility upon men to come forward if called upon for duty watching by day and warding by night. The old system had, however, fallen into disuse. It was now (in February 1812) revised and brought up to date. An Act of Parliament, the Nottingham Peace Bill, was passed, at the request of the Nottingham authorities. Its provisions were based upon their resolutions and upon the suggestions of Colonel Eyre, Member of Parliament for the county. A system was instituted whereby, in the event of disorder, and after a decision by the county Lieutenancy or Justices in Sessions, the constables might draw up a list of names of men liable to serve, from which a sufficient number of constables might be drawn by ballot whenever it was desired to institute a general system of watch and ward.

[1] Ibid.

[2] Coldham admits as much in his letter to the Mayor of Leicester.

This system, despite the Act, whose scope was extended, at the special request of the Leicestershire Justices and Members, to other counties, was little used. Meetings were held in Nottinghamshire, Lancashire, Cheshire, and the West Riding in April and May 1812 in order to apply the provisions of the Act to those counties. In Nottinghamshire nothing was done further than the taking of names. In other places, and particularly in the West Riding, an attempt was made to use the system. There was, however, great prejudice against it, both because of the expense, which fell upon the poor rates, and because the inhabitants were either afraid or unwilling to serve. We have noted, for instance, the northern villages whose inhabitants petitioned in April and May 1812 that no such system be applied to them.[1] In two places only in the West Riding, in Huddersfield and Halifax, and there only with difficulty, by special order of the Lord Lieutenant and at the request of a resolute minority, was a sufficient Watch actually recruited.[2] It was usually, in 1812–13 and again during later disturbances, found preferable to keep this power of compulsory levy in reserve and to depend upon volunteers, on whose loyalty more dependence could be placed.

The favourite system in the north, and particularly in the Spen Valley, where magistrates were as unwilling to act as the inhabitants to come forward and enrol, was that of voluntary defence associations. These could be instituted by any loyal minority. Their expenses were covered by voluntary subscriptions. They relieved the normal legal authorities in fact, though not in law, of some of their responsibilities, and they provided the military, and the national government, with effective instruments of action when the normal ones had failed. They were besides, in disturbances such as Luddism, considered preferable, both on the score of expense and otherwise, to extensive use

[1] Huddersfield Committee's Memorandum, dated April 1812, in H.O. 40. 1.

[2] Coulhurst to Fitzwilliam, May 1812, in H.O. 42. 123.

of special constables or of a compulsory Watch and Ward. As General Maitland remarked, and tried to impress on the local authorities in Lancashire and Yorkshire, the only real defence against a combination of workers to attack property was a combination of the owners of property to defend themselves.[1] Sometimes such associations confined themselves to the business of procuring information and prosecuting offenders.[2] At other times they organized a nightly patrol.[3] Sometimes they even took the form of a semi-military force.[4]

While special constables were being enrolled, or a substitute system of police was being instituted, dependence had to be placed upon the militia and yeomanry. These bodies could provide a large force, there being, for instance, four militia regiments in Nottinghamshire, with a total strength of about 3,000. The Yeomanry Cavalry, though less numerous, were still a powerful force, highly mobile and of the greatest use in dispersing disorderly mobs. A troop of yeomanry (consisting of from 50 to 60 men) or a regiment of militia (600 or 700 strong) would make a considerable impression upon the most tumultous of meetings and the most disorderly of districts. For a brief period these local forces, whose use the Government always approved and whose expense it bore, were a great standby of the local authorities, at whose command they acted.

Various troops of Nottinghamshire Yeomanry,[5] some of which were out more than once for a day or so at a time, and one of which was continuously on duty for nearly a fortnight, were of the greatest use in dispersing the 'angry

[1] Maitland to H.O., May 4 and 6, 1812, in H.O. 40. 1.

[2] As at Nottingham; for particulars see local press, esp. *Nottingham Journal* for July 1812 and *Nottingham Gazette* for April to Oct. 1814.

[3] As at Huddersfield; see letters from Radcliffe, in H.O. 42. 121 et seq. and 40. 1. and local press.

[4] As at Newcastle-under-Lyme and also in Nottinghamshire; see Baker to H.O., enclosing letter from Wm. Kirby of Gotham, Jan. 28, 1812, in H.O. 42. 119.

[5] Particulars of yeomanry and militia arrangements in the midlands, in H.O. 42. 117 et seq. and 52. 129.

mob' of which reports were reaching the Home Secretary in November 1811. The entire county force was called out on November 14. Although only three of the four regiments actually saw sufficient service to entitle them to a remission of annual training, even that meant that a powerful force was available. The 1st or Nottingham Militia provided an infantry garrison to Nottingham from November 15 to 27, when it was relieved by the 2nd or Southwell regiment, of which two companies had already been out for one week, which served until December 9, when it was replaced by the Berks. Militia, a regular infantry regiment which had by now arrived.

Similar use was made of the local forces in the north. The Manchester magistrates towards the end of April 1812 called out 500 men from Colonel Sylvester's regiment of Militia and 20 men from each company of Colonel Cook's and Colonel Kenyon's regiments, a total force of nearly 1,000 men.[1] At Bolton a force of nearly 250 yeomanry and militia was available at the same time, 20 men from the permanent staff, 50 from recruiting parties, and 132 ordinary members from Colonel Fletcher's regiment.[2]

It was often planned to call out the local forces in order, so that an adequate force might be available permanently over an extended period without any individual being called upon for more than the usual period of service. Thus at Bolton[3] the sections were so arranged that a force would be available for 15 weeks, while in the West Riding the militia was divided into four sections, making a force of 3,000 men available for several months.[4]

Here and there suggestions were made that the local forces could not be trusted. For this reason, or from other prejudice, the Sheriff of Cheshire refused to accede to the request of the Stockport magistrates and call out the local

[1] Manchester magistrates to H.O., April 28, 1812, in H.O. 42. 122.
[2] Fletcher to H.O., April 22, 1812, in H.O. 40. 1.
[3] Fletcher to H.O., May 1, 1812, in ibid.
[4] Maitland to H.O., May 16, 1812, in H.O. 42. 13.

force there in April 1812.[1] The West Riding authorities talked a little later of the calling out of the militia as being a means of 'putting arms in the hands of the most powerfully disaffected'.[2] In the event, however, both militia and yeomanry in all areas and at all times were found absolutely trustworthy and were invariably commended by the authorities on their dismissal. Their members were also, again contrary to general rumour and expectation, usually safe, a very, very few cases of shots at militia members, or of damage to their property, being reported.

Although great use was made of the local forces, with the approval in each case of the Home Office and the War Department, this great dependence upon this arm of defence was deprecated. It was said in the midlands in November 1811 that the local force had been called out to a much greater extent than was really necessary.[3] The same complaint was made generally in the following June.[4] The Government, though it did not stint this force, felt that it should be sparingly used. It agreed with General Maitland that for a handful of Manchester magistrates to call out a force of 1,000 men (as they did in April 1812) was wholly unnecessary and improper.[5] It felt with him that the local force should be a third line of defence, coming after use of constables and voluntary associations, and being very conservatively and economically used.[6]

The fourth line of defence in theory, though the first in practice and in magnitude, was the Regular Army. Very great forces were used against the Luddites. The forces at first available were small. At Nottingham, when the

[1] Lloyd to H.O., April 13, 1812, in H.O. 40. 1.

[2] Clerk of the Peace at Wakefield, April 23, 1812, in H.O. 40. 1.

[3] See correspondence between Newcastle and Ryder for Nov. and Dec. 1811, in H.O. 42. 117–19.

[4] See correspondence between Maitland and Sidmouth, in H.O. 42. 123–5 and 40. 1.

[5] Maitland to H.O., May 4 and 6, 1812, in H.O. 40. 1.

[6] H.O. circular to Lords Lieutenant, May 12, 1812, in H.O. 43. 20.

framebreaking recommenced in November 1811, there was only one troop of Queen's Bays available at the barracks.[1] The commanding officer, when applied to for a military force, had to confess that his command consisted principally of raw recruits, that their horses were raw and incapable, and that not more than ten or twelve dragoons could be efficiently mounted. Even the area commander, writing from area head-quarters at Lichfield, having dispatched one troop of Greys (consisting of a subaltern and 24 other ranks) said that he had no means of sending further reinforcements, the depleted garrison consisting now only of 2 men sick, 3 in charge of horses, and a sergeant and 13 other ranks on escort duty with French prisoners. Similarly in the north[2] in February and March 1812 the troops locally available were few in number so that continual marching and counter-marching was necessary and it was impossible for the area commander to meet more than a small proportion of the requests that were made of him.

Very soon, however, very great reinforcements were sent to each of the disturbed districts. Between November 13 and December 9, 1811, two regiments of regular militia and ten troops of regular horse, a total force of 1,000 infantry and between 800 and 900 cavalry, were concentrated in and near Nottingham, under the command of General Dyott, the commander of the Lichfield District, who had been ordered personally to take charge of operations against the Luddites.[3] A further infantry regiment was brought to this area later in December.[4] Two more regiments arrived in February 1812.[5] This was a tremendous force, totalling nearly 4,000, of whom 3,000 were regular infantry. When it is remembered that the much

[1] See correspondence between Dyott and Torrens, Dec. 1811, in H.O. 42. 119.

[2] See correspondence between Grey and H.O., in H.O. 42. 120 et seq. and 40. 1.

[3] Correspondence chiefly in H.O. 42. 119.

[4] *Nottingham Journal*, Dec. 1811.

[5] Ibid., Feb. 1812.

smaller force of less than 2,000 sent to Nottingham between November 13 and December 9, 1811, had been referred to by Secretary Ryder[1] as 'a larger force than had ever before been necessary for the quelling of any local disturbance', it will be understood how grave the situation was felt to be, and how liberal the Government had been in sending reinforcements.

While a large part of this body of horse and three of the infantry regiments were moved away from Nottingham to the north in April,[2] when the midland disturbances had ceased and the Lancashire and Cheshire disorders were at their height, this loss was quickly made up. It was announced in May 1812 that the Government intended to maintain a permanent camp in Sherwood Forest, some seven miles from Nottingham, for a force of 3,000 infantry and 500 cavalry, a force just equal to that then available in the area.[3] These troops were kept in the district throughout the summer, only being moved away to the north when it had become clear, from the long period of quiet, that the disturbances had been entirely, if temporarily, quelled. A portion of them were kept in the area for nearly two years more, the last detachment being about to be moved away in April 1814, when renewed disturbances indefinitely postponed this step.[4]

The two northern districts, Manchester and Yorkshire, under the command respectively of General Maitland and General Grey, were equally strongly reinforced. By the beginning of May Maitland had under his command, distributed throughout Lancashire and the adjacent part of Cheshire, no less than 79 companies of infantry, 18 troops of horse, and two detachments of artillery, a total force of probably nearly 7,000, 5,500 infantry and about 1,400 horse.[5] General Grey had at the same time

[1] *Parl. Debates*, xxi. 808.

[2] *Nottingham Journal* and *Review* for April 1812.

[3] *London Times*, May 18, 1812. [4] Nottingham press, Sept. 1812.

[5] For disposition of Maitland's troops see enclosure in letter of May 9, 1812, in H.O. 40. 1.

about 1,800 men, 1,000 infantry and 800 cavalry, under his command in the West Riding, a force equal to that in the midlands in 1811, and therefore by itself greater than had ever before been needed in such circumstances, except during these recent, unprecedented disturbances.[1]

There were, therefore, available for the suppression of the Luddites in the summer of 1812 more than 12,000 troops in the disturbed districts between Leicester and York. This tremendous force was more than six times as large as that which Secretary Ryder had spoken of as unprecedented. It was a veritable army, larger than many actual armies with which British Generals had waged and won important foreign campaigns.

This huge force, though increasingly concentrated in the north, and especially in the West Riding, where disturbances persisted longest, was not withdrawn from the disturbed districts as a whole until the spring of 1813. Even after that larger forces than usual were left in the manufacturing districts and the inland commanders were more interested in civil disturbances, and more quick to respond to local requests than they had been in the easy days before 1811, and before the army had become the police force of industrial England. In each of the later periods of disturbance, and in all of the other smaller centres of disorder, immediate and ample use was made of the regular forces locally available. They and some ships from the fleet had to be used to suppress disorders in Hull, Sunderland, and South Shields in October 1815.[2] Troops as well as yeomanry and militia were used in Staffordshire in the same year on an occasion of sharp, though local and temporary, disorder.[3] They were needed again, in several places, and especially in East Anglia and the Isle of Ely, in 1816.[4] In later Luddite outbreaks, in 1814 and 1816–17, the military commanders, Generals

[1] Grey to H.O., May 2, 1812, in H.O. 42. 123.
[2] H.O. 42. 146. [3] Ibid. [4] H.O. 42. 151 and 152.

Byng and Fane, were as active and as ready to help the civil power, as Generals Maitland, Grey, Dyott, and Hawker had been in 1811–13. They were equipped, as the area commanders in 1811 had not at first been, to come quickly and strongly to the support of the magistrates on the occasion of any disturbance, and they did not therefore need, like their predecessors, to use the tremendous forces that were required to put down the 1812 disturbances, in which the spirit of riot had time to take a general hold of the population before adequate measures could be concerted and adequate forces assembled. Thereafter, and largely because of the lesson the authorities had learnt in 1812, the army in England was kept ready for internal and civil duty at a moment's notice.

These military forces, which were used to replace the local militia and yeomanry which served in the first days or weeks of any disturbance if and when regular forces were not available, were under the command of their own officers, but at the disposal of the civil power. The area commander was supposed to plan his campaign in consultation with the civil and local authorities. He sent detachments of his force wherever and whenever they requested it. And these detachments were supposed to co-operate equally closely with the responsible local authorities in the places where they found themselves, acting only at their request. It was even necessary for parties of military, out to disperse noctural meetings or to apprehend offenders, to be accompanied by a magistrate (who could read the Riot Act) or at least by a constable (who could make legal civil arrests). The military did not, at least in theory, supersede the civil power. There was no declaration of martial law. The army merely served as if it were a police force, at the request and subject to the orders of the civil authorities, and it had to observe the normal legal procedure.

The soldiers were used in various ways. Detachments of them were cantoned out in the various villages and towns where disturbances were feared.[1] Smaller parties of them were used as guards of individual establishments.[2] Others were kept available in the chief centres for sudden action, forming a reservoir upon which the civil authorities could draw when a force was quickly needed anywhere.[3] Others again were employed, especially in the north and in the latter part of 1812, as a moving patrol, proceeding from village to village, staying only a night or two, or even less, at each place, and co-operating with the civil power in maintaining a spy system.[4] This latter practice was found to be far the most effective. To place guards in each village required the use of a tremendous force, as the area commanders more than once remarked in reply to criticisms of their action; if they were to accede to every request 'the entire army would be insufficient'.[5] The same objection applied to the policy of providing guards for individual houses and factories, though this was frequently done, which was also deprecated on the grounds that it would be made 'a means of reducing the wages of the workers even below their present level'.[6] Merely to have troops available upon call was ineffective, there being many instances, such as the attack on Rawfolds Mill in April 1812, when ample forces were within a mile or so of the scene of disorder, without the Luddites being deterred from making, and often completing, their attacks. The only really effective solvent to disorder, which was also the most economical way of using the available military

[1] e.g. the Berks. Militia in Dec. 1811 and the South Devon Militia in Feb. 1812 were thus distributed in the disturbed villages around Nottingham, and Gen. Dixon was said (Fletcher to H.O., May 1, 1812, in H.O. 40. 1) to wish to provide a detachment in every Lancashire village where disturbances might be expected.

[2] As at Rawfolds, W. R., in April 1812 (Peel, op. cit.), and at Basford, Notts., in Oct. 1814 (H.O. 42. 41).

[3] As in the two guard-rooms at Nottingham (H.O. 42. 119).

[4] For details see report of the activity of Capt. Raynes and a detachment of the Stirling Militia around Stockport in June and July and in the West Riding in Aug. and Sept. 1812, in H.O. 40. 1.

[5] Grey to H.O., May 23, 1812, in H.O. 42. 13.

[6] Maitland to H.O., May 9, 1812, in H.O. 40. 1.

force, was to have parties of military moving about the country, especially by night, so that the Luddites would never know whether or no the coast was clear. In this way noctural meetings of the disaffected could be prevented from collecting, and the sense of security, which had been the Luddites' chief advantage, might be transferred from them to the peaceable inhabitants. The same method could be, and sometimes was, employed in the towns, where rapidly moving and frequently changing nightly patrols were found the best means of preventing disorders, from the alarm they created amongst the disaffected, who never knew when they might not run into the very arms of the watch.[1]

The effect of this general use of the military was to give almost an appearance of a state of war to the disturbed districts. As it was more than once remarked, both as regards the midlands and the north, the great bodies of troops, the continual coming and going of parties of cavalry, the frequent and ubiquitous military patrols, the garrisons of soldiers, large and small, in the different centres and factories, gave to the district a most warlike appearance.[2] Some towns were literally bursting with troops, there being, for instance, no less than 1,000 billeted in the thirty odd public-houses of Huddersfield in September 1812.[3] Every village inn in the disturbed localities had its quota of troops billeted upon it. In addition there were the two great garrison camps, that in the Forest near Nottingham, and that on Kersal Moor, near Manchester.

Maitland kept 18 of his 79 companies of infantry in reserve in this latter camp.[4] He had 16 companies apiece under the immediate command of his two subordinate

[1] For particulars of the system employed in Nottingham and of the alarm thus created amongst the Luddites see report of Conant and Baker, in H.O. 42. 119.

[2] e.g. *London Times*, Feb. 1, 1812, with regard to Nottingham, *Leeds Mercury*, April, and *Intelligencer*, May 4, 1812, with regard to the north.

[3] *London Times*, Sept. 1, 1812.

[4] Maitland to H.O., May 9, 1812, in H.O. 40. 1.

district commanders, Major-General Dixon at Liverpool and Major-General Acland at Manchester. General Dixon had also 8 troops of horse available to him at Liverpool and Chester and in the intermediate country. General Acland had 5 troops at Manchester. Smaller garrisons were on duty in other places, varying from a single troop of horse at places like Shrewsbury or Chester or Blackburn, and 2 at Bolton, to the 2 troops of horse and 10 companies of infantry on duty at Macclesfield.

General Grey kept his forces similarly distributed.[1] The bulk of his force in May 1812, both cavalry and infantry, was at Leeds, under the command of Colonel Campbell, or at Huddersfield under Major Gordon, and in the intervening country. But he had in addition other smaller contingents in the places where they were most likely to be needed. There were also under his command a squadron of dragoons at Wakefield, troops of dragoons at Burnley, Halifax, and Bradford, 2 companies of infantry each at Barnsley and Penistone, and 3 troops of dragoons and 2 companies of infantry at Sheffield. All these forces were greatly reinforced in the months following.

The midland forces were similarly distributed prior to the spring of 1812 when, the disturbances being over, the district command was collected at the garrison camp near Nottingham. During the winter of 1811–12, when disturbances were ragings, while a strong reserve force was kept at Nottingham, and other lesser reserves at Mansfield, Derby, and Leicester, the bulk of the force was widely distributed throughout the whole area.

The command of the whole district, of Yorkshire, Lancashire, Cheshire, and the midlands, was given to General Maitland in June 1812. General Grey was given leave to get married so that Yorkshire was brought directly under Maitland's command.[2] General Dyott at Lichfield, though

[1] May 2, 1812, in H.O. 42. 123.

[2] The formal union of the two commands was not consummated until November; Sidmouth to Maitland, Nov. 10, 1812, in H.O. 42. 129.

somewhat independent in his command, was still under Maitland's general supervision, referring requests for help to Maitland, and using the necessity of getting the latter's consent as an excuse for refusing the excessive help sometimes asked of him, as, for instance, by the Mayor of Leicester.[1] This unity of command had not existed in the early part of the disturbances, nor did it exist after 1813, responsibility for the different districts being normally divided between the various area commanders.

Maitland had a very scientific conception of his duty.[2] He was very clear that the military should be the last and not the first resort of the civil authorities, to be used only on occasions of emergency.[3] He tried hard to stimulate non-military defence arrangements, even going so far as to make the grant of military force dependent upon suitable local and civil arrangements having already been made. The basis of the machinery of order in his opinion should be voluntary associations for defence. He wanted to meet the Luddite combination against machinery by a property-owners' combination in defence of machinery. He believed in the use of special constables and advocated their being divided into groups of from fifty to a hundred, each with its own commander, badge, and time and place of meeting. Yeomanry and militia, and even more the regular Army, should, he believed, never be made a substitute for other measures.

He, and to a lesser extent other military officers, spent therefore almost as much time devising, and trying to get the local authorities to adopt, civil measures, as he did planning a military programme. So much was this the case that he even found it necessary to assure the Government that he had no intention of passing the proper limits of his military responsibility.[4] He was, however, forced

[1] Dyott to Maitland, June 16, 1812, in H.O. 40. 1.

[2] Maitland to H.O., especially May 4 and 6, 1812, in H.O. 40. 1.

[3] He comments in Aug. 1812 (in ibid.) on the fact that soldiers are only to be used in a crisis.

[4] May 16, 1812, in ibid.

almost to supersede the local authorities in many places. The hiring of spies, the searching for arms, the making of arrests, the filling of vacancies upon the bench and the making up of the serious shortage of peace officers, the keeping informed of the Home Office, and other normally civilian responsibilities absorbed a growing amount of this time.[1] He more than any other official in the north in 1812–13 was responsible for the suppression of disorder, the detection of offenders, and the break-up of the Luddite conspiracy. He more than any one was responsible for preventing the authorities losing their heads and believing alarming, baseless rumours. His moving military patrols, more than any other single factor, were responsible for the restoration of order.

This sort of military activity might have been expected to provoke criticism. In Maitland's case it does not seem to have done so. Criticism of military officers in his area was directed against other men and other measures. General Grey had occasion to talk of jealousies between himself and his officers and some of the magistrates.[2] Although the Vice-Lieutenant went out of his way to remark that the area commander had done all that was asked, or could be expected of him, other local officials were not so considerate.[3] It would, as the General complained,[4] have been impossible to meet all their requests, their alarm being out of all proportion to the actual necessities of the situation, and being kept up more from the memory of past outrages than from any present trouble.[5] There was similar and even more bitter criticism of the military for inactivity in the midlands, both in 1812 and

[1] The correspondence of Maitland and Ryder, and Maitland and Sidmouth in H.O. 40. 1 and 2; H.O. 42. 123 et seq., and H.O. 43. 20 et seq., is one of the best sources of information with regard to every matter connected with northern Luddism.

[2] Grey to H.O., May 23, 1812, in H.O. 42. 123.

[3] Wood to Fitzwilliam, June 1812, in H.O. 40. 1 and 42. 123–4.

[4] Grey to H.O., May 23, 1812, in H.O. 42. 123.

[5] Campbell to Grey, May 1812, in ibid.

in 1814. It was said that officers would refuse to act, even though they could hear the noise of framebreaking, without a magistrate's warrant.[1] This caution, though eminently correct in normal times, was, as one magistrate remarked, rather out of place at a time of crisis.[2] There was similar criticism of the Lancashire commander who, being warned that the mob was attacking Westhoughton Mill near Bolton in April 1812, would not return there to see if it were so without a magistrate's orders, there having been several previous false alarms.[3] There was also a plaintive criticism of the military by the Duke of Newcastle, who, in commenting on a rumour that the Nottingham garrison had no cartridges, said that such evidences of unpreparedness, if true, were almost incredible.[4]

This slowness of the military to act without express orders was the natural result of incidents such as that which happened in Nottinghamshire in February 1812. General Hawker, who had been sent down at the end of January to take special, personal command of military operations against the Luddites, got into a controversy with Mr. Becher, a magistrate of Southwell, for having sent troops into that town without magistrate's orders.[5] The General complained that one magistrate, like Becher, would criticize him for doing what another magistrate, like Sherbrooke, would order. The affair was smoothed out but the General nursed his grievance and it was again impressed on the army officers that they must not act without definite orders from a magistrate.

Upon the whole there was much more criticism of the civil authorities by the military than of the military by the civil. The latter were too happy to get a military guard, and too willing to devolve all their responsibilities upon the military, to be over critical of the way the latter acted. The military upon the other hand were disgusted at the

[1] See correspondence with regard to such incidents in H.O. 42. 119.
[2] H.O. 42. 120. [3] H.O. 40. 1. [4] H.O. 42. 119.
[5] Correspondence in H.O. 42. 121.

inactivity of the civil power. They found the local magistrates and gentry cowardly, inactive, overthinking the whole situation and finding deep revolutionary designs which never really existed.[1] They tried their hardest to induce the local and civil authorities to stir themselves, to get the manufacturers to defend their own property. They were disappointed in the way the whole burden of defence fell upon them, the way the state of alarm persisted long after the need for it, the way the manufacturers neglected the real distresses of the workers and tried to profit by military support and to oppress their employees still more. The army seems in this instance to have been more level-headed, more just, more generous, as well as infinitely more active and efficient, than the civil power. It carried out its difficult and thankless duties, which soldiers never like, with restraint. And it succeeded, rather surprisingly, in avoiding criticism, except from a few disgruntled magistrates.

The military, when upon civil duty such as this, were subject to the civil authorities, and to the Home Secretary, and not to the War Office and the Commander-in-Chief, who acted as the Home Department requested. It was with the Home Office and with the civil authorities that soldiers like Maitland chiefly corresponded and co-operated. And the Home Office continually and urgently requested the magistrates to appeal not to it but to the local military commanders, in whom it had absolute confidence, and who were empowered to give localities all the help they needed.

The actual measures taken, when all these various forces had come together, varied from district to district. The most efficient and highly organized system, and that in which the military had the smallest share, was that of the town of Nottingham.[2] The Corporation of Nottingham

[1] See especially Maitland's comments, especially in letters in H.O. 40. 1.

[2] Letters of Coldham to H.O., and Conant and Baker to H.O., especially in H.O. 42. 119.

was always quick to act. It enrolled special constables and organized a nightly watch of six special and six regular constables in March 1811. It revived this watch and enrolled further constables in November 1811. It enlarged this watch by stages during November and December, until it consisted of a double watch of sometimes as many as thirty-six constables. It proceeded towards the end of January 1812 to take even more ambitious measures, dividing the town into five districts, establishing a regular nightly watch in each district by a corporal's guard of five or six soldiers under a peace officer, and changing these guards, and their districts and itineraries, frequently, so that the members might always be fresh, and so that the Luddites might never know who would compose, or where they might meet, the nightly watch. In addition the force which had been established at the two guard-rooms in the town, one of which was next to the Police Office, and which consisted of constables and soldiers always ready for instant action by night or day, was much increased. The magistrates also, as they had done from the beginning of the disturbances, took it in turn to attend at the Police Office night and morning to receive reports from and give orders to this watch. A further special patrol of constables was kept on the move to watch and report upon the activity of the other detachments. This system seems to have been completely successful, striking terror into the Luddites and putting a speedy end to framebreaking in the town. It was continued until April, when the civil watch was dismissed and the whole responsibility turned over to the soldiers. A similar, though less extensive system was adopted in Nottingham in 1814 and in 1816. In these latter years also, both in the town and county, the magistrates and constables were more quick to act, so that disorder had no time or chance to get so hopelessly out of hand as it had in 1811–12.[1] The final instance of disorder during our period, in June 1817, when

[1] Newcastle to H.O.

the Derbyshire rioters from Pentridge were expected at Nottingham, found the town as well prepared as ever, the magistrates and a great force of constables and yeomanry being on duty all night, ready for any eventualities.[1]

Much less was done in the county of Nottingham, where reliance was placed first on the militia and yeomanry and then on the army rather than on constables, though a few of the latter were enrolled, and though some towns, like Mansfield and Southwell, were successful in concerting adequate measures of their own to prevent trouble. The town was much safer than the county, so much so that the military were busily occupied during November and December 1811 bringing frames into Nottingham under guard. There were a few voluntary associations, like that mixed group of farmers and yeomen who were reported to be patrolling a part of the county in November,[2] or like the villages which kept up a nightly watch by turns during December 1811.[3] But they were few in number, and informal and temporary in character, and contributed little to the suppression of Luddism. The major burden fell upon the soldiers, who provided patrols, garrisons, escorts, and parties for the pursuit of offenders.

In the north, as we have seen, some towns like Leeds had an ample number of magistrates and soldiers to maintain order without the aid of an elaborate system of watch like that at Nottingham. Manchester enrolled a great number of constables, and had a strong military garrison. Constables were enrolled, and the local forces employed, in other places. But the main burden here, in Lancashire and Cheshire, in the towns as well as in the country, fell upon the military. It was with their help that disturbances were put down everywhere, at Manchester, Macclesfield, Oldham, Middleton, Bolton, Stockport, Ashton-under-Lyne and elsewhere. It was their garrisons, and their

[1] Lockett to H.O., June 11, 1817, in H.O. 42. 166, and local papers.

[2] Baker to H.O., enclosing letter from Wm. Kirby, Jan. 28, 1812, in H.O. 42. 119.

[3] *Times*, Dec. 16, 1811, and letters in H.O. 42. 119.

moving patrols, which restored order and prevented renewed trouble.

The same was true of the West Riding, in spite of the great effort that was made to establish voluntary defence associations. Something was done. Various towns did have some sort of watch, while two, Huddersfield and Halifax, had instituted a compulsory system of Watch and Ward. But even at the end of the summer, in September 1812, when the Lieutenancy made a second attempt to institute the Watch and Ward generally in the Wapentakes of Agbrigg and Morley, and despite the making of such measures a condition precedent to the grant of military assistance, the system was wofully incomplete. Captain Raynes, who was charged with the duty of making a report upon it, noted on September 15 that out of eleven separate towns, some of them as important as Dewsbury or Batley and Morley, the Watch and Ward was in operation in none of them.[1] Five of them had no sort of voluntary watch or patrol of any kind. At Dewsbury three men patrolled the streets 'but not to the extent of the town'. At Adwalton and Tonge fourteen constables patrolled twice a week while the churchwardens searched the public-houses every night for suspicious characters. At Falnuth, Lawton, and Stanlingham an association met twice a week. Forty special constables formed a patrol, which was usually out twice a week, though recently an alarm and the breaking of some windows had caused a watch to be kept every night. At Morley there was a patrol on duty two or three nights a week. At Batley an association patrolled occasionally. If this survey is typical of conditions generally, and there is reason to believe that it is, it will be realized that even after eight months of disorder and the passage of five Acts of Parliament the local machinery for the maintenance of order was very casual and incomplete.

Things were better later on. It was reported in 1816

[1] Raynes to Acland, Sept. 15, 1812, in H.O. 40. 1.

that many attacks that had been planned by the Nottinghamshire framebreaking gang had not taken place because there was 'such strict order in Bulwell, Basford and Arnold by the Watch and Ward'.[1] The chaotic situation which had existed in 1812 seems to have had one good effect, it stirred the authorities up so that on future occasions of emergency they could act quickly and efficiently.

Some sort of watch there was in many places, even in the West Riding and in 1812. We have noticed reports of a nightly watch at Skipton, Wakefield, and other places even before the first Yorkshire attacks in January of that year.[2] Here and there a town would enrol a few special constables, or employ one or two watchmen, as a precaution against disorder. On the whole, however, except in a few large towns, these patrols were very small, occasional, and ineffective. The real burden even of watching and warding, universally throughout the country districts, generally in the towns, fell upon the military. If a watch had to be kept up continuously for very long, even towns like Nottingham, which had commenced with a civil watch, were content to hand the responsibility over to the military. It was quite a typical policy for a local body to pursue, for it to do as the Huddersfield Committee for Suppressing Disorders did in March 1812, to ask for Bow Street officers and regular soldiers who might compose a nightly watch.[3] Most towns and associations, however, would be less eager than the Huddersfield Committee to say that they would bear the expenses of such a system. Most localities were content to get men, measures, and money from above.

The lessons of 1812 seem, however, to have been learnt. In 1814 things were much better organized. There was, as we have seen, an efficient watch. There was an effective spy system which succeeded, as the informers of 1811–12

[1] Enfield to H.O., Dec. 9, 1816, in H.O. 42. 156.

[2] *Leeds Intelligencer*, Jan. 20, 1812.

[3] Radcliffe to H.O., March 1 and 17, 1812, in H.O. 42. 121.

had not been able to, in uncovering the Luddite plans. There were ample military forces locally available. And there were magistrates and private prosecuting committees, like that of the Nottingham hosiers,[1] ready and willing to act, to organize patrols, collect information, and advance prosecutions.

That so large a burden should have fallen upon the military in 1812–13, that they should have had to serve as leaders as well as servants of the responsible local authorities, detecting as well as preventing disorders, and presenting prisoners to, as well as guarding the judges of, the Special Commissions of Assize, was due to the general alarm, making local authorities and civilians generally afraid to act, and to the fact that the country was not prepared for such an emergency and took time to adopt adequate measures.

The Luddite disturbances, requiring an army to put them down, had shown conclusively what the lesson of the Regency disturbances as a whole was to drive home, how ill-adapted the system of English local government was to the strains that were imposed upon it. The system was archaic. The officials were too few and too inactive. They were provided with an wholly inadequate force. English local government, on the administrative side no less than on that of the poor law, had broken down. The Luddites had started a riot. The forces of order could hardly have been more strained if they had started a revolution.

[1] There were three committees at Nottingham. (1) A Secret Committee of the Corporation established by resolution of the Corporation, Dec. 17, 1811, mainly to collect information. (2) A committee of hosiers established in June 1812 to prosecute framebreakers and hosiers paying 'truck' and to protect the industry against legislative or other interference, and (3) a committee of hosiers formed in 1814 to oppose the strike and the renewed framebreaking and, later, to employ informers. The Town Clerk and his deputy and successor served as secretary to each of these committees, the hosiers and the town officials and magistrates being in close agreement.

XIV

SPIES AND INFORMERS

In the dark years that followed Waterloo, moving mysteriously about the country, appearing here and there in the manufacturing districts as disaffection showed itself, spreading abroad suspicion and alarm among the reformers and Luddites of the north, were an obscure band of government informers. Suspected long before, the existence of this group of spies flamed into notoriety in 1817. The name of Oliver[1] became for a brief period one of national reputation and ill fame. The columns of the press in Leeds, Manchester, and London, the debates in Parliament, the trials in the country, echoed the talk of the ale-house and the street corner. Oliver and Castles[2] were made the scapegoats of every disorder. 'The March of the Blanketeers', 'The Pentridge Revolution', and the rising at Huddersfield were all attributed by opponents of government to the same agency as the Spa Fields Riots, to the activity of the *agent provocateur*. Oates and Beddow were rivalled at last. It was imagined that in the activity of the informers might be found an explanation of the whole complicated story of disorder.

The Debates in the House of Commons in July 1817, repeating the revelations then appearing in the *Leeds Mercury*, and substantiated by documents in the files of the Home Office,[3] show that Oliver was in the midlands and the north in March and May 1817. Just before the two outbreaks, at Pentridge in Derbyshire, and at Huddersfield in the West Riding, on June 8, 9, and 10, he had been talk-

[1] For the activities of Oliver see Hammond, *The Skilled Labourer*; Peel, *Risings of the Luddites*; and *Leeds Mercury*, issues for July 1817.

[2] The Government witnesses in the case against the Watsons for the Spa Fields Riots and projected attack upon the Tower of London in December 1816.

[3] See especially letters from Nottingham and West Riding magistrates in H.O. 42. 151–6, especially those dated in June and July 1817.

ing with the disaffected in these two areas. When Brandreth, Turner, and Ludlam paid the penalty of their 'treason' at Nottingham they attributed their downfall to Oliver.[1] When Fitzwilliam was reporting the disturbances at Huddersfield he said that all Yorkshire attributed their origin largely to Oliver.[2] It was not surprising that radicals generally should be inclined to attribute blame for the whole system of disorder also to Oliver.

But Oliver, though the most notorious and successful, was by no means the earliest or the most regular of the government's rota of spies. Although the spy system was largely concerned in the disaffection and disorder of 1817, it had been hardly less concerned with the whole long period of disturbance that had gone before. Informers had been employed before the first frame had been broken by the Luddites in 1811. They were still to be employed long after the last Luddite had been swung off the gallows in 1817. They were an integral and essential part of the system of internal government. Whether or no their employment was systematically and permanently organized by the Home Office, they were at any rate always sure of a job whenever any locality was in a state of alarm.

Some of the local magistrates both in London and in the provinces were empowered by the Home Office to maintain a permanent system of information.[3] The Home Department itself was approached by volunteers, convicts, soldiers, labour leaders, and anonymous members of the public, who were anxious to be employed as spies. Magistrates and other authorities wrote frequently to Whitehall to ask either for Bow Street runners and other persons to procure information or for authority to incur expense in hiring their own informers. The Government itself sent

[1] Sutton, *Date Book . . . of . . . Nottingham*, p. 241.

[2] To H.O. June 14 and 17, 1817, in H.O. 42. 167.

[3] Especially Colonel Fletcher of Bolton-le-moors. His correspondence with the H.O. from 1811 to 1817 is the best single source of information with regard to the contemporary spy system.

down, either on its own initiative,[1] or at the request of the appropriate authorities[2] its own agents and spies. Large sums of money were spent in this manner.[3] When money was not spent directly in payment to secret agents it was offered in rewards to people who should give information. The procuring of secret information was almost the major activity of many of the authorities.

Spies were responsible for many of the arrests and convictions in connexion with the Special Commissions at Lancaster and Chester in 1812.[4] They were responsible for most of the convictions at York in 1813.[5] It was a secret agent employed by the Town Clerk who penetrated into the organization of the society of the framework knitters in Nottingham in 1814.[6] It was a secret agent who exposed the activities of the midland framebreaking gang in 1816.[7] It was on informers' evidence that the case against the Watsons and Thistlewood for their part in the Spa Fields Riots rested.[8] It was informers' evidence which enabled the authorities to penetrate the organization of the Derbyshire and Yorkshire rioters in 1817.[9]

In the absence of any organized system of police, lacking the most rudimentary detective staff, the only way in which the authorities could discover what was going on in the country was by the employment of informers or by the confession of accomplices. Not merely was it only by such means that arrests and convictions were possible after

[1] e.g. Oliver in 1817. [2] e.g. Maitland in 1812.

[3] See in instance of this the two accounts appended to this chapter.

[4] See particulars sent up to Mr. Whitbread, some of which are in H.O. 42. 132, and which prove the spies to have been very often promoters of offences, if not inventors of the charges they advanced. See also Prentice, *Hist. Sketches of Manchester*, pp. 55 et seqq.

[5] See Hansard's reports of the Trials and letters from Hobhouse, in H.O. 42. 132.

[6] See correspondence between Coldham and H.O., especially for June and July 1814; H.O. 42. 139, 140; 43. 23; 79. 2.

[7] See letters from Nottingham magistrates in Home Office letters, H.O. 42, for period Oct. 1816 to July 1817.

[8] See letters from Conant, Stafford, and other London magistrates in ibid. [9] Letters from Nottingham in ibid.

offences had been committed, but it was upon such expedients that the Government depended that it might be forewarned as to impending trouble. The maintenance of order, the development of habits of obedience, have always been recognized to depend largely upon the swift and certain action of justice. When crimes are quickly followed by the capture and punishment of the criminals, the population will tend to be law-abiding. But swift and certain justice depends upon an efficient system of police, upon an organized and elaborate system of detectives. In the absence of such a system in the early nineteenth century the authorities had to improvise some alternative. The most obvious, the most immediate, the least ambitious system to their hand was that of secret information. The spies and informers of Ryder and Sidmouth were the detective department of the government. Oliver was a sprig from which the Criminal Investigation Department of New Scotland Yard has grown.

If riot and disturbance were to be not merely punished but prevented it was necessary that the proceedings of the rioters should be discovered. Apart from the granting of their terms, or from such ambitious state action as would have been needed sufficiently to relieve the distresses which provoked disorder, the only way in which the Luddites and other rioters could be put down was by the discovery of their plans and leaders. It was to penetrate their meetings and committees, and to discover their leaders and their plans, that informers were sent to mingle with the Luddites in 1811–12. Similarly, according to Lord Castlereagh, it was 'to see what was going on in the country' that Oliver was sent out in 1817.[1] Information was notoriously difficult to obtain. Accomplices were reluctant to come forward. The public seemed to sympathize with the disaffected rather than to be willing to give them away. Only by the use of spies could the organization of the Luddites and informers be discovered,

[1] *Parl. Debates*, xx, July 1817.

such was the secrecy and dispatch which characterized their actions.[1] Only on informers' evidence could the guilty be arrested and punished. Only in the light of their information could the government know what was going on and devise an appropriate policy.

There was, however, the danger that informers would exceed the original limits of their mission and from being reporters become instigators of disorder. There was the difficulty that it was not easy to assess the worth of informers' evidence. There was such a temptation for the spy to find what he had been sent to find, what he would be paid for finding. It was easy for him, knowing the wild rumours of sedition and even revolution that were circulating, and not being trained in the taking of evidence, to confuse Luddite mobs with Reform meetings, and both with more serious political designs. He was tempted to find alarming situations because it was alarm which created the demand for his employment, and evidence justifying alarm which would make his employers willing to pay him liberally. He was apt both from ignorance, and because the situation was in fact confused and obscure, as well as from deliberate malice, to present exaggerated and even unfounded reports. Natural credulity, self-interest, professional pride, as well as the low cunning which was natural to the men who were willing to take on so thankless a task, all combined to warp the outlook, and cast doubt upon the trustworthiness of the informer, He was certainly entitled to no absolute or uncritical belief, nor could he safely be allowed a wide scope of action.

That the evidence of the informer is to be taken with a good deal of caution is suggested by the fact that, although the actual situation undoubtedly differed from time to time and from place to place, throughout this whole period, both before and after the actual machine breaking and other overt acts of disorder, the stories of the spies were

[1] There was continual comment on the unexampled secrecy of the Luddites, e.g. by Coldham in many letters, in H.O. 42. 119 et seq.

the same. It is suspicious, too, that while machine breaking was the most prominent feature of the actual disturbances, and while machine breaking, raids for arms, and provision riots were the only overt acts of disorder (apart from common robbery), these aspects of the situation received far less emphasis in the spies' reports than revolutionary plans which never materialized. The informer 'B' in 1812 and Oliver in 1817 were telling the same tale. They were talking of vast numbers enrolled throughout the country in a seditious conspiracy. They were detailing the various plans that were current whereby this great mass should rise simultaneously throughout the country and assume the government. They even passed on similar rumours as to the organization of this provisional revolutionary government, and of the part that Whitbread, Cartwright, and Sir Francis Burdett were to play in it. They ventured more than once on actual and specific prophecies of an armed rising. It was on their reports that the Secret Committees of Parliament based their conclusion that there was such an alarming, seditious basis to the disaffection. And yet these prophecies were always confounded. The story was always the same while the actual conditions, revealed by definite evidence, differed widely. The actual facts discovered in the few places and instances in which it was possible to check the truth of the spies' stories were so modest as compared with their exaggerated tales. In several instances a careful search failed to reveal any of those proofs of guilt, such as stores of hidden arms, about which the spies had spoken so precisely. It is difficult to resist the conclusion that a large part of this so-called 'evidence' was purely fabrication.

Still more damaging to the credit of the spies were the actual revelations of the time. It had been feared that the informer might degenerate into the *agent provocateur*. Clearly in certain cases he did. Stones in 1812 and Oliver in 1817 were undoubtedly not merely privy to the plans of the disaffected. They actually encouraged them. They were accomplices, and major accomplices, 'before the fact'. What they had done it was possible, if not probable, that other spies, whose record we cannot so precisely trace, had done elsewhere.

The first sign of the spy system in this period comes from Bolton. So early as April 19, 1811, long before Luddism was to make its appearance in Lancashire, one James Hamill, secretary to a group of petitioning weavers in Bolton, being accused by his fellows of irregularities in connexion with his position, turned around, unknown to them, and offered to give information to the authorities.[1] The endorsement on this letter, 'May be paid £10 if trusted—has been useful before,' shows both the generosity with which the Government was willing to reward its agents and the routine character of such a practice. In May the Home Office was accepting a bill drawn upon it by Colonel Fletcher and was authorizing 'further expenditure in the public service'.[2] In October, although there was still no actual disorder in this district, the Home Department wrote to say 'you will continue to avail yourself of the means of which you are now in possession to procure information of their further projects'.[3] In November the report of the spy 'B', whom we know from other evidence as Bent, a cotton spinner and treasurer of the so-called Secret Committee of the disaffected at Manchester, and who was to be a very regular informant, shows that Mr. Fletcher was following these instructions.[4] 'B's' report, moreover, by its references to 'L.F.' and 'Stones', shows that these further spies, to whom reference was continually to be made, were already active. The cost of these men was paid initially by Colonel Fletcher. Apparently it was already fairly heavy. 'B' received £4 1s. for his time from September 29 to November 11, as well as expenses to the

[1] Hamill to Ainsworth, April 19, 1811, in H.O. 42. 115.
[2] H.O. to Fletcher, May 17, 1811, in H.O. 79. 1.
[3] H.O. to Fletcher, Oct. 28, 1811, in ibid.
[4] In Fletcher to H.O., Nov. 21, 1811, in H.O. 42. 117.

amount of £3 7*s.* 7*d.* (of which 9*s.* was on account of 'subscriptions' at Stockport and Manchester).[1] Ultimately the cost was defrayed by the Government, the local authorities being authorized to draw upon the Treasury solicitor.[2]

The practice continued. On March 26, 1812, Mr. Ryder wrote to say that it appeared to him 'very inadvisable to take any step which would have the effect of interrupting that Channel of Information through which' they had been in the habit of 'coming at the knowledge of the proceedings of the disaffected in the neighbourhood of Bolton'.[3] In June one of Lord Sidmouth's first official acts was to confirm the practice and the authority which had been granted for the expenditure of public money.[4] At the same time Colonel Fletcher was sending up accounts totalling more than £200.[5]

From these accounts and from other information it appears that the officer in direct charge of this spy service was the adjutant of the local militia. Many of the spies, including the notorious Stones, were themselves members of the militia. At the same time, apparently in conjunction with Colonel Fletcher, Captain Chippendale, adjutant of militia at Oldham, was also arranging for members of the militia and other people there to procure information.[6] In July Major Seals from Sheffield was asking authority to do the same thing, and his request was referred to General Maitland with a favourable minute.[7]

Maitland had indeed become very closely concerned with the system of information. As early as May 9, within a week of taking up his command, he was writing to say that magistrates stopped generally 'just where they ought to begin'.[8] Informers ought not merely to discover com-

[1] Ibid. [2] H.O. to Fletcher, Dec. 2, 1811, in H.O. 79. 1.
[3] Beckett to Fletcher, March 26, 1812, in H.O. 79. 2.
[4] Same to same, June 15, in ibid.
[5] Fletcher to H.O., June 15, 1812, in H.O. 42. 124.
[6] Beckett to Chippendale, May 26, 1812, in H.O. 79. 2.
[7] H.O. to Maitland, July 13, 1812, in H.O. 43. 21.
[8] Maitland to H.O., May 9, 1812, in H.O. 40. 1.

mittees but by remaining quiet to get to the bottom of the whole proceedings, to the real 'nature of the whole conspiracy'. He had his own plan.

'I am persuaded the best mode of doing it would be to select in London through the means of some confidential Police Officer some ten or twelve men of the lower orders of the Community who are thoroughly to be relied on, and to send them down, unknown to each other, to this neighbourhood for the direct purpose of getting on to these Committees, and with instructions to come near nobody till they have got introduced, and had something serious to communicate.'

He wanted to distribute these men over the area at Stockport, Macclesfield, Oldham, Bury, Rochdale, Huddersfield, Halifax, and Warrington. Later he developed his views. He wanted men from Wiltshire (as had earlier been suggested by the West Riding authorities) and he arranged a channel of communication with them at Buxton.[1]

'The general object of their Instructions might be, to get sworn in and to become active and efficient Members of the committee, to conceive merely being sworn in is nothing, but to endeavour to come to a thorough knowledge of what is at the bottom of all this, who are their real Leaders, what their ultimate object, and not to hazard any discovery of themselves by communicating with me or anywhere too frequently unless the information they have is of real importance.'

The places to which they were to be sent he now specified as 'at least two to Huddersfield, one to Halifax, one to Bradford, one to Saddleworth on the borders of Lancashire, and two to Leeds'. His last proviso was important. Where two spies were sent to the same place they were on no account to be known to each other.

Sidmouth replied immediately to this request.[2] It was difficult to find suitable people.

'It will not be possible, I fear, to find in Wiltshire such a number of competent persons as you have named. But I hope

[1] Same to same, June 17, in H.O. 42. 124.

[2] Sidmouth to Maitland, June 20, 1812, in H.O. 42. 124.

the deficiency will be supplied by a contribution from some of the Manufacturing parts of Gloucestershire . . . but the Inhabitants of those parts have not the sharpness of understanding nor the determination of Character which belong to those of the North and it is therefore very difficult to find amongst them Persons fit for the purpose.'

This difficulty of getting effective people was a serious one. As Maitland himself recognized, a trustworthy spy was almost a contradiction in terms.[1]

'Those who are willing to undertake mixing with the Disaffected are generally of a Character whose information must be received with extreme Caution, and certainly in the instances of those on whom we could rely, they very much to their credit feel extreme difficulty in going to the lengths they must necessarily do to be of any real utility.'

Apparently Wiltshire was even more barren than Lord Sidmouth had feared. Maitland wrote on July 18 to say that 'the only person who came from Wiltshire was totally disinclined, when he learnt the state of the case, from a feeling of personal Danger, to undertake anything, and he of course was completely useless'. He had made an attempt to get men from Scotland, but that also had failed. He was now trying again.[2]

There had been a suggestion of sending down from London two men, Playfair and Reynolds, who 'happened to be in Gaol at the time that General Ludd and his companions (i.e. the condemned Nottingham Luddites) were brought in', and who volunteered for service as informers.[3] In the event, however, Playfair refused to go down alone, and Maitland refused to allow him to be accompanied by an associate. He was a total enemy to co-partnership upon such a duty. The informer must be under some one man's sole control.[4]

'Unless he is put under some Rule, and that a strict one, he

[1] Maitland to Beckett, July 18, 1812, in H.O. 42. 125. [2] Ibid.

[3] H.O. to Maitland, June 24, 1812, in H.O. 79. 2.

[4] Maitland to H.O., June 25, 1812, in H.O. 42. 124.

will infallibly become a general Operative under Government instead of being what he ought to be, a man limited within the narrowest bounds of jealousy and suspicion with regard to his conduct.'

Though Playfair did not come down other similar volunteers did. A man called Lawson (alias Montgomery), a sergeant in the militia stationed at Chelmsford, was moving about in the north during August, September, and October 1812. For a while his stories were believed. Early in September Maitland actually went up to London and a number of warrants were issued on his indictment, and as a result of Lawson's information. In the end the failure of anything substantial to appear to substantiate his charges and rumours, together with the remarkable fact (discovered by some bright young A.D.C.) that according to his own reports Lawson was travelling more than 100 miles a day even over almost impassable trails in the Lake District, discredited his character, and he was sent back to duty at Chelmsford.[1]

Another informer, in this case an accused man confessing in the hope of pardon and reward, by name Barrowclough, raised great hopes in July. He gave apparently specific information with regard to dumps of arms hidden by the Yorkshire Luddites. Unfortunately, though his stories were definite and convincing, there were no arms, and no signs of arms ever having been hidden there, in any of the hiding-places he had listed, and which were searched by the military upon his information. It was impossible thereafter to have any confidence in any part of his story.[2]

The two spies whose information had lead to Barrowclough's arrest, and attempt to win a pardon by giving away information about the Luddites, had been themselves at first under similar suspicion. They had been examined

[1] Letters referring to Lawson in series H.O. 42, letters for July, Aug., Sept., and Oct. 1812, and letters to Major Chamberlain from H.O. in H.O. 79. 2.

[2] Letters in H.O. 42. 125; especially Hay to H.O., July 7, 1812.

and had confessed their complicity in the so-called secret committees at Manchester and Stockport. These men, Taylor and Whitehead,[1] were sent into Yorkshire early in July 1812. At the same time two other men, McDonald and Gosling, like so many other spies apparently connected with the militia, had been sent from Manchester to Huddersfield. These four men were acting under the orders of Mr. Hay and the magistrates of Manchester, and of Nadin, Deputy Constable of that town.[2] Mr. Lloyd of Stockport was also apparently concerned in their employment.[3] Mr. Hay also had two other men from whom he was getting secret information.[4] One of these was a young man who had offered to serve and who was a Luddite only because it was part of his duty as an informer. The other was an older man, at one time genuinely connected with the disaffected, who had become disgusted with what his fellow conspirators were doing (or disappointed with the treatment he was receiving at their hands) and was giving information secretly to his employer.

At this time also was being perfected the semi-military intelligence service. Captain Raynes of the Stirling Militia, acting in conjunction with General Acland, and with his A.D.C., Captain Thornhill, was in command of a moving band of military operating around Stockport on the borders of Lancashire and Cheshire.[5] He was using some men under his command as spies. He was reporting, for instance, on September 2, that Sergeants Todd and Tomlinson were doing well at Delph.[6] He was swearing in constables, one of whom he notes had been 'frequently mentioned as an active spy'.[7] Some of his new recruits had themselves

[1] Depositions in Maitland to H.O., July 15, 1812, in H.O. 42. 125 and in document dated May 7, 1812, in H.O. 42. 123.

[2] Letters in H.O. 42. 125.

[3] Lloyd to H.O., July 17, 1812, in H.O. 42. 129.

[4] Hay to H.O., May 1, 1812, in H.O. 40. 1.

[5] Reports in H.O. 40. 2.

[6] Raynes to Acland, Sept. 2, 1812, in H.O. 40. 2.

[7] Same to same, Aug. 31, in ibid.

previously been 'twisted in'. These men, whether old soldiers, old spies, or genuine former Luddites, were sworn as special constables, and paid as such.[1] They were stationed in the various villages throughout the district and ordered to worm their way into the plans of the disaffected. Rayne's force, which was moving rapidly about the area, and which was accompanied by further regular constables or magistrates, was thus able to get secret information upon which to base its movements. As Raynes reported his only difficulty was regarding the pay of his spies, who they were to get it from, and what sums should be allowed them. From the accounts which survive,[2] it appears that the finances went through the hands of General Acland and his subordinates, and that the expenses for September 1912 amounted to more than £50.

This practice, at first operated only in the triangle of country about Stockport, was later introduced into the West Riding. In this area a similar suggestion had been made at the very beginning of the riots. On February 4, 1812, Mr. Joseph Radcliffe wrote to the Home Office to suggest that some of the soldiers at Huddersfield, who had been west country drapers in private life, should get employment among the shearmen in order to learn the 'origin and course' of the disturbance.[3] It is not clear whether this was done. At any rate there was not any information about the conspiracy in this area until July. Then, following rapidly upon the arrival of the spies from Lancashire, some arrests were made.

These arrests of Yorkshire men, mainly for giving or receiving illegal oaths, which have been discussed before in connexion with the organization of the Luddites, followed too closely upon the arrival of the spies, and depended too much on the spies' uncorroborated testimony, to appear altogether convincing proof that the actual organization

[1] Same to same, Aug. 31, in ibid.
[2] Printed in full as appendix to this chapter.
[3] Radcliffe to H.O., Feb. 4, 1812, in H.O. 42. 120.

of the disaffected was really, as the authorities fondly believed, at last being discovered. These cases, like those in which the spies Stones and Fleming were concerned in Lancashire,[1] appear to the fair witness, in the light of all the available evidence, to prove rather that the spies were instigators than that they were honest reporters of disorder. Clearly these informers were more eager to secure convictions than to prevent offences.

Especially is this true of the Bolton informers. We have in their case very ample evidence. Some of the Bolton weavers who came in October 1812 to take the Oath of Allegiance told a convincing story of the course of events in Bolton and Westhoughton in March and April.[2] In the autumn also a number of people, including the spy Stones and other members of the local militia who had worked with him, were examined and their dispositions were sent up to Mr. Whitbread.[3] The evidence given before the Lancaster Special Commission in June 1812 also tended in the same direction, as do all other contemporary accounts.[4]

From these it appears that it was only in February 1812 that seditious meetings began to be held in Bolton. There were then two or three meetings and delegates from Stockport attended. These meetings were small, furtive, and unrepresentative. Stones and his father, the 'Young S' and 'Old S' of many reports, took the lead. The father, Simeon Stones, was said to have had the oath administered to him by his son, John. Thereafter father and son were active in swearing people in. John Stones took the lead in meetings, choosing captains of sections and giving them picturesque names, such as Oliver Cromwell and Colonel Wardle. Stones called himself Samuel Whitbread and his contingent, Whitbread's men. He went about collecting

[1] See accounts of Stones's activities in Chap. IX and below, and of Fleming's in Chap. IX.

[2] Depositions in Clayton to H.O., Oct. 18, 1812, in H.O. 42. 128.

[3] Depositions in H.O. 42. 132.

[4] Ibid. and such books as Prentice, op. cit., and Cowdroy's *Manchester Gazette*.

subscriptions from the various houses in the district, threatening people who were unwilling to contribute. Evidence appears of his inviting men into ale-houses and trying to 'twist them in'.[1] He induced some of them to attend the meetings that were held occasionally at night on the moors outside the town. Those who were unwilling to do so he threatened. 'Those who did not attend would be in greater danger than those who did attend and would be torn out of their beds.' He was said to have distributed firearms. At a meeting on April 8 there was an alarm and the nervous crowd broke up in disorder, Stones's father among them. John Stones, before hurrying away to rescue his father from the deep pool into which his frightened parent had fallen in his hurry to get away, tried to rally the crowd, 'damning their souls for running away.'

Finally a meeting, which was later to be notorious, was held on April 19. A body of ten or more members of the local militia, containing at least one of the Stones, was instructed to attend. They received their orders directly from Colonel Fletcher and Adjutant Warr. They turned out with blacked faces, disguised and armed. They seemed, according to the reports of the handful of weavers and other frightened workers who also attended, to 'conduct the meeting'. When one man tried to slip away home he was prevented from doing so by Stones. A rearguard of the disguised militiamen kept the others together, threatening 'to shoot them if they did not go forward'. It was this crowd, thus dominated, that was accused of administering an illegal oath to Sergeant Holland Bowden, another militiaman, who, by some strange coincidence, they happened to meet on the moor.

It was at these meetings under Stones's domination that the plan to attack Westhoughton Mill was developed. First discussed as early as April 7 and at once reported to the authorities, this project was apparently finally decided upon on the 17th. It actually took place on the 24th. It

[1] Undated documents, in H.O. 42. 132.

was clearly largely at the spies' instigation that the mob proceeded to such a length. The weavers are said merely to have complained about low wages and starvation prices. They wanted to send in petitions. It was the disguised men, Stones and his fellow militiamen, who said that that was 'all damned nonsense' and that 'no Justice would be done except they did it themselves'.[1] It was reported that the spies were equally to the fore in the actual attack. Prentice, the historian of Manchester and a contemporary, reported that the mob was driven to the attack by just such a collection of disguised men, and that the troops, when arresting some of the assailants after the attack, arrested some of these men, with white caps and blacked faces, and dismissed them immediately, discovering that they were spies.[2]

The militia spent a great deal of time the next few days harrying the district and taking up men against whom these spies had presented evidence.[3] There was a veritable reign of terror. Unfortunately most of the arrests were vain since convictions could only have been obtained on spies' evidence, which would have involved exposing the system of the authorities and have rendered the spies themselves useless in the future and liable to attack. The Government agreed with Colonel Fletcher that, even at the expense of having to dismiss many of its prisoners without trial, it must at all costs keep its informers in the background.

Although many of the prisoners were therefore dismissed, and the spies not used as witnesses in court, news of their activity seems to have leaked out. The two Stones, having aroused the suspicions of their associates, thought it wise to get out while the going was good. Colonel Fletcher was soon writing to say that he hoped the Govern-

[1] Depositions in Clayton to H.O., Oct. 18, 1812, in H.O. 42. 128.

[2] Prentice, op. cit., p. 56.

[3] 'Cases showing the manner in which arrests are made in the night by the Bolton Local Militia of which Colonel Fletcher the magistrate is Colonel', dated May 8, 1812, preserved in H.O. 42. 132.

ment would feel their services to have been sufficiently valuable to entitle them to some reward, even though the suspicion now attaching to them made them useless for the future. It is not clear how much reward they did receive, but they had already done well. They got a very fair share of the £120 that Adjutant Warr spent on spies, and on food and drink for his parties of militia, during March, April, and May 1812.[1] The very first entry in these accounts is an item of £3 to 'Young S' on March 6. One of the latest is that of June 22 'for clothing "Old S" and "Young S" £2 5*s*.' Altogether during these three months father and son seem to have received from Adjutant Warr alone more than £13, besides allowances for expenses, such as that for clothes which we have just quoted. When it is remembered that 'Young S' had been active for many months, during which he was being paid at least as liberally as during those for which we have precise accounts, it will be realized that he found informing a not unprofitable business.

In the midlands there is not the same evidence of spies being the driving power behind the mobs committing disturbances, nor of them presenting false and exaggerated reports such as those of McDonald, Stones, Fleming, and others, some of which lead to unjust convictions.[2] Very many fewer spies seem to have been employed. And they were, so far as the first period of Luddism were concerned, very much less successful than the northern spies in penetrating the rioters' designs.

Even there, however, the system of secret information was an integral part of the defence measures employed. One of the earliest requests of the authorities, in March

[1] In Colonel Fletcher to H.O., June 11, 1812, in H.O. 42. 124.

[2] Compare the case of *Rex* v. *Baines* and others at York (see Hansard and letters of Hobhouse in H.O. 42. 131–2), in which even the crowd expected an acquittal, with that of *Rex* v. *Knight* and others at Lancaster (see letters in H.O. 42. 123–5) in which an acquittal was secured. In the former case there was no independent witness, in the latter there was one, the accusing evidence of the spy being equally strong in each case.

1811, was for Bow Street runners to spy out the Luddites' plans, and several such men seem to have been thus employed in the Nottinghamshire villages at that time.[1] A similar request was made in the following December, but was refused by the Home Office.[2] A month later, however, when disturbances seemed to be getting more serious, this refusal was reconsidered, and several Bow Street runners were sent down. Meanwhile the local authorities had already been taking similar measures of their own. Since December 1811 the Duke of Newcastle had been employing an informer at his own expense.[3] The Home Office endorsed this plan as soon as it heard of it and instructed the Duke to draw for such purposes privately and secretly on Secretary Ryder.[4] In January 1812 authority was advanced to the police magistrates whom the Government had sent down for them to advance money in a private way for procuring information.[5] Mr. Coldham and the secret committee of the Corporation had been spending money in the same way since the middle of December. One of the purposes of the county subscription taken up in January was to enable the authorities to employ informers.

It does not appear that these midland spies were, like their northern counterparts, imported from outside. They do not seem to have received so much money. They were probably, at this early period in the midland disturbances, amateurs or free lances, rather than regular employees of government. They did not succeed in providing sufficient information to allow the authorities to make a single arrest. They seem also, unlike the northern spies, to have had some scruples. It was frequently reported to be next to impossible to get any one to incriminate an accomplice. The midland population was too united in its aims to provide many traitors or much opportunity for such

[1] *Nottingham Journal*, March 1811.

[2] Newcastle to H.O., Dec. 14, 1811, in H.O. 42. 118.

[3] Same to same, Dec. 16, in ibid.

[4] Ryder to Newcastle, Dec. 18, 1812, in ibid.

[5] H.O. to Conant and Baker, Jan. 31, 1812, in H.O. 43. 19.

informers. Even the few informers that were employed seem to have had scruples. They were, as Mr. Coldham remarked, much less willing to give him information after the passage of the Framebreaking Bill, when their evidence might result in the death of a fellow being.[1]

Not even the provision of rewards and pardons for accomplices who should come forward and confess their offences and turn King's Evidence sufficed to get the midland Luddites to betray one another. Again and again the various authorities emphasized the impossibility of procuring information and the absolute loyalty of the Luddites to one another. In the north, apart from the spies' activities in Lancashire and Cheshire, the same difficulty was experienced in the beginning and for many months. In that area, however, the activity of the spies gradually broke down the confidence of the disaffected. Soon the latter did not know whom they could trust. Arrests began to be made and the various men at large could never know from day to day whether their arrested colleagues were not going to save their own skins by accusing their accomplices. It was in this way, by the confession of Benjamin Walker, in a desperate attempt to save his own skin, that the authorities were able to solve the murder of Horsfall, the attack on Rawfolds Mill, and other long-standing mysteries of Yorkshire Luddism. Usually, however, and taking the country as a whole, this alternative method of procuring information was not of much value. It was generally throughout this period easier to get spies to invent than accomplices to confess offences.

The Government maintained its system even after the disturbances of 1811–12 had been entirely quelled. In Nottingham it was handled by the Town Clerk. In February 1814 Mr. Coldham was writing to the Home Office to recommend the employment of some informer to become a member of one or two of the societies for Obtaining Parliamentary Relief, the so-called Nottingham

[1] Coldham to H.O., Feb. 24, 1812, in H.O. 42. 119.

Union.[1] He advised the appointment of some person 'on the distinct understanding he will not be used as a witness'. It was, he said, impossible to get a suitable person upon any other terms. The Government seems to have endorsed the scheme and declared its willingness to co-operate in measures for 'penetrating the Efforts' of the disorderly. It met in March of the next year, 1815, the very heavy bill, for more than £600, that the Nottingham Committee sent in.[2] An interesting item in this account was that of £2 2*s*. a week to the secret agent and 'other expenses on the same head'.

This, or some other similar secret agent, seems to have been employed continuously right through the summer of 1817 until long after the last signs of Luddism had disappeared. In 1815 he was so far in with the disaffected (whether Luddites or otherwise) that there was talk of their sending him as their delegate to London.[3] In the next month the Mayor of Leicester asked for Bow Street officers to procure information, feeling the need there for the security that a continual supply of secret information was giving to Nottingham.[4] While his request was refused the habit of using secret informers in this area persisted. In April 1816 Mr. Enfield, Mr. Coldham's successor as Town Clerk of Nottingham, announced that the Committee's funds were exhausted.[5] But at the same time he suggested some reward for their secret agent and said that the committee was trying to raise funds to continue their 'secret service'. In 1817, when the Government was agreeing to pay a reward of £525 in connexion with the Heathcote and Boden case it was noted that 'Mr. Enfield's Secret Informer' was to get £10.[6] This agent had sent in a revealing series of reports. The exposure of the framebreaking gang

[1] Coldham to H.O., Feb. 20, 1814, in H.O. 42. 137.
[2] Same to same, March 21, 1815, in H.O. 42. 143.
[3] Same to same, June 1815, in H.O. 42. 144.
[4] Mayor of Leicester to H.O., July 1815, in ibid.
[5] Enfield to H.O., April 6, 1816, in H.O. 42. 149.
[6] Lockett to H.O., Feb. 4, 1817, in H.O. 42. 152.

was largely due to his efforts. It was natural that he should confuse their last, desperate efforts with those of the radicals who were forming Spencean Societies and Hampden Clubs, in whom the authorities were interested in 1817, and into whose activities the informers were to pry in the years following the last collapse of Luddism. But in spite of such misunderstandings, to which even the best informers were liable, this Nottingham agent continued to be of use. His reports are important evidence of the planning of the 'Pentridge Revolution' and they expose the presence and activities of that 'delegate from London', whom we can identify as Oliver.

A similar permanent spy system existed in other areas. Colonel Fletcher continued to be very active in and near Bolton throughout this period. He kept many of his old spies on his pay-roll. In December 1813 he sent up a bill of £144 3*s.* 3*d.* for expenses on this account and said that he had drawn upon Government for this sum.[1] Most of the old names reappear on this account. 'L.F.' had received £26, 'B' £46, and other agents such as '1' and 'A.B.' lesser amounts. Even the notorious pair of Stones were back upon the list again, receiving rather more than £4 apiece. The Government in accepting this bill asked Colonel Fletcher to reduce the expense of the system in the future. On the 18th Lord Sidmouth wrote to ask if Colonel Fletcher thought the expenses needed to be continued under the circumstances while on the 25th he begged Fletcher 'to reduce the expense of the Missionary System'. In doing so he took occasion to say how 'much to his satisfaction' the whole system had always been conducted.[2]

At the same time other expenses of this kind were gradually liquidated. Some money had already been distributed to spies after the York trials, Mr. Hobhouse having spent at least £70 on this account before leaving

[1] Fletcher to H.O., Dec. 10, 1813, in H.O. 42. 136.

[2] H.O. to Fletcher, Dec. 18 and 25, 1813, in H.O. 79. 2.

the city.[1] Later in that year Captain Raynes received £200 on account of his efforts and expenses.[2] Allowances were also made to Nadin and Fleming.[3] Taylor and Whitehead, having been rewarded and offered jobs in Glasgow, were insolent enough to ask for Commissions in the army and it was with much difficulty that they were ultimately got rid of.[4] Similarly informers like Benjamin Walker were importunate, though they were less successful in obtaining any concession.[5]

The system was kept in operation even during periods of quiet. Contact was kept up with some at any rate of the spies. Though a number of new names appear upon the pay-rolls in 1817, some of the old names, such as 'A.B.', 'B', and Fleming reappear. In 1816 both Colonel Fletcher at Bolton and Captain Chippendale at Oldham were employing informers just as if disturbances were raging.[6] Fletcher indeed had already, in November 1816, exceeded his estimate of £50 for the year.[7] In 1817 spies were active at Manchester as well as at Oldham and Bolton. In each case the adjutant of the local militia was in direct charge of the system.[8] Even in Sheffield similar arrangements were made, Mr. Stuart Wortley writing up in January 1817 to report upon the activities of the person whom they employed to give them intelligence of some working-class movement which they called 'the Union'.[9]

Manchester seems to have had an especially elaborate

[1] Hobhouse to H.O., Jan. 1813, in H.O. 42. 132.

[2] H.O. to Montrose, Dec. 24, 1813, in H.O. 79. 2.

[3] Fleming got £100.

[4] H.O. to Lloyd, Jan. 23, 1813, in H.O. 79. 2.

[5] Walker was never told, what the Government believed, that he had a good legal claim against the Huddersfield Committee for the reward they had offered for information leading to the arrest of the murderers of Horsfall. Hall and Sowden, two other York witnesses, were rewarded, Sowden getting £50 and Hall being given employment in the Treasury Solicitor's Office. (H.O. to Lloyd, May 8, 1813, in H.O. 79. 2.)

[6] Chippendale to Byng, Dec. 8, 1816, in H.O. 42. 156.

[7] Fletcher to H.O., Nov. 5, 1816, in H.O. 42. 155.

[8] See Fletcher and Ethelston to H.O., various letters in H.O. 42. 158.

[9] Wortley to H.O., Jan. 15, 1817, in ibid.

system. Mr. Ethelston, a magistrate of the district, writing on January 5, 1817, to acknowledge the directions he had received from Lord Sidmouth to employ Campbell and Fleming as spies 'on a moderate scale', said that there were several secret agents in the employ of the constables of Manchester. He himself had 'for some months been at considerable expense in paying different spies from whom I receive regular accounts of the proceedings of the disaffected', and he urgently wanted authority to draw on the Home Office for such purposes up to £100.[1] The Borough-reeve and Constables were writing at the same time and forwarding information from their agents '1' and '2'.[2] In an accompanying schedule of Manchester papers reference is made to no less than five different spies.[3] The Borough-reeve and Constables had decided to send up regular reports from all these informants. Indeed it was announced that the Manchester authorities had decided to form themselves into a Board.[4] Each magistrate was to submit to the Board all communications he received before forwarding them to London. In this way it was hoped to check the value of each report by comparison with others. So valuable was this pooling and checking of information found that it was almost immediately decided to introduce it at Stockport.[5]

At London, in Scotland, and elsewhere the same, or a similar system of secret information was in effect. Sir Nathaniel Conant, the most trusted and experienced of the metropolitan police magistrates, acting in conjunction with another London magistrate, Mr. Stafford, was employing informers to spy into the activities of the Spencean Societies and Hampden Clubs in the capital. Bundles of documents in the Home Office files marked 'Thistlewood Papers' contain these and other similar letters and reports.

[1] Ethelston to H.O., Jan. 29, 1817, in ibid.

[2] Feb. 10, 1817, in H.O. 42. 159.

[3] 'Schedule of Manchester Papers', in H.O. 42. 164.

[4] Hay to H.O., Jan. 27, 1817, in H.O. 42. 158.

[5] Lloyd to H.O., Jan. 21, 1817, in ibid.

In Scotland the spy system was managed through the Lord Advocates' Office.[1]

Another method of acquiring information that was employed was the tapping of the mails. Instructions were issued in February 1812 for intercepting the letters of suspicious characters in Nottingham.[2] At the same time the Post Office sent down a man called Grotrian Hart to watch the mails and the people who should come to the local post offices for signs of communication between the Luddites in Nottingham and elsewhere.[3] The organization of the Post Office seems indeed to have been regularly used as a part of the system of intelligence. Mr. Freeling was continually writing from the General Post Office to the Home Office, forwarding reports from sub-postmasters. The latter were expected to keep a look out for suspicious circumstances and to report them immediately to London to be passed on to the Home Office. There seems to have been some system in the procedure. In 1817 Mr. Freeling was writing to say 'our circulating system is proceeding famously'.[4] It does not appear that this 'circulating system' was very complicated. Nor did it reveal anything startling. Only the actual warrant of a Secretary of State would entitle letters to be opened. Ordinarily all that the system would do would be to provide the Government with a number of correspondents and informants about the country, men well able because of their position to keep a check upon communications between known radicals and rioters in different parts of the country, and therefore valuable sources of information as to local conditions.

This habit of the Government and of local authorities to rely upon secret information, and to pay very liberally for it, was well known. It provoked some criticism in Parliament, in the columns of papers like the *Leeds Mercury*, and

[1] Letters between H.O. and Lord Advocate, in H.O. 79. 2.
[2] H.O. to Fowke, Feb. 5, 1812, in H.O. 43. 19.
[3] H.O. to Conant, Feb. 2, 1812, in H.O. 79. 1.
[4] Freeling to Addington, Jan. 6, 1817, in H.O. 42. 158.

in some contemporary works, although it was accepted upon the whole as necessary and unavoidable, as indeed it was. It also induced many individuals to volunteer for service. There was actually competition to be employed. We have noted the cases of Playfair, Lawson, and other spies in 1812 who volunteered for, and received, employment. Other similar offers, not all of which could be taken advantage of, were then and later received. A George Brifac of Gloucester, for instance, wrote up in July 1812 to tell Lord Sidmouth that he was going to get 'twisted in' as a Luddite in order to ingratiate himself with the disaffected and thus acquire information.[1] Lord Sidmouth cautiously replied that he could not become a party to any particular method of acquiring information but left it to Mr. Brifac to use his discretion as to the best way of acquiring such information as he felt disposed to communicate to the Government. Another man, signing himself anonymously 'An Englishman', offered himself as a spy wherever he should be needed on condition that his name should be kept secret, and that he should be paid all expenses and given a pension if injured, and a reward if successful.[2] Offers continued throughout this whole period, there being a larger number of volunteers than usual in periods of especial anxiety, such as 1817.

It was then a continual policy of the local authorities and of the Government to spend money on acquiring secret information. Great numbers of spies were employed. Some magistrates and local committees employed semi-permanent agents on a regular weekly salary. Other spies were employed from time to time as occasion required, or were paid in the form of rewards for specific pieces of information. The Home Office was always willing to meet such expenses and to empower local authorities to draw upon it for such a purpose. Spies were maintained in all the disturbed districts. They were often, though not always,

[1] Brifac to H.O., July 8, 1812, in H.O. 42. 125.

[2] Anonymous in ibid.

managed through the medium of the local militia staff. They were sometimes a part of the military arrangements. They were maintained in 1811. They were still maintained in 1818. They were one of the most important, and not the least expensive, instruments of Government in its attempt to work a medieval system of local and internal government under modern conditions.

Spies played an important role in Regency disturbances. What they discovered, and even more what they failed to discover, was important evidence as to the real character, gravity, and extent of the disaffection. Nothing is more reassuring as to the general security of the country than the fact that, after so much effort, and after acting so often as positive promoters of disorder, the spies should have discovered so little real ground for alarm.

APPENDIX

Expense Accounts of Adjutant James Warr of the Bolton Local Militia.

(Enclosed in a letter from Colonel Fletcher to the Home Office, Bolton, 11 June, 1812; in H.O. 42. 124).

Cash Paid by James Warr for Secret Service.

1812			£	s.	d.
March	6	Cash to /S/	3	–	–
	16	,, ,, and old /S/	1	7	6
	21	,, ,, to buy shoes and breeches	1	–	–
	,,	Expenses at Isherwood's; meat, liquor, etc., for the above and others concerned	1	7	7
	26	Cash to /S/		10	–
	30	,, ,,		3	–
	31	,, ,,		7	–
April	4	,, ,,	1	–	–
	8	,, ,,		3	–
	11	,, ,, and old /S/		7	–
	,,	Expenses since the above		13	–
	10	Cash to Joseph Wainwright from Leigh		5	–
		Carried forward	£10	3	1

1812		Brought forward	10	3	1
April	10	Cash to William Orrell on journey to Leigh		2	–
		Meat and liquor for Orrell and Wainwright		3	–
	11	Cash to /S/	1	–	–
	13	Packing Arms and conveying them to Westhoughton		18	2
	16	Liquor to men with arms		8	–
	17	,, ,, in arranging districts		15	–
	18	Cash to /S/	1	–	–
	,,	,, ,, Joseph Wainwright	2	–	–
	20	Expenses at Westhoughton; meat and liquor for the guard		14	4
	21	Paid Orrell, Hardwoon, Schofield, and Wood	2	10	–
	,,	Horse hire to Manchester 6/-; expenses 5/-		11	–
	,,	Cash to /S/		4	6
	25	To Isherwood for liquor to guard-room; meat and liquor for scouts since 21 March	6	2	3
	,,	Cash to Joseph Wainwright		13	–
	,,	To local militia man who lost 3/- when pursuing a man at Chowbent		2	–
	,,	Cash to /S/		16	6
	,,	Meat and liquor at Westhoughton	4	4	6
	29	Liquor at George and Dragon on assembling to go to Bolton Moors as per Bill	3	3	4
	,,	At Sergt. Grimes' after returning	2	15	4
	,,	Cash to old /S/		13	–
May	2	Cash to /S/	1	–	–
	,,	,, old /S/		7	–
	,,	,, Joseph Wainwright	1	13	7
	3	,, Abraham Hay, Hayward and Walker	1	16	–
	,,	Liquor, etc.		10	–
	5	Cash to S		3	6
	9	,, ,,		15	–
	11	Liquor at Rainers after returning from Rag End		11	7
	,,	Cash to Grundy, Heywood, and Fletcher	1	16	10
	,,	,, Abraham Hay for going after Lever	2	4	–
		Carried forward	£49	16	6

1812		Brought forward	49	16	6
May	14	Cash to /S/	1	3	4
	15	William Hardman; loss of time and expenses		6	–
	19	Cash to Roger Ward for meat; liquor for Kay while sick		8	–
	21	Cash to old /S/ and young /S/	3	2	–
	22	Joseph Shelton's Bill for eating as ordered by G. M. Lever	1	4	10
	,,	Fletcher's Bill for clothing old /S/ and young /S/	2	5	–
	,,	Capt. Langos Law's Bill for guard expenses at Lane Ends on Sunday evening, April 19		9	–
	,,	Quartermaster Lever's Bill. Sundry expenses	14	12	6
	,,	Paid Enoch Sankey for horse hire		5	–
	,,	Cashing a Bill		6	–
June	9	Expenses of Adjutant Warr	10	10	–
	,,	Compensation of 60 men of Bolton Local Militia on nights of 19, 20, and 21 April assembled by Colonel Fletcher and Magistrates and Deputy Lieutenants 60 men at 3/- per man	9	–	–
	,,	Mr. Nelson's Bills as particularized	28	13	1
			119	2	3½ [1]

Accounts presented by General Acland to General Maitland for Secret Service Expenditure.

Including payments to Raynes, Thornhill, and MacDougal and smaller payments by Acland and by subordinates.

(in H.O. 40. 2.)

Money Expended on Secret Service.

				£
1812	18	August	Lawson	4
	20	,,	Smith and Downes	4
			Carried forward	£8

[1] This bill is not added up correctly. The total should be £122 1*s*. 3*d*.

		Brought forward .	8
1812	24 August	Munro and Robinson	1
	26 ,,	men of Norfolk	3
	28 ,,	Smith and Downes	5
	29 ,,	John Brookes	2
	,, ,,	men of Stirling	1
	30 ,,	Blythe, Constable of Holmfirth .	1
	,, ,,	John Ferraby, Special Constable .	2
			£23

Transmitted to General Maitland, 31st August, 1812.

1812	2 Sept.	Shipley	2		
	5 ,,	Smith and Knowles	6		
	6 ,,	Cooper	3		
	7 ,,	Thornhill to Lawson . . .	3		
	8 ,,	Sergt. Todd	1		
	9 ,,	George Brookes	2		
	,, ,,	3 men of Norfolk	1		
	11 ,,	William Cooper	2		
	12 ,,	Parties of Suffolk & Stirling .	2		
	,, ,,	Smiths and Downes	5		
	17 ,,	John Knight	5		
	,, ,,	Shipley	5		
	,, ,,	William Cooper	5		
	19 ,,	Colcher?	3		
	20 ,,	per Wm. Cooper	2		
	,, ,,	per Shipley	2		
	22 ,,	John Gosling alias Downes . .	2		
	,, ,,	Whitehead	2		
	,, ,,	Sergt. Gilderwater	1		
	28 ,,	John Gosling alias Downes . .	2		
			£56		
		Balance overpaid last month .	2		
		Remains due to General Acland .	54		
		This amount delivered to T . .	21	10	6
		Gen. Maitland, 30 Sept. to McD. .	10	–	9
		Rec.d £100, 14 Oct. R. . .	44	13	6
			130	4	9

1812	1 Oct.	Sergt. ?	3	–	–
	2 ,,	,, Gilderwater	1	–	–
	5 ,,	Knight	2	–	–
	6 ,,	Corporal Allsopp	3	–	–
	,, ,,	Gosling paid up & discharged	3	–	–
		Knight	3	–	–
		Jones	2	–	–
	7 ,,	Cooper by Lt. Col. Rapier	3	–	–
	8 ,,	Farnley Constable	2	–	–
		Pd. up ? and Stirling	4	10	3
		For Information		15	6
	22 ,,	Knight	5	12	–
		For expenses	2	–	–
		Balance	3	16	–
		For expenses	2	–	–
			38	13	9[1]

[1] Another instance of faulty Regency arithmetic. The total should be £40 13*s*. 9*d*.

XV

THE DANGER OF REVOLUTION

It was a matter of anxiety to the authorities at the time and has been one of interest to students ever since, whether there was in fact any serious danger of revolution in nineteenth-century England. During the half-century following the French Revolution, from the fall of the Bastille to the final collapse of English Chartism, the danger of revolution was never entirely absent from any European country. English people might think, as they always have since their peaceful Revolution of 1689, and since the Hanoverian dynasty was finally and safely seated on the throne, that violent revolutions were foreign to their character. Few people in England, even in the midst of the alarm occasioned by events in France, seriously expected the continental example to be copied in the British Isles. Neither the Tories who took events abroad as an excuse for repression at home, nor the radicals who were encouraged in their domestic agitations by the success of foreign revolutions, really believed that conditions in England and on the continent of Europe were comparable. Only a handful of alarmists, and they only on a few occasions of crisis, felt that an English revolution was probable.

No one, however, could know for certain how far the radical movement could be safely opposed, and changes blocked, without provoking a violent opposition to the existing order. No one can ever know for certain whether a revolution might not have been attempted, and been successful, if the structure of British government had not been gradually and peacefully adapted to the needs of the new situation. No one could know then, or can know now, what might have happened if a political crisis had developed in England, and if events had been allowed to drift beyond control, as has happened in the case of other revolutions. It is difficult to tell in advance whether the seeds of a revolutionary situation exist, still more difficult to tell whether, though there be ground for a revolution, any particular revolutionary attempt would be successful. Many revolutions which have been successful might, perhaps, have been defeated, avoided, or at least postponed, if the revolutionaries had been a little less lucky, or the established authorities a little more skilful and firm. Many further revolutions might have occurred if things had happened a little differently, if the revolutionaries or the authorities had pursued slightly different tactics. A revolutionary situation, the sort of situation which provoked, for instance, the French and Russian Revolutions, does not always lead to actual revolution, or at least such a situation can exist for a long time before an actual revolution occurs. Some revolutions like that in France in 1830 have occurred without any such pronounced revolutionary situation existing. History seems often to depend too much on chance.

It was, therefore, impossible for English people in the early nineteenth century, though they might think a revolution unlikely, to know that it would not take place. It is equally impossible for us to argue, because a revolution did not take place, that there was no danger of revolution. The slight doubt in British minds a hundred years ago lest reaction, if it were pressed too far, or reform, if it were allowed too free a scope, might not lead to revolution, was a factor of great importance. It accounted for much of the moderation exhibited alike by advocates and opponents of change, a moderation which was largely responsible for the peaceful consummation of those great changes which in fact constituted, without violence, the English Revolution, political, industrial, and social, of the nineteenth century. The danger of revolution was in some degree as much a cause of change in England as the fact of revolution was abroad. The head-on collision between one section of society and another, from which revolutions issue, was never allowed to occur in England. We shall, therefore, never know how great the danger of revolution was.

We can, however, make an estimate. We can study the contemporary conditions in order to see how far there was in England at that time a situation comparable to that which had, and has, produced revolutions elsewhere. We can study the disturbances short of revolution which did occur in England, and by seeing how they arose and were handled form some sort of estimate of what chance there was of more serious disturbances still, of revolution.

The period and the disturbances which we have studied in the foregoing chapters are particularly significant from this point of view. There was between 1810 and 1818, and especially in 1811–12 and 1816–17, a more severe depression of trade, and more sudden and severe distress, and therefore more widespread discontent, than at any other time between 1790 and 1850. There occurred during those years the most widespread, persistent, and dangerous disturbances, short of actual revolution or civil war, that England has ever known in modern times. A greater force, and more exceptional measures, had to be employed to restore order than had ever been used before, or than have ever been needed since. There was never a time, moreover, in which a revolution would have had a greater chance of success than during those years in which the greater part of the army was engaged in foreign service, and when the energy of the authorities was absorbed in the problems of two foreign wars. Then, if ever, the seeds of a revolutionary situation existed. Then, if ever, a revolutionary attempt would have had a real chance of success.

The chances of a revolution occurring, or being successful, grew less every year after 1818, and especially after 1822. The army was home again. The Government was free to give all its attention to the internal situation. There was no longer a chance of revolutionaries getting foreign aid. The terrible distress of the war and immediate post-war years diminished, despite a few setbacks, and periods of acute business depression, and the rising tide of the Industrial Revolution, vastly swollen by the railway boom, though it wrought terrible hardships, carried the bulk of the nation forward too far and too fast for there to be an opportunity for political revolution. The governing class, moreover, began to compromise, to give up the attitude of rigid reaction that had characterized it during the war years. While it was not until the shake up of the Liverpool Ministry in 1822, and after the accession of Canning, Peel, and Huskisson to power, that the period of reform legislation began, and while the years 1817 to 1822 were a period of stormy conflict between the Government and the discontented elements in the community, already at the end of the war a political and industrial opposition was developing, and great changes attained by legal means began to appear possible, as they had not been for a quarter of a century. Political and industrial leaders, Brougham, Cobbett, Place, and many others, were getting the ear of the country. Those who were opposed to the existing order were no longer left inarticulate and desperate. They were being given a legal outlet for their energies and hopes.

As soon as the stream of modern legislation began the incentive for, and the chance of success of, a revolution became rapidly less and less. On the one hand, the creation of a police force, of modern efficient units of local government, lessened the chances of the disorderly. Riots had far less opportunity to grow into revolution. On the other hand, the repeal of the Combination Acts, the passage of Factory Acts, the movement towards Free Trade, the parliamentary reform programme, all had a moderating effect upon popular discontent, and removed the incentive for revolution. It became credible, as it had not been credible before, that a redress of grievances might be obtained, gradually but still effectually, by peaceful means.

It was then before 1817, while the attitude of the governing class was set firmly against all change, while there was no legal outlet for the discontents of the people, while there was no reasonable hope of ever achieving by normal, peaceful means any substantial redress of grievances, that the danger of revolution was greatest. It was while the army was occupied abroad, while English governmental machinery was still antiquated, before there was any regular system of police, that revolutionaries had their real chance.

This chance was greatest towards the end of this period, after rather than before 1810. The burden of the war was greatest towards its close, the campaign on land against Napoleon, on the sea against the United States, was costly in money and men. The Continental System on the one hand, the American Non-Intercourse Act upon the other, bound in the trade of Britain, and restricted the employment of the people, both of which had previously been expanding rapidly in spite of, and in some cases because of, the war. The sudden closing of foreign markets during the winter of 1810–11, the sudden slump after the war, were almost unprecedented in their severity. They accentuated, they made matters of acute personal knowledge to all the people, the cost of the war. The shoe began to pinch when the foot was idle and had a chance to swell.

The Industrial and Agricultural Revolutions, moreover, proceeding rapidly during the war years, on the strength of an inflated war demand, had by 1811 begun seriously and adversely to affect some sections of the people. Displacement of labour, reduction of wages, owing to the introduction of labour-saving machinery, had begun, but only recently, to be seriously felt by some classes of workers. The ultimate effects of these revolutions, urbanization, industrialization, division of labour, the separation of the worker from his market, from his machine and from the land, the dependence of industry and agriculture upon distant and foreign markets, were becoming obvious, and they made the average Englishman in 1810 more vulnerable to trade depression than he had been before. He was also less sensitive to the old restraints, being often uprooted from his original village, a new-comer in a strange, new town, missing acutely the old personal relationship he had enjoyed with his neighbours, his employer, and the local authorities. The growth of population and its changed distribution had, moreover, begun by 1810 seriously to affect the adequacy of the old system of local government, which was no longer, as we have seen, able to stand up to its responsibilities.

There was a further reason why conditions should be particularly serious during the Regency of George IV. It has been often remarked what an element of security it was in eighteenth-century Britain that the King and the Prince of Wales should almost always have been on unfriendly terms. The Opposition was always tempted to await the normal accession of the Heir whom it liked rather than go to extremes against the Monarch whom it hated. The Whig party had been friendly to George IV during his days as Prince of Wales. It, and the country, still expected in 1812, when the restrictions upon his power were finally removed from the Prince Regent, that there would be a change of ministers. It was a matter of acute disappointment to many people, who really had no good reason for hoping for better things from Whig than from Tory ministers, that the Perceval Government should have been kept in office. If various threatening and anonymous letters are to be believed,[1] and also the lesson of certain riots, like that at the Manchester Exchange Hall on April 8, 1812, such disappointment was actually a factor in some of the disturbances of the spring of 1812. The disillusionment which followed the Prince Regent's full accession to power was a measure of the hopes that many people had held that his rule would bring about an improvement in conditions generally, hopes which had

[1] e.g. letter received by Mr. Smith of Huddersfield in May 1812 (in H.O. 40. 1), quoted in Chap. VI.

apparently kept some discontented people quiet during the preceding years.

There was therefore in 1811–12 an accumulation of causes for discontent, as well as a most unusually favourable opportunity for disorders, if they occurred, to be successful. It should not be a matter of surprise that this year, and to a lesser extent the period 1811–17, should have witnessed such extensive disturbances, and should have been accompanied by such unusual alarm. Then, if ever in nineteenth-century England, there were grounds for revolution, hopes for improvement only in revolution, chances for the success of revolution.

For a brief period in April and May 1812, while the more than 12,000 troops employed were being distributed about the disturbed districts, and while rumours of a general armed rising were circulating, it might well have appeared that a revolution was likely and might succeed. Officials who should have known what they were talking of, men like the Vice-Lieutenant of the West Riding, wrote[1] up to the Government to say that 'except for the very spots which were occupied by Soldiers, the Country was virtually in the possession of the lawless . . . the disaffected outnumbering by many Degrees the peaceable Inhabitants'. According to him the disturbances were taking the 'direct Road to an open Insurrection'.[2] The authorities, apart from the military, were clearly scared. And even the military were swamped with the requests for help that they got from frightened villages. It is hardly credible, if similar disorders had broken out, as they well might have, in the other manufacturing districts, all of which were terribly distressed, and if the disaffected had proceeded from simple attacks upon machinery or markets to general disorder, that the existing military and civil force in the kingdom would have been able, except slowly and with great difficulty, to put them down. For a time

[1] Wood to Fitzwilliam, June 17, 1812, in H.O. 40. 1.

[2] Same to same, June 7, in ibid.

the whole country would definitely have been at the mercy of the disaffected, and real revolutionaries, with or without foreign help, would have had a wonderful chance to profit from this situation. A relatively small force, well led, could have seized its opportunity, while the Government and its forces were extended by the disturbances in the manufacturing districts, and could have assumed the reins of power. The machinery of order, which was so hard pressed to put down very limited disturbances in parts of five counties only, could hardly have tackled a real revolutionary movement, if it had come on the top of general disturbances in every manufacturing region.

The spring of 1812 was, therefore, the time when the English Revolution should have occurred if it was to have had any real chance of success. If there had been any able leaders of a revolutionary movement they would have seized that opportunity. They could, as a few anonymous papers suggested they would,[1] have provoked disorders similar to Luddism in the other manufacturing districts, all of which were petitioning against the Orders in Council. They could have recruited from amongst the disaffected, some of whom were clearly in a mood to join in any sort of destructive campaign,[2] some detachments of storm troops with which to seize strategic places, at the right moment when they were left exposed to attack by the departure of their normal garrisons to the disturbed manufacturing regions. They could have arranged as some of the spies and agitators said they had arranged, for an insurrection in Ireland and for an invasion from France to have coincided with their rising. Such a situation, which would seem to have been within the bounds of possibility, would have been as good a setting for revolution as any which has ever existed.

[1] Various such papers are included in the Home Office in Letters (series 40 and 42).

[2] For instance the colliers who joined with the cotton weavers in attacking steam looms in Lancashire and Cheshire in 1812.

It does not appear likely that the Government could have coped with such a situation, if it had occurred, without bringing home its troops from the Peninsula. It would have had its hands full trying on the one hand to repell the foreign invasion which would have immediately threatened and on the other to put down internal disorders which, like a prairie fire, would have burst out again elsewhere each time they were extinguished in any one locality. It would certainly have lost the war. It might have been unable to prevent invasion and crushing defeat and revolution.

It is astonishing really that the advantages of this situation were not more apparent to Napoleon. Had he known the real gravity of the situation in England in the winter of 1811–12 he would hardly, surely, have led his troops off on a wild goose chase into the marshes of Russia. It is easy to appreciate, when one remembers the alarm which the actual restricted disorders of 1812 created in England, the terror which would have affected the country if at the same time a serious foreign invasion had been threatened.

As it happens there is no evidence, and strangely enough there was no suggestion, that the English disorders were even encouraged by the French. The latter were then, as the Russian Communists have been recently, the bogies of Tory England. But no suggestion was made, as it often is in cases of internal or industrial disorder in England to-day, that the foreign bogy was responsible. The French missed a real chance in not spending a little money employing agitators and otherwise encouraging and assisting disorders in England. Even if they had not wished to attempt a concurrent invasion, or expected any considerable success, they might have found some advantage in tying up in England the larger number of troops that would have been needed if the Luddite and other disorders had not been so restricted. At best the French, if they had backed the English rioters, might have started a revolution, which would surely have ended, if it succeeded in overthrowing the existing British Government, in allowing Napoleon to nominate a pro-French one, since no provisional English government could have been expected to stand against him. At worst, if the revolution had failed, or if there had been no revolution but only slightly more serious and protracted local industrial disorders, the French would at any rate have greatly embarrassed the British Government at a critical stage of Wellington's campaign.

The British were, however, spared all danger of such outside interference. And without that the chances of successful revolution would probably have been slender. There is no evidence, moreover, that the disaffected possessed leaders, or a plan, which would have enabled them to launch a revolution, still less establish a stable provisional government. The real weakness of all these movements of disturbance, and the great source of stability to the established order, was the fact that disorders were confined to the lowest orders of the people. There is no trace anywhere or at any time during this period of the disaffected possessing a single middle or upper class leader, or any one with the experience and ability necessary to carry through even a simple positive campaign. There was no one to weld the many discontented groups of English workers into an effective national force, no one to win this mass of scattered, isolated, discontented people, from mere attacks upon machinery or markets to a constructive revolutionary or reform campaign. The few leaders of the radical movement, Cobbett, Cartwright, Whitbread, Sir Francis Burdett, none of whom would have served very effectively as a revolutionary leader, were in fact all opposed to violence, even to the restricted violence of the Luddites.[1]

The Luddites and other disaffected people lacked, as we have seen, not merely leadership but organization. There was nothing to connect the disorderly in the different

[1] e.g. letters from Cartwright in *Nottingham Review*, Dec. 1811.

districts, no machinery for promoting in other districts the disorders which had had such great, though temporary, success in the few regions where they had occurred, and which might be so much more successful if they were more general throughout the country. Mere discontent in different districts, among different classes of workers, will not produce a revolution unless there is organization to unite the different groups and localities, as well as a plan to secure their action in unison. There was no such organization amongst the Luddites, or amongst the other discontented groups, nor was there any agreement among them on positive, general objects which they wished to achieve.

One of the things, indeed, which made Luddism so difficult to suppress, made it also ineffective as the basis for a general revolutionary movement. The aims of the rioters were so limited and so local. The machine breakers, even the collectors of arms, did not want to overturn the Government. They only wanted to coerce this or that employer, to get this or that particular, local, industrial concession. They used only sufficient force for the limited objects they had in mind, and they used it only when, where, and against whom they had some special grievance. Luddism was made a means of coercing particular employers, even the employers' group in general, into granting certain general trade concessions. But it was not made, as it might well have been, a means of trying to coerce the Government into regulating the industry and preventing abuses, or into repealing the Orders in Council, bitterly though these general objects were desired by all the workers. Disturbances in Regency England, though very widespread and serious and calling for all the effort of the Government for their suppression, were not directed against the Government. The agents of Government, magistrates, members of the local force, constables, though they became in effect, since to put down the disturbances would play into the hands of the employers, the agents of the latter, were almost always perfectly safe. The authorities might be eluded and their commands ignored, but they were not resisted or directly attacked. The Luddites' quarrel was not with the Government but with particular employers.

There is no evidence anywhere, except amongst a few irresponsible agitators like the Watsons, of a desire to overturn the Government. It is highly doubtful whether the Luddites, or other rioters, if they saw that their campaign was being made a means of overturning the Government, would have tolerated this distortion of their original purpose. Just as they carefully refrained from taking the very many opportunities for easy robbery that were open to them during their campaign of violence so they might have been expected to refrain from taking opportunities for treason and rebellion if such had occurred. The Luddites, though opponents of existing authority in so far as that stood in the way of their objects, were not revolutionaries. They were very typical loyal Englishmen. They would probably have opposed a French or Irish invading force as eagerly as the Government itself. A foreign invasion, or foreign interference in domestic English matters, might have been a means, not of dividing and defeating, but of uniting the nation. There is no evidence of the talk of some of the spies and Irish delegates, about great numbers enrolled in a national conspiracy against government and of the possibility of French and Irish help, having affected many people, or any of the leading Luddites.

General Maitland, the person best placed to form an accurate estimate of the situation in 1812, was certain that there had never been any serious intention among the rioters to stage a general rising, nor did he think that their numbers or state of organization were such as to permit of such a venture, had it been intended.[1] The rumoured intention of the northern workers to stage a general rising

[1] Maitland to H.O., May 4, 1812, in H.O. 40. 1.

in the spring of 1817 was received with equal scepticism by authorities such as General Byng. The only acts of any of the disaffected throughout this whole period which can be construed as having any revolutionary tendencies are those of the Huddersfield and Derbyshire rioters in June 1817, acts which show how vague were the plans, and how few the adherents, of the revolutionary movement. The Luddites, when they confined themselves to attacks upon the machinery of unpopular employers, were very difficult to suppress. They had the sympathy of the whole working population. But projects of a more ambitious political character, like these 'risings' or 'revolutions', attracted only a very insignificant support, and that only from amongst the poorest, most ignorant section of the people, and were easily put down.

The invariable loyalty of the troops, the militia, and the constables; the fact that the population as a whole, though it would not proceed against the Luddites, yet refrained from openly opposing the authorities; the divisions of opinion even amongst the workers themselves about Luddism, half the trade opposing violent measures, even during the height of the disturbances, and continuing to put their trust in negotiation; the unanimity with which the middle and upper classes, even where they sympathized with the distresses which were causing disturbances, opposed disorder; all go to show, what all but a few contemporaries never seriously doubted, that the fundamental state of the country was sound. The fact, indeed, that, at a time of unexampled distress, during the most severe protracted disturbance, when the machinery of order was taxed to the uttermost to prevent events getting beyond control, there should have been no attempt, and little disposition, to profit by the emergency and seek broad political or social objects, shows emphatically how little chance there was of a revolution occurring in Regency England, even though the chances for its success, if it should occur, were in many ways so great.

For all the distress and discontent in Regency England, and despite the willingness of particular groups of workers, like those concerned in Luddism, to join in violent movements, there was no material for a revolution. There was no unity amongst the discontented, no concentration of their hopes and despairs upon a particular national object, like the overthrow of the dynasty, or the Government, or the established political or social system. There was no movement, or even tendency, of revolt against the established system as such; no disposition to see in the system the cause of the very many grave evils from which great bodies of people were suffering, and against which they were protesting sometimes by violence. Individuals, groups, localities, had objects of grievance. Many were driven on occasions almost to despair and were the ready prey of the agitator. But there was no general dissatisfaction with existing conditions, no deep prejudice against the monarchy, or against the landowners, or against employers, as a whole. The prejudice of the disorderly was against particular ministers, measures, employers. Their objects were limited ones, to secure this or that industrial, local, sectional concession. There was not even, as there was to be later on, a concentration of popular hopes and aims upon some one general object, such as the Reform Bill or the Ten Hours' Act or the Charter, a concentration which might make possible a revolution if those in power were too unyielding in their opposition to a cause which was uniting all, or a great part, of Britain's discontented people under its banner.

There was no cause, and no banner, for the discontented and disorderly manufacturing population in Regency England. Each of the disorderly districts had its own cause, and its own banners. It was for particular limited objects—their old conditions—and not for the general causes of the time, repeal of the Orders in Council, peace or parliamentary reform, that the riotous mobs in 1812 were willing to fight. Until some general cause should arise with a powerful enough appeal to rally all these different elements in the nation's life, and to make them forget their particular selfish objects, there was, despite all the discontent and the restlessness of the workers, and despite the weakness of the forces of order, no serious danger of revolution.

XVI

THE STATE OF PUBLIC OPINION

ONE of the most surprising features of the situation which we have been studying was the very slight attention that was popularly given to disturbances and to problems of internal order generally. Partly, of course, this was due to the war, which naturally absorbed the nation's energies and interests to the exclusion of all other matters. The fact that a much greater amount of attention should have been given by Parliament and public to the, in fact, much less serious disturbances of the period after 1816, is proof of the extent to which the foreign emergency cast a shadow over domestic matters of all kinds. The overwhelming importance of great world issues connected with the close of the Napoleonic Wars is a sufficient explanation for much of the neglect that was shown to internal matters at the time, and which has been shown by students ever since.

Even so, however, it is surprising that so little attention should have been given either by contemporaries or by posterity to disturbances which required a fair sized army to put them down. It is astonishing that twenty years only after the French Revolution, when all its excesses were freshly in the public mind, people in England should have been so little scared of a similar collapse of the established order, and should have allowed to pass almost without comment the most destructive and difficult to suppress of all the internal disorders from which the country has ever suffered in modern times. Great though the demands of foreign questions were upon every one's attention one would have thought that the unprecedented measures that were taken for the suppression of Luddism would have aroused some considerable public comment. It is an interesting example of the state of public opinion at that time that they should not have done so.

There is no sign of Parliament or press, or of very many of the public, being concerned about the danger of disorder, or the weakness of the machinery of order, except upon occasions of actual immediate crisis. It was not until long after disorders had been threatened, and might have been confidently expected by every impartial observer acquainted with the facts, not until actual disorders had been raging for some time, that more than minor and local attention was given to the Luddite situation. Even then emergency measures were rushed through Parliament almost without debate, before very meagre houses, and were neglected by all but the members and ministers directly concerned.[1] Very little attention was given to them, except by persons intimately acquainted with the situation in the disturbed districts. The local press, and, so far as one can judge, local opinion generally, in other than the disturbed districts themselves, gave practically no attention, and the national press gave only minor attention, to a situation which might honestly have been thought to threaten a general collapse of order. The moment actual serious disturbances had stopped, the moment the Government's measures had gone through Parliament, even though nothing material or permanent had been done to alter the situation out of which disturbances had arisen, or to improve the machinery of order, even the local press and the local members of Parliament from the disturbed districts, were content to put such dull topics as the internal situation out of mind. Disturbances and the weakness of the system of internal order were matters of interest only to those directly concerned in the business of suppressing disorders, and to them only when and where actual disorders were raging.

Even those few people who were strongly concerned about the matter were, upon the whole, interested only in its superficial aspects. To most people the only important matter in connexion with civil disturbances was

[1] See description of Parliamentary action in Chap. XII.

the necessity of putting them down. A very few people indeed were concerned to do more than note the causes of disorder, of which popular distress was universally held to be the chief. Hardly any one believed that there was anything material that could be done, at any rate by the state or by the local authorities or outside the trades concerned, except take such measures, legal and military, as might be needed to restore order. These tremendous internal convulsions, the effects of war, of the Industrial Revolution, and of the way in which England had outgrown its previous structure of society and government, though they prepared the way for much greater attention to such matters in the post-war period, did not give rise at the time to more than a rare momentary interest in these fundamental questions. Disorders, which were only a symptom of much deeper social diseases, were generally taken at their face value. They were not expected. They were given a minimum of attention during their zenith. They were soon forgotten.

This general neglect of the matter is no doubt the reason why the country never lost its head. There is little sign in 1812–13, though the situation was much more serious then, of the tendency to panic which was becoming evident in 1816–17. It was because they had more attention to give to them, rather that because the danger was greater, that the authorities were more alarmed by the confused, aimless disorders of the period 1817–20, than by the fierce, concentrated disorders of the period 1811–13. It would otherwise have been astonishing that it was in the latter rather than in the former period that the Habeas Corpus Act was suspended (for the last time in British history) and that the Government proceeded to its famous policy of repression, the notorious Six Acts. One would gather by comparing, for instance, the Circular Letters sent out by the Government to the Lords Lieutenant in May 1812[1] and January 1817,[2] that the situation on the latter occasion

[1] Copy in H.O. 43. 20.

[2] Copy in H.O. 42. 158.

was much more alarming than on the former. In point of fact in January 1817 there was not a single serious act of disorder, whereas in May 1812, despite the presence of more than eight thousand soldiers and several thousand constables and militia, great parts of Lancashire, Cheshire, and the West Riding were, in the words of a contemporary authority, 'in the hands of the disaffected', the scene of nightly raids and robberies.

The general calmness of the authorities, and, except in the actually disturbed regions, of the public, is indeed as surprising a feature of the situation in the period of war-time disturbances, when one might expect the alarm to have been greatest, as the exaggerated alarm that was general on the occasion of the foolish, limited post-war disorders, such as the 'March of the Blanketeers', 'The Pentridge Revolution', and 'Peterloo', is of the post-1816 situation. One wonders why the Liverpool Government should have been so frightened, and should have proceeded to such repressive measures in the period 1817–20, when there was nothing as bad as the Luddite situation to threaten the safety of the country. One wonders even more, in the light of that later alarm, at the level-headed moderation of the Government, and of most authorities, during the really exceptional disorders of 1812.

There were, of course, a few individuals who lost their heads, and a few occasions of great alarm. Mr. Giddy, a local member of Parliament, was speaking for some of his contemporaries when he said in May 1812, during the debate on the Unlawful Oaths Bill,[1]

'But, good God, when men were thus associated by thousands to murder those who differed from them was it a time to be sitting there debating upon systems? . . . Was it a time to hesitate when Parliament saw diabolical designs carried into execution, which could not from their nature proceed from an ignorant multitude but must be planned by higher talents, whether foreign or domestic he could not say, but which,

[1] *Parl. Debates*, xxiii. 40–1.

unless they burnt the standing corn before the harvest, were better calculated than any others which could be adopted to bring misery and starvation upon the people.'

Another northern member was similarly panicky when he exclaimed a month later, when Whitbread was trying to prove the broad suggestions of the reports of the Committees of Secrecy unfounded, that those actually exaggerated accounts of the northern disorders, understated rather than overstated the actual danger.[1] The Vice-Lieutenant of the West Riding himself almost lost his nerve at the same time, talking of the 'total Insecurity' of the country, and of the disturbances taking a 'road to open insurrection'.[2] Here and there a scared magistrate would write to London at different times during these disturbances, in 1812, 1814, and 1816, to pour out his fears lest the disturbances might not presage a general collapse of order.

There were particular occasions of alarm. Nottinghamshire was scared towards the end of 1811 and at the beginning of 1812. *The Times* reporter, commenting on the situation in the county, reported that the great garrison and the continual coming and going of the military gave the district 'an appearance of warfare', an appearance which he 'hoped to God' might not become a reality.[3] The West Riding was so scared in June 1812 that in a hundred townships only two could be found bold enough to institute a system of Watch and Ward.[4] The Mayor of Leicester, although there were no actual disturbances there, was terrified enough to talk in January 1812 of 'the flood gates' being open, and of 'the bands of Society' being 'unloosed'.[5]

Such instances of alarm were, however, exceptional. There were always people, even on occasions of greatest

[1] Ibid., p. 1028.
[2] Wood to Fitzwilliam, June 7, 1812, in H.O. 40. 1.
[3] *The Times*, Feb. 1, 1812.
[4] Wood to Fitzwilliam, June 17, 1812, in H.O. 40. 1.
[5] In letter to Coldham, Jan. 23, 1812, in H.O. 42. 119.

difficulty, who were willing to present a calm, truthful account of the situation, to state, as Colonel Eyre did with regard to Nottinghamshire accounts in January,[1] and General Maitland and other officers with regard to northern accounts in May and June 1812,[2] that many reports of the disorders were frankly exaggerated, that a number of the magistrates, because of their fear, 'had rather overthought the whole situation',[3] and that the alarm was kept up more from the memory of past disorders than from any actual present danger.[4] The London daily and weekly newspapers, and journals like *The Annual Register*, though they report the disorders, and even go so far as to say 'that the public interest was never so anxiously, permanently, or generally excited as by the domestic and foreign events and transactions of the year 1812',[5] and to refer to the 'great alarm and apprehension'[6] which the disturbances had created, dismiss such matters in a few lines in their news rather than in their editorial columns, and do not suggest by their treatment that they felt any real anxiety as to the national situation.

There was, of course, great alarm in the actual disturbed districts, amongst some magistrates, and amongst the general public, as well as on the part of employers and merchants who felt themselves to be in danger of attack. Even level-headed authorities like the Town Clerk of Nottingham could report great anxiety. As he said in November 1811 with regard to the midland framebreaking:[7]

'Since I have been resident in Nottingham we have had many dangerous and alarming Riots, some of which for a very short period have assumed a more dangerous character than the present state of the surrounding country exhibits, but I regard them all as having afforded infinitely less cause of serious

[1] Jan. 23, 1812, in H.O. 42. 119.

[2] Various letters in H.O. 40. 1, and H.O. 42. 122 et seq.

[3] Maitland to H.O., May 4, 1812, in H.O. 40. 1.

[4] Campbell to Grey, May 9, 1812, in Grey to H.O., May 10, 1812, in H.O. 42. 123.

[5] *Annual Register*, 1812, pp. 305–8.

[6] Ibid.

[7] Coldham to Newcastle, Nov. 28, 1811, in H.O. 42. 119.

alarm and permanent danger. . . . The state of Manufacturers who are spread in every direction . . . and united by one common feeling of distress and one common desire of forcing upon the Hosiers or upon the Public some decisive measures for their relief, gives the present disturbances a most serious aspect.'

The Duke of Newcastle, another usually calm official, reported a similar anxiety on two occasions, in January 1812[1] and November 1816,[2] on which latter occasion he even reported the disturbances to be more alarming, although the police arrangements were better, than in 1811–12. This anxiety stirred the authorities to great efforts, and induced the Government to adopt exceptional policies,[3] though it also caused the public, especially at first, to stay at home and to give up in terror the practices to which the rioters objected.[4]

But this terror was terror of Luddite vengeance. The anxiety was as to the security of the persons and property of the particular people against whom the Luddite campaign was directed. There was no terror, and little anxiety as to the general safety of the country. No one seriously expected that machine breaking was going to lead to rebellion, though many people wondered and feared what the collection of arms and the rumoured drilling of the Luddites portended. It was generally believed that people were safe when they discontinued using machinery or committing other frauds (as the Luddites considered them). It was never doubted that it was within the power of the authorities to restore and to maintain order, once their

[1] Jan. 10, 1812, in ibid.

[2] Nov. 6, 1816, in H.O. 42. 155.

[3] Ryder in House of Commons, Feb. 1812, referred to the Government's measures as being exceptional, Government conduct of prosecutions, for instance, not having been resorted to since 1778 (*Parl. Debates*, xxi. 11, 808).

[4] The Home Office, in Letter Books, are full of depositions and letters showing traces of the lively terror created by the Luddites and of the effect that it had had in persuading employers to give up the unpopular practices.

arrangements had been completed. It was not the general maintenance of order, that was never threatened longer than it took to conclude a Luddite attack, but the suppression of isolated instances of machine breaking or robbery, that was such a difficult and anxious responsibility of the authorities.

Local forces, of which great numbers were employed, as militiamen and constables, and members of juries, were always found in fact, and contrary to rumour, wholly trustworthy. They seldom if ever incurred any real danger from doing their duty, the rioters often eluding but never openly opposing the agents of the Government. Three men were killed, a few more shot at or threatened, a somewhat larger number troubled by petty nuisances, the injuring of their farms or cattle, on account of their exertions against the disaffected. But on the whole, despite the fear that many people had of taking any prominent part in the suppression of disturbances, there was no real danger in such duty. Nor was there any unwillingness, except on the part of a few magistrates and in connexion with the institution of the Watch and Ward, especially in the West Riding, of people in the last resort and when called upon, to come forward.

The Courts, the whole machinery of internal government, though inadequate from the point of view of the suppression of Luddism and obviously in need of improvement, were nevertheless adequate, even during these disturbances, for their other duties. They might not be able, except slowly and with the assistance of the army, to prevent Luddite offences being committed. But they were not prevented by the Luddites from fulfilling their other functions. It was not against them, not against established authority, even when employed against them, that the Luddite campaign was directed. There was no need for, and there was little evidence of, alarm for the safety of the general public or of the agents of government, or for the general security of the country.

The astonishing thing about all the early Regency disturbances was not that they should have provoked anxiety on the part of the authorities and terror on the part of some manufacturers and members of the public but that this anxiety and terror should have been so restrained.

When one leaves these general questions, as to the amount of attention given to, and the extent of the alarm occasioned by, these disturbances, and proceeds to discuss in detail the attitude of the different classes of society to the disorders and to the measures taken against them, the record is more complicated. The lower classes outside the disturbed districts do not seem to have been much interested in disturbances elsewhere. They probably knew little about them. They shared in similar distress. They would surely, if they had understood them, have sympathized with the Luddites' objects. But there was nothing, no organization on the part of the Luddites, no adequate press publicity, to win for the disorderly in one district the sympathy or help of the distressed in others. Within the disturbed districts virtually the entire working class, whether or no they were themselves engaged in the affected industries, sympathized with the rioters. Many of them were willing to engage personally in disorder, like the Lancashire colliers who helped the Oldham spinners break looms at Middleton in 1812. They all condoned violence, even where they did not take part in it, or believe that it could be successful. They never obstructed or gave evidence against, or showed any signs of opposition to, or disapproval of, the Luddite campaign of violence, though some of them, by their continued reliance upon peaceful methods, proved that they had no confidence in direct action. They all sympathized with the rioters' objects, which, indeed, even the pacific elements amongst the labouring population were continually, before, during, and after the rioting, trying to achieve by non-violent means. They all saw the whole cause of their distress in such obvious factors as the use of new machinery, frauds in the manufacture, reduced wages, &c., the abuses against which the rioters' campaign, like the others' petitions, were directed. They none of them recognized the fundamental causes of their distress. And they, therefore, none of them demanded fundamental remedies such as the ending of the war, the halting of the new industrial advance, the regulation and planning of industry, the only measures which could really and permanently have helped them.

The agitation for peace and parliamentary reform and against the Orders in Council continued to attract much working-class attention even during the height of the disturbances, and much more after their suppression. Similarly negotiations with the employers, trades union activities, and petitions to Parliament, won, even during the period of worst disorder, a great volume of support. The workers were never wholly converted to a policy of attempting to secure redress of grievances by direct violent action. The latter was a method to which some of them resorted in desperation at a period of acute distress, after the break-down of negotiations, and with which most of them at such times were in sympathy. But it was not the only, or even the favourite, method of all, or indeed of a majority of the workers even at such times, and it was definitely the method of a small minority at normal times, or taking this period of the Regency as a whole. It cannot be doubted that far more energy and interest was put by the body of workers, even during, for instance, the years 1811 and 1812, into trades union activities, into petitions to Parliament, and the organization of a body like the 'Nottingham Union', than into framebreaking. It is interesting also that no attempt was made to use violence as an instrument in the campaign for these other legitimate, peaceful, political, or industrial objects. Disturbances or the danger of them were never made an argument for repealing the Orders in Council or granting parliamentary reform. They were never made a sanction for the policy of the 'Nottingham Union'. They were always used merely as a means of intimidating particular employers and merchants and of coercing them into particular limited concessions.

Authorities, witnesses before the House of Commons inquiry into the effect of the Orders in Council, officers like Colonel Clay (commanding at Manchester in 1812), even bodies like the Corporation of Nottingham (in an address to Parliament in April 1812), speak of the 'exemplary patience of the working classes',[1] of their praiseworthy moderation in the face of great distress and provocation. It was remarked more than once, as, for instance, by one of the members of Parliament for Nottingham in the House of Commons in February 1812, that the blame for the disturbances lay as much with the masters as with the workmen.[2] It is clear, therefore, that violence had not become the policy of the majority of the workers even under the distresses of this difficult time.

The majority of the workers did, however, share with the rioters what the Government considered the misguided notion that the use of new labour-saving machinery, or the employment of cheap methods of manufacture, or wage-cutting, or the charging of excessive prices in the markets, were abuses on the part of the masters and merchants which the latter could and should have avoided, and which were responsible for the prevailing distress. It was, in the labourers' opinion, whether they were Luddites or no, not the necessity of the situation, because of the war or the Industrial Revolution, but the tyranny and misjudgement of particular employers and merchants, which was the prime cause of popular suffering.[3] The workers almost invariably believed that those abuses could be corrected, and the distress relieved, either by regulations within the trades concerned or by the action of the

[1] Borough reeve and constables of Manchester to H.O., April 25, 1812, in H.O. 42. 121.

[2] Mr. Smith, M.P. for Nottingham, in House of Commons, Feb. 1812 (*Parl. Debates*, xxi. 11. 813–15).

[3] See evidence before Parliamentary Committee, June 1812 (*Parl. Papers*, 1812, ii. 204 et seq.).

authorities, of the magistrates or Parliament. It was in default of such action that they resorted to violence.

A great many of the smaller manufacturers, even including some of those who themselves had been forced by the pressure of competition into using the new machinery or making use of the new methods, also looked upon these matters from the point of view of the workers. They also doubted the value of these practices, especially at a time when goods were in any case a glut upon the market. They also thought that these various evils of which the workers complained were largely responsible for the prevailing distress. They, too, would have been glad to have seen these matters regulated by agreement within the trades concerned or by state action.[1] They, too, if they did not positively condone violent methods, were at any rate disposed to profit by them, and were not sorry to see the ends in which they believed attained by direct action after it had become obvious that there was no possibility of achieving them by peaceful or normal means. They, too, would do nothing to obstruct the rioters or to give them away to the authorities.[2]

Middle-class people with such opinions were accused more than once during these years of giving positive encouragement to the disorderly. The ultra-Tory *Nottingham Gazette*, for example, in 1814 bitterly criticized those employers who excused the framebreakers, and pleaded with them to spare their frames.[3] It was necessary, so the *Gazette* thought, to make it clear to the framebreakers that their actions were wholly reprehensible and misguided. It was from a similar point of view that the *Nottingham*

[1] Note in *Parl. Papers*, 1812, ii. 204, and also in Felkin, op. cit., evidence as to attempts of some of the hosiers to establish regulations for the trade, and as to acceptance by some of them of the workers' petition to Parliament (*Parl. Papers*, 1812, ii. 264).

[2] Many of the victims of attacks must have recognized some of the members of the attacking mobs, which often included their own apprentices and employees, yet they seldom gave evidence against them.

[3] *Nottingham Gazette*, Aug. 12, 1814.

Review, and its editor, Sutton, and leader-writer, Blackner, were criticized on several occasions. It was said that their reports of the Luddite outrages had been in such a tone as to excuse, and therefore to encourage them.[1] In 1815 this paper was actually cited for seditious libel and fined for comparing the acts of the military in England against the Luddites and in North America against popular liberty there.[2]

It does not appear to have been fair to have accused Sutton or Blackner or *The Review*, or any of the manufacturers and other middle-class commentators, of having given any encouragement to actual violence. That they always condemned, though some of them may have felt that the workers had been driven to it, and should not be judged too harshly. It was with the objects and not with the methods of the Luddites that they sympathized. They, and other friends of the workers, men like Cartwright[3] and Whitbread, were quite certain that no good could come of violence, it was doomed to failure and would only jeopardize other more useful causes, peace, parliamentary reform, trade regulation, &c. Most of the middle class, like some of the workers, and especially the group following Gravener Henson, distrusted violent methods and pinned their hopes, even in the face of continual disappointments, to negotiations and petitions.[4]

Not all the middle class, also, by any means, sympathized even with the objects of the rioters. On the one hand, of course, were the merchants and masters against

[1] *Nottingham Review*, Jan. 3, 1812. The *Review* was voted out of the local news room because of the local feeling that it had encouraged the Luddites by the tone of its reports.

[2] *Nottingham Review*, June 1815.

[3] See letters in Nottingham papers for Dec. 1811 and Jan. 1812.

[4] The history of the framework knitting industry is throughout one of continual and usually fruitless negotiations between hosiers and framework knitters, the latter and many of the former persisting in the face of continual failures, due to the refusal of a minority of the hosiers to come into line, and in spite of occasional outbreaks of Luddism or of strikes and other violent expedients, which sometimes attracted a minority of the men.

whose practices the rioters were protesting, those who drove up the price of foodstuffs by speculation, who undercut their competitors, who drove down the rate of wages, who used machinery and otherwise economized in production, and who defended their practices on the score of necessity. There were some who realized, though they might not admit, that these practices were harmful to the country, and to the trade at large, but who employed them because they were profitable to them as individuals. There were others who, though they saw hardships thus inflicted upon some workers, felt that these measures were necessary in the existing state of trade. If production were not cheapened in every possible way how could even the small remaining market be kept open?[1] There were others again who believed these practices to be positively sound, new machinery, cheaper production, were the means by which industry as a whole, including in the end the employees who thought they were being hurt, would achieve a higher prosperity.[2]

Upon the whole, though a section of the masters agreed with the men's analysis of the situation, the majority attributed to the war and the Orders in Council, and to changes in fashion and demand, evils which the workers attributed to fraudulent work, 'cut-ups', and new machinery. The great majority of the masters also, though some might have wished to see the men's objects achieved by pacific means, were content to join in attempts to put down disorder, in so far as they felt it safe to do so.

There was considerable difference of opinion also amongst such people as to the advisability and possibility of regulating such matters. A great many employers believed, like those who appeared before the House of Commons Committee on the Framework Knitters' Petitions, that it would do more harm than good for Parliament to meddle

[1] See evidence of hosiers before Parliamentary Committee, June 1812, especially that of Thomas Nelson and others (*Parl. Papers*, 1812, ii. 290 et seq.).

[2] Ibid.

with industrial matters. Wages, they believed, as the new economics taught, should be left to find their own level. Manufacturers should be left free to vary their products and their conditions of work as occasion demanded. Any fixed or parliamentary regulation was, as the majority of the masters thought, and as they successfully persuaded Parliament, sure to be to the ultimate harm of the trade, and therefore of the very workers whom it was hoped to help. The minority of masters which was willing to see some matters, as, for instance, frame rents, subject to regulation, and some trades, such as lace, supervised by Parliament, was overborne by the majority.

The upper and governing classes, including the responsible local officials, were similarly divided in their attitude. Even more universally than the middle class they were opposed to violence and ready to adopt any measures needed to put it down. Mostly they tried to be impartial as between the masters and the men, in whose disputes most of the disorders of the time were recognized to be rooted. They realized that the masters were very often as much to blame as the men.[1] They were, like General Maitland, on the look out lest their defence measures, the placing of guards in factories and so on, should be made a means of reducing the wages of the workers even below their existing level.[2] They were as quick to subscribe to funds for the relief of distress as to those for the suppression of disturbances.[3] They gave themselves as willingly and energetically to measures for the public relief, like the Charitable Society which was organized in the summer of 1812 and of which the Duke of York was President, as to measures of public order.

They differed, however, in their attitude towards the causes of the trouble, and as to the measures which should

[1] e.g. statement of Smith, M.P. for Nottingham (*Parl. Debates*, 1812, xxi. 11. 813–15). [2] Maitland to H.O., May 9, 1812, in H.O. 40. 1.

[3] See accounts of subscriptions in local and national press for May, June, and July 1812.

be taken to deal with it. Some of them, including, significantly enough, a few of the most energetic local officials, were eager not merely to put disturbances down but to remove their cause. Many magistrates and officials wished that some way could be found to raise wages and reduce prices. The Nottingham magistrates tried to mediate between the framework knitters and the hosiers, only to be rebuffed by the latter.[1] The Stockport magistrates felt very aggrieved when rioting commenced, having, as they thought, done all that they could to meet the just grievances of the workers[2]. Colonel Fletcher of the Bolton bench even went so far as to suggest that the justices might revert to their old function and rate wages, as he said had recently been done in Kent. He believed an increase in price of 5 per cent., which would have little effect upon demand, might allow an increase in wages of 15 per cent., which would have a great effect upon distress and discontent.[3]

There was similarly a demand in Parliament that something should be done to inquire into the causes of the disturbances, and to remove the chief of them, the unprecedented popular distress. The Earl of Moira during the debate on the Framebreaking Bill in February 1812 said that it 'undoubtedly became the justice of the House to endeavour to extirpate such a dangerous species of offence, but it no less became their justice to endeavour to prevent those distresses which gave rise to them, and to try to ameliorate the situation of the starving manufacturers'.[4] Mr. Hutchinson in the House of Commons took the same line. 'What had been the immediate cause of these outrages? Distress perhaps unparalleled. Did not this involve a consideration that bound them to reflect upon the measures that had created that distress?'[5]

These attempts to help the distressed and disorderly

[1] Conant and Baker's report, in H.O. 42. 119.

[2] Letters from Lloyd to H.O., in H.O. 40. 1 (especially for March 1812).

[3] Fletcher to H.O., April 11, 1812, in ibid.

[4] *Parl. Debates*, xxi. 11. 1167.

[5] Ibid., p. 859.

labourers did not, however, get very far.[1] The *laisser-faire* philosophy, which was especially powerful in the House of Lords and amongst the intelligentsia, who might otherwise have wished to help the poor labourers, prevented any action being taken. In 1811, when petitions had been presented to Parliament from distressed cotton weavers, the Committee appointed to consider them reported:[2]

'While the Committee fully acknowledge and most deeply lament the great distress of numbers of persons engaged in the cotton manufacture . . . they are of opinion that no interference of the legislature with the freedom of trade, or with the perfect liberty of every individual to dispose of his time and of his labour in the way and on the terms which he may judge most conducive to his own interest, can take place without violating general principles of the first importance to the prosperity and happiness of the community, without establishing the most pernicious precedent, or without aggravating, after a very short time, the pressure of the general distress, and imposing obstacles against that distress ever being removed.'

In 1812 the Committee appointed to consider petitions from the framework knitters reported:[3]

'The Committee is confirmed in the belief that the Workmen suffer considerable inconveniences and are liable to deductions in various ways in payment for their work . . . but they have found it very difficult to suggest measures that can meet or obviate all those abuses, being of opinion that legislative enactment alone will not have that effect; and that trade of every kind should be left as much as possible to find its own level.'

In response to this feeling the Committee struck from the Bill the clauses relating to Hosiery, an old-established industry, and only recommended for a limited term, as an experiment, and because of the obvious importance of some relief being given to what otherwise looked like becoming a bankrupt trade, some regulations of Lace.[4]

[1] There was no motion for inquiry in the House of Lords and that in the House of Commons was defeated by 40 votes against to 15 for.

[2] *Parl. Debates*, xx. 609.

[3] *Parl. Papers*, 1812, ii. 208 et seq.

[4] Ibid.

The Bill thus amended, which had the backing of some of the lace manufacturers and all of the men, was carried through the House of Commons, in spite of a stern defence of the orthodox *laisser-faire* position by Hume. It was, however, rather surprisingly, overwhelmingly defeated in the House of Lords, in which the landowners (who were generally throughout the century more favourable to the regulation of industry, and especially to Factory Acts, than the manufacturers, who were more powerful in the Commons) were in control. Lauderdale, Liverpool, Holland, and Sidmouth, usually bitter opponents, were all in agreement in condemning this attempt to meddle with the affairs of industry. Lord Sidmouth 'trusted in God that it would never again be attempted to introduce a Bill founded on those principles in the House of Lords'.[1]

There were other reasons why, despite a general sympathy with them, it was felt that little could be done to help the workers. Many people felt with William Lamb (afterwards Lord Melbourne) 'that it was nothing less than wilfully deluding the country to hold out a hope that greater commercial embarrassments, greater severity of distress, than the country had hitherto felt, were not yet to be endured'.[2]

Not very many people really believed, what some of the Whigs, especially in the House of Lords, tried to suggest, that the whole cause of the distress was rooted in the policy of the Government which had, as the Earl of Lauderdale remarked, reduced 'the commerce of the country to a gambling speculation' in which wages were first higher, then lower, thus driving men to discontent and disorder.[3] Most of them believed, either, like Lamb, that distress was part of the inevitable cost of the war; or, like Liverpool, that it was the natural result of ups and downs in trade, and of a depression like that which had followed the speculative boom of 1807 and 1808, and which had produced a

[1] *Parl. Debates*, xxiii. 1191, 1240–50. [2] Ibid., xxi.
[3] Ibid., 11. 603.

collapse in 1810. They did not see what could really be done to relieve it. In any case they felt, with Premier Perceval, 'whatever the causes of the disorders did any one deny the necessity of putting them down'. It was the most obvious course, despite much genuine sympathy for the distressed and disorderly workers, to restrict government action legislating against offences.

People were the more willing to do this in that, at any rate in Parliament, they generally confused the objects of the rioters, believing Luddism to be directed essentially against new machinery on the grounds that it economized labour.[1] Very few upper-class people agreed with Lord Byron, who made a biting, brilliant maiden speech criticizing the Government's policy, and arguing that labour-saving machinery was of little value when the trouble with the country was a surplus, and not a deficiency, of goods and of labour.[2] Most people agreed with the Cabinet, which ordered pamphlets to be issued proving how misguided it was to oppose the introduction of machinery. It was as absurd, so such people thought, to oppose the introduction of a steam loom, as it would have been to have opposed the introduction of a spade or a plough, and as vain, since destruction of machinery in one district or country would only ruin it by driving the trade to others. It was, therefore, necessary, as Lord Liverpool suggested, to give legislative protection to machinery in the hosiery and lace trade, as it had previously been found necessary to protect by law the machinery used in every previous manufacture in which it had been introduced to the detriment of manual labour.[3]

The few measures that were taken for the relief of distress, the proposal to regulate the lace trade and the repeal of the Orders in Council, were in fact not considered in relation to disturbances. It was recognized after the event

[1] See Report of House of Lords Secret Committee, June 1812, in *Parl. Debates*, xxiii.

[2] *Parl. Debates*, xxi. 11. 966–71.

[3] Liverpool in *Parl. Debates*, xxi. 11. 972.

that the defeat of the former, and the passage of the latter, proposal had had an effect upon the situation in the disturbed districts, the former worrying and unsettling the Nottingham framework knitters, the latter encouraging and setting to work the northern operatives. But the defeat of the Lace Regulation Bill and the Repeal of the Orders in Council were both decided upon by Parliament without thought of any such results.

On the whole, therefore, although the upper and governing classes sympathized with the labourers who were rioting, they felt them to be misguided, and they did not see how they could do anything material to help them. A small minority only asked for an inquiry into distress. An almost negligible minority agreed with Lord Byron in thinking the Luddites' objects to be sound.

A few authorities did, by implication, recognize the truth of Lord Byron's position. Becher, Coldham, Cartwright, Conant, and Felkin all admit that the hosiery and lace trades were overexpanded and would in any case have had to suffer a decline. They admit that the trades were overstocked with hands and frames. They state that there were still more than sufficient frames surviving even after all the destruction. But not even they, and indeed not even Lord Byron, were for this reason willing to defend machine-breaking, even if they doubted whether its actual effect had been as harmful as some critics suggested. Most people, moreover, were wholly convinced that a campaign against machinery was an unqualified disaster from every point of view.

The upper and governing classes were, therefore, forced back upon a policy of mere repression. So far as such matters were concerned they were upon the whole willing to follow the advice of the Government. They gave the administration, as that was usually willing in the end to give the local authorities, the support it requested. There is little evidence of any independent thought upon the matter.

There was sharp opposition to certain aspects of the Government's policy. The Whig party in the House of Lords, for example, which made no attempt to excuse the Luddites, and no serious attempt to press for an inquiry into the causes of disturbance and distress, did put up a strong opposition to the Framebreaking Bill.[1] They argued, as did Mr. Coldham and other Nottingham authorities, that it was vain to increase the penalty against framebreaking when even the lesser penalty had not yet been put into effect. Surely it was the wiser policy first to apply the existing law, and sentence some framebreakers to transportation, before proceeding to pass a new law making framebreakers liable to capital punishment! They foresaw, what ultimately proved to be the case, that it would become even more difficult than before to secure information, or to get one offender to give away another, when the consequence might be the death of a fellow creature.

The whole of the Tory party in both Houses of Parliament, and many of the Whigs, especially in the House of Commons, took, however, a contrary view. They felt, as Lamb suggested, that the new law making framebreaking punishable with death would operate, by reason of the terror of the penalty, to prevent the offence. It would at least make clear to the public the sense of Parliament as to the enormity of the crime. It would be following precedent, which had applied to other instances of machine-breaking, as they occurred, as it had to other crimes, the death penalty. They did not agree with Lord Holland and Sir Samuel Romilly that this policy had defeated its own ends, that the 'Statute Book was too thick set with penalties of death to make that a very explicit declaration of the sense of Parliament as to the enormity of the crime'.[2] They did not appreciate what a few reformers were beginning to suggest, that it was a wiser policy of criminal law to graduate penalties and to refrain from antagonizing juries, and discouraging the public from co-operating with

[1] See debate in *Parl. Debates*, 1812, ii. 960 et seq. [2] Ibid.

the police, by having extreme penalties for what the public regarded as moderate crimes.[1]

The other aspect of the Government's policy which was criticized was the spy system. Mr. Whitbread in 1812, and other Whigs and Radicals with more vigour and persistence in 1817, attacked the Government for its dependence upon informers, many of whom had clearly become agents and instigators of disorder. Strangely enough, however, considering what a good case the Opposition had in this matter against the Government, the Whig party as a whole was not willing to press this charge strongly. It left the question to a few Radicals. It apparently felt, what was really the case, that spies and informers, distasteful and untrustworthy though such agents and methods might be, were in fact, and in the absence of an effective system of police detectives, the only instrument available to the authorities. Only in that way could they find out 'what was going on in the country'.

Similarly it was left to the Radicals, and especially to Mr. Whitbread, to criticize the reports of the Secret Committees of Parliament, and the measures that were founded upon them. The bulk of the Whig party was not willing, even in 1817, to make these internal questions a major issue. They mostly, especially at the beginning of our period, accepted the Tory Government's contentions. They did not bother to go behind the Committees' reports. There seems to have been, apart from the natural desire of the Opposition to oppose, and from the presence in the Opposition ranks of a few individuals, Holland, Whitbread, Brougham, Marriott, Romilly, who had a real interest in and knowledge of progressive principles of criminal law, which produced an occasional and half-hearted opposition to a few of the Government's measures and arguments, no sign in the Whig party of any different attitude to these

[1] It is significant that those actually experienced in applying such laws, men like the Town Clerk of Nottingham, were often opposed to them.

matters from that which was characteristic of the Tories. Leading Whigs, like Grenville and Moira, were apparently as wholly convinced as Tories like Liverpool, Castlereagh, and Sidmouth, that disturbances must be put down in the old way, the only way they then knew of, by the use of greater force, by increased penalties, by enlarged and emergency powers to the Government and local officials.

There was little sign in Parliament of any recognition that this old policy of order was inadequate. In the country, on the part of local officials in every disturbed district, on the part of soldiers like Maitland and Byng, and on the part of the general public, which swamped the Home Office with letters urging the establishment of a system of regular police,[1] there was growing realization of the fact that the only effective solvent of disorder was a regular police establishment. There were several requests from responsible local officials, especially in Manchester and Nottingham, for the creation of such a body. There was no reflection of these requests, or of this tendency of public and local opinion, in Parliament. It was not until the next decade, after a long, fruitless attempt to maintain order with the old system, that the reform of the machinery of public order was seriously taken in hand.

It is indeed rather astonishing that Parliament, which contained many members, peers and commoners, who had been personally concerned in the suppression of disturbances, and who knew at first hand the weakness of the existing system, should have been content to neglect this matter and merely to endorse the policy of the Government. It is surprising that there was not any suggestion from any quarter of any but emergency measures, of anything more far-reaching than a slight modernization of the old system of Watch and Ward.

[1] Some unsolved murders in the east end of London at Wapping created great alarm at the beginning of 1812, in some ways greater alarm even than the national disturbances, and for some weeks the Home Office was deluged with letters urging the organization of a more efficient police (see London Press and H.O. 42. 119).

It is similarly surprising that no suggestion should have been made as to the need for recasting the system of local government, and for developing a new policy for the state regulation of industry. Both these things were obviously necessary. The state was going to be forced continuously throughout the century to expand the sphere of its authority, to intervene in industry for the protection of women and children, and finally of men, against the evils that seemed to be inseparable from industrial advance, and to set up a complicated new series of governmental agencies, national and local. The whole programme of nineteenth-century domestic legislation, Reform Bills, Poor Law and Factory Acts, &c., the readjustment of the nation's political and social structure to accord with the needs of the new situation created by the industrial and commercial revolutions, could have been deduced to be necessary and inevitable by any fair student of Regency conditions. And yet there was no sign of recognition that any such far-reaching changes would be necessary. The very Parliament which was dealing with Luddism was casting overboard the last remnants of the Elizabethan system of industrial regulation.

This period was, indeed, an interlude. It was significant that the repeal of the Statute of Artificers and the passage by the House of Commons of the Lace Regulation Bill, should have been so nearly contemporaneous. It was significant that almost at the same moment a local magistrate should have been recommending that the justices should rate wages and that Parliament should have been declaring that any interference with the natural laws of trade would be pernicious. English opinion was at the parting of the ways. The old system was dying, though a few country people still wished to cling to it. The new system had not yet come in, though a few people were already proposing measures similar to those which were to characterize it. The last of the Elizabethan Statutes was being repealed just at the time that the first of the nineteenth-century Acts was being passed. *Laisser-faire*, which was rapidly becoming the ruling policy, was being proved impossible of complete application even while it was making rapid strides towards supremacy.

It was because of this, because of the confusion which therefore existed, in fact, in conditions in the country, and in thought, in the state of public opinion, that Regency England stumbled so haltingly through this period of disorder and discontent. It was, though few people knew it, a time of preparation for the period of feverish activity which was to follow. Public opinion was being prepared for its ninteenth-century tasks. The workers were being taught that an attempt to put back the clock of industrial advance was doomed to failure, and were being won to a policy of ameliorating the conditions of the new industry by industrial and political action. The middle classes were being taught to recognize the possibilities, and the dangers, of the new industry and of unrestrained competition. The upper classes were learning that a new England existed, an England which was in need of a new suit of government. Disturbances were a symptom of those varied social diseases which were going to force upon each class in the community an attitude of mind, and a policy of action, far different from those in which they had believed, and to which they still clung. But they were not as yet at all generally recognized to be anything so fundamental or significant.

Public opinion was poorly equipped to understand the problems of Regency England. Eighteenth-century minds were dealing with a nineteenth-century country. It was therefore natural that some people, like the magistrates who wished to rate wages, and the workers who wished to prevent the introduction of machinery, should look backwards to the old England; while others, like the workers who formed the 'Nottingham Union', and the officials who pressed for a system of police, should look forward to the new one. It was natural that effective action with regard to problems of disturbance and of public order should have been lacking. It was fortunate that no irreparable damage was done while Regency Englishmen were being taught to understand Regency England.

BIBLIOGRAPHY

SOURCES

Primary

Parliamentary Debates (especially volumes for 1812 and 1817).

Journals of the House of Lords and House of Commons.

Parliamentary Papers.

Reports of Committees.

'Report on the state of the Woollen Manufacture in England and on the use of Machinery', 1806.

'Report of the Committee on the Petitions of Several Weavers', 1811.

'Report of the Committee of Secrecy of the House of Lords into the Disturbances in the Northern Counties', 1812.

'Report of the Committee of Secrecy of the House of Commons into the Disturbances in the Northern Counties', 1812.

'Report of the Committee on Framework Knitters' Petitions', 1812.

'Second Report of the Same', 1812.

'Report of the Committee of Secrecy of the House of Lords', 1817.

'Report of the Committee of Secrecy of the House of Commons', 1817.

'Second Reports of same', 1817.

'Report and Minutes of Evidence of the Framework Knitters and their Petitions respecting the making of stockings, &c.', 1819.

'Report and Minutes of Evidence of the Committee on the Orders in Council', 1808.

Ibid., 1812.

'Report of the Committee on Artisans and Machinery', 1824.

'Report of the Committee on Handloom Weavers' Petitions', 1834.

'Report of the Committee on the Framework Knitting Industry', 1845.

Accounts and Papers.

1809, ix, Exports to the U.S.A.; Real Value of British Produce and Manufactures.

1812, x, p. 25; An Account of the Real Value of Exports from Great Britain in the Years 1805–11, respectively.

Ibid., p. 59; Real Value of Exports, Distinguishing British Produce and Manufactures from Foreign and Colonial Merchandise.

Ibid., pp. 79–99; Account of the Several Items from which the Gross Sums in the Export and Import Lists are made up.

1817, xiv, p. 243; An Account of the Official Value of Exports from Great Britain, 1792–1816.

1831–2, xxxiv, p. 152; Exports of British and Irish Produce and Manufactures from Great Britain; 1799–1830.

Departmental Papers. (Preserved at the Public Record Office.)

Home Office.

H.O. 40. Disturbances:

1, 1812, Luddite Riots.
2, 1812–13, Military Reports.
3, 1816–18, Précis of Information, Reports, &c.
4, ,, ,, ,, ,,
5, ,, ,, ,, ,,
6, ,, ,, ,, ,,
7, ,, ,, ,, ,,
8, ,, ,, ,, ,,
9, 1817, Miscellaneous Correspondence.
10, ,, ,, ,,

H.O. 41. Disturbances. Entry Books:

1, 1816, April–Dec., Miscellaneous.
2, ,, Dec.–1817, April, ditto.
3, 1817, April–1818, Jan., ditto.

H.O. 42. Domestic Letter Books. Letters and Papers:

100–109, 1810.
110–118, 1811.
119–131, 1812.
132–136, 1813.
137–141, 1814.
142–147, 1815.
148–157, 1816.
158–172, 1817.

H.O. 43. Entry Books. Domestic Letter Books:

18, 1809, Dec.–1811, Feb.
19, 1811, Feb.–1912, Feb.
20, 1812, Feb.–July.
21, 1812, July–1813, July.
22, 1814, April–1815, May.
23, 1815, May–August.
24, 1815, Aug.–1816, June.
25, 1816, June–1817, Feb.
26, 1817, Feb.–Dec.

H.O. 47. Judges' Reports. Original Letters and Reports from Judges with Petitions for commutation, &c.

46, 1811.
47, ,,
48, ,,
49, 1812.
50, ,,
51, 1813.
52, ,,
53, 1814.
54, 1815.
55, 1816.
56, 1817.

H.O. 48. Law Officers. Reports and Correspondence:

15, 1811–12.
16, 1813.
17, 1814–18.
22, 1809–18.

H.O. 49. Law Officers. Letter Books.

6, 1809–17.

H.O. 50. Military Correspondence. Original Correspondence with the Commander-in-Chief, the Secretary at War, &c., on questions of internal defence.

H.O. 51. Military. Entry Books. Appointments, Commissions, &c., relating to the Militia, Volunteers, &c.

H.O. 65. Secret Service. 1811–20. General Letter Book.

H.O. 79. Private and Secret. Letters relating to secret service, postal censorship, alleged criminal acts, and other matters of a confidential nature.

1, 1806–12.
2, 1812–17.

Newspapers and Periodicals.

London.

Times,
Morning Herald,
Courier.

Provincial.

Nottingham Journal,
,, *Review,*
,, *Gazette* (1813–16 only).
Leeds Mercury,
,, *Intelligencer.*
Manchester Exchange Herald,
,, *Cowdroy's Gazette.*

Periodicals.

Annual Register,
Cobbett's Political Register,
Gentleman's Magazine.

SECONDARY

Contemporary Publications.

The Beggar's Complaint against rack rent Landlords and some Observations on the conduct of the Luddites in reference to the destruction of Machinery, anonymous, J. Crome, Sheffield, 1812.

History of Nottingham, J. Blackner, Nottingham, 1815.

Report of the Proceedings under Commissions of Oyer and Terminer, Jan. 12–22, 1813 at York, Gurney, J. and W. B., 1813.

Report of Proceedings under Commissions of Oyer and Terminer and gaol delivery for the County of York, held at the Castle of York . . . 2nd to 12th Jan. 1813, pub. by Luke Hansard, 1813.

An Appeal to the Public—containing an account of the services rendered during the disturbances in the North of England in the year 1812, Francis Raynes, London, 1817.

Digest of Evidence of the Committee on Artisans and Machinery, Geo. White, London, 1824.

Letter on the Subject of the Lancashire Riots in the year 1812, Dr. Robert Eveleigh Taylor, Bolton, 1813.

HISTORICAL WORKS WRITTEN BY FIRST HAND AUTHORITIES

History of the Framework Knitters in Europe and America, Gravener Henson, Nottingham, 1831.

Date Book of . . . remarkable events . . . connected with . . . Nottingham and neighbourhood, J. F. Sutton, London, 1852.

History of the Machine Wrought Hosiery and Lace Manufactures, William Felkin, London, 1863.

Account of the Machine Wrought Hosiery and Lace Trade, Wm. Felkin, London, 1845.

History of the County Palatine and Duchy of Lancaster, E. Baines, London, 1836.

The Manufacturing Population of England, Gaskell, London, 1833.

Historical Sketches of . . . Manchester, Archibald Prentice, 1851.

Manchester; its political, social, and commercial history, ancient and modern, J. Wheeler, London, 1836.

History of Preston, D. Whittle, 2 vols., Preston, 1821–37.

The Blackfaces of 1812, consisting of D. Taylor's Letter regarding the disturbances in Bolton in 1812; William Moor's Letter to the late Colonel Fletcher, with an introduction containing some notice of the spy system in 1812, 1817, and 1819, Bolton, 1839.

History of the Cotton Manufacture, Edward Baines, 1836.

The British Cotton Manufacture, Richard Guest, 1828.

Compendious History of the Cotton Manufacture, Richard Guest, 1823.

Cotton Manufacture of Great Britain, D. Ure, 2 vols., 1836.

SECONDARY WORKS

The Risings of the Luddites, Chartists, and Plug-drawers, Frank Peel, Heckmondwike, 1888.

Spen Valley, past and present, Frank Peel, Heckmondwike, 1893.

An Historical Account of the Luddites of 1811, 1812, and 1813; with a report of their trials at York Castle from the 2nd to 12th January, 1813, before Sir Alexander Thompson and Sir Simon Le Blanc, Knights, Judges of the Special Commission, Cogwill, Huddersfield, 1862.

The Luddites, J. Russell, Thoroton Society Publications, 1906, vol. x, pp. 53–62.

Annals of Nottingham, Bailey, 1853.

Yorkshire, past and present, Thomas Baines, 2 vols., London, 1877.

Lancashire and Cheshire, past and present, Thomas Baines and William Fairbairn, 2 vols., London, 1869.

An Historical Account of the towns of Ashton-under-Lyne, Stalybridge, and Dunkinfield, E. Butterworth, Ashton, 1842.

Annals of Bolton, J. Clegg, Bolton, 1888.

The Story of Old Halifax, T. W. Hanson, Halifax, 1921.

The Annals of Yorkshire from the earliest period to the present time, J. Maynall, 3 vols., London, 1874.

The Pentridge Revolution, J. Neal, 1895.

Huddersfield, its history and natural history, C. C. P. Hobkirk, London, 1859.

History of Colne Valley, D. F. E. Sykes, pub. F. Walker, Slaithwaite, 1906.

History of Huddersfield and Its Vicinity, D. F. E. Sykes, Advertiser Press, Ltd., Huddersfield, 1898.

Bad Times, a tale of the Luddites, A. Lodge, pub. Woodhead, Huddersfield, 1870.

Ben O' Bill's, the Luddite; a Yorkshire Tale, D. F. E. Sykes and G. H. Walker, pub. by Advertiser Press, Ltd., Huddersfield.

The Chartist Movement, Mark Hovell, ed. T. F. Tout, Manchester University Press, 1919.

The Machine Wreckers, a play, Ernst Toller, London, 1923.

Life of Thomas, 1st Lord Denman, Sir J. Arnold, 2 vols., 1872.

Life and Correspondence of Henry Addington, 2 vols., Pellew, London, 1847.

The Town Labourer, J. L. and B. Hammond.

The Skilled Labourer, J. L. and B. Hammond.

History of Trade Unionism, S. and B. Webb.

English Local Government, S. and B. Webb.

The Industrial Revolution in the Eighteenth Century, Paul Mantoux.

History of the English People, Elie Halevy, vol. i.

The Progress of the Nation, G. R. Porter, London, 1847.

Wages in the United Kingdom in the Nineteenth Century, A. L. Bowley, London, 1900.

An Economic History of Modern Britain, J. H. Clapham, vol. i; *The Railway Age*.

Commercial Statistics, John MacGregor.

The Cotton Industry, J. L. and B. Hammond.

The Cotton Trade in the Revolutionary and Napoleonic Wars, G. W. Daniels.

A Century of Fine Cotton Spinning, McConnel and Kennedy, 1915.

Early English Cotton Industry, G. W. Daniels, Manchester, 1920.

Life and Labour in the Nineteenth Century, C. R. Fay.

England's Foreign Trade in the 19th Century, A. L. Bowley.

High and Low Prices, Thomas Tooke, London, 1823.

Handbook of Silk, Cotton, and Woollen Manufactures, W. Cooke Taylor.

Six Centuries of Work and Wages, Thorold Rogers, London, 1884.

Nottinghamshire in the Eighteenth Century, J. D. Chambers, London, 1931.

The Framework Knitters Company, J. D. Chambers, Economica, Nov. 1929.

INDEX